The
NEW CRITICISM
IN FRANCE

The

NEW CRITICISM
IN FRANCE

Serge Doubrovsky

Translated by
Derek Coltman

With an Introduction by
Edward Wasiolek

THE UNIVERSITY OF CHICAGO PRESS
Chicago and London

Originally published as *Pourquoi la nouvelle critique: Critique et objectivité*, © Mercure de France, 1966.

The University of Chicago Press, Chicago 60637
The University of Chicago Press, Ltd., London
©1973 by The University of Chicago
All rights reserved. Published 1973
Printed in the United States of America
International Standard Book Number: 0-226-16040-8
Library of Congress Catalog Card Number: 73-78664

Serge Doubrovsky, both a literary critic and a creative writer, was educated at the Sorbonne, where he received his *doctorat d'Etat* in French literature. He is now a full professor at New York University. His works include *Corneille et la dialectique du héros* (Gallimard), *La Dispersion*, a novel (Mercure de France), and numerous articles in scholarly publications. [1973]

To
Smith College and to Th. C. Mendenhall
with all gratitude, and with my warmest
thanks to the John Simon Guggenheim
Foundation
S.D.

The function of the critic is to criticize, which is to say to engage himself for or against and to situate himself by situating.

Jean-Paul Sartre

Situations I

CONTENTS

INTRODUCTION

by *Edward Wasiolek*

I

IT WAS a bitter foe, Raymond Picard, who brought the French New Criticism to the attention of the general literate French public and ultimately to the attention of the English reader by his attacks in 1964 and 1965 on Roland Barthes. He did this first in the pages of *Le Monde* in 1964 and in a full-scale attack on Barthes's *Sur Racine* (1963) in a small polemical book entitled *Nouvelle critique ou nouvelle imposture?* in 1965. Barthes answered Picard in *Critique et vérité* in 1966. Between 1964 and 1966 the Parisian literary scene was rocked by the fury of defense and attack on each man in articles and books. The vehemence of passions that an argument about the function of criticism and the teaching and reading of literature aroused in the French reader will surprise the American reader, who is accustomed to look upon literary criticism as a slightly dreary and surely an arcane matter. *L'affaire Picard*, as the quarrel has come to be known, engaged for a time a good segment of the Parisian literary life, and also the attention of some ordinary citizens, who gave vent to their feelings in letters to the editors. Roland Barthes has catalogued some of the things he was called in his *Criticism and Truth*, and the appellations seem more apt to characterize someone who has betrayed his country or recommended mercy killing for everyone over fifty. Picard himself has called *la nouvelle critique* a fraud, its language pathological, Barthes's *On Racine* a revolting book, and the recent trends of French criticism monstrous. In an article in the *New Statesman* ("Magical Criticism," 15 July 1966, p.

1

88) he characterized the "New Critics" and their position in the following manner: "They multiply contradictions, philological nonsense and jumbles, they extrapolate wildly. The need for logic, clarity, and coherent thought strikes them as silly. One of them has just had the courage, or ignorance, to erect a theory round their own unreasoning. Clarity, he assures us, is no more than a reactionary prejudice; what stands to reason is commonplace and banal; objectivity is an empty illusion." He characterized the difference between the New Critical position and his own in the following manner in his *New Criticism or New Fraud*: "In opposition to this intolerant, neo-magical nihilism, a parasitic criticism which at best considers the literary work as a dunghill where flowers can be made to grow, I, for my part, defend another kind of criticism, one preoccupied with intelligibility, inspired by a flexible, humanistic neo-positivism" (Towne translation, p. 26; see Bibliographical Note).

The French New Criticism did not begin, of course, with the quarrel; Picard spoke of "the flowering of monstrosities that has taken place in French criticism in the last ten or fifteen years" (ibid., p. 27), but he chose correctly to attack Barthes, who is without doubt the most distinctive representative of the movement and its most articulate spokesman. Those among the group who are loosely associated with the movement — Goldmann, Mauron, Richard, Starobinsky, Poulet, among others — have tended to elaborate and defend special and partial views; Barthes alone has exposited the general theoretical bases that support these views as well as his own position. To read Picard, the issue is between reason, moderation, intelligence, and sanity on the one hand, and irrationality, frenzied and irresponsible excess, and magic and obscurantism on the other. Underneath the rhetoric, real issues divide the men and the traditional and the new criticism that they personify. The quarrel and the ensuing clamor both hardened and obscured the differences. It is unfortunate and incorrect to moderate these differences, in a spirit of academic reconciliation, as one American commentator has done: "All clear-cut distinctions between New Criticism and university criticism are false, and theses along the lines of New Criticism are being accepted in increasing numbers by French universities" (Laurent LeSage, *The French New Criticism: An Introduction and a Sampler*, 1967, pp. 10–11). Both Barthes and Picard have used the term *critique universitaire*, and neither in the literal and institutional way the author uses it in the quotation above. The term "university criticism" is used by both for a set of attitudes toward the reading of literature, similar in many respects to those embodied in the term "academic criticism" in America. University criticism, as explained by Picard, sees itself as self-effacing before an objective text, the nature of which may be apprehended by patient accumulation of historical evidence and the analysis of such evidence according to the generally accepted norms of rational discourse. It does not necessarily mean, as academic criticism in this country has meant at times, a procedure that avoids the text and talks only about the author's life or the historical evidence surrounding the work. Picard has clearly rejected the charge that he is a blind follower of Lansonian criticism, and he has agreed with Barthes in rejecting an old-fashioned biographism. Picard, it must be repeated, is as interested as are the New Critics in elucidating the text; his argument with Barthes is about how this is to be done.

It was perhaps inevitable that the term "New Criticism" would be misunderstood in America. The coincidence of the term "New Criticism" with the name of the movement that exercised such lasting influence on American reading habits for more than a generation prepared the way for our understanding to flow along the grooves of settled critical habits. We have become so accustomed to think about criticism in terms of those who are for the text and those who are against it, for "intrinsic" criticism and "extrinsic" criticism, that it was perhaps inevitable that some of the American commentators have understood the issue between Picard and Barthes in this way. In the introduction to translated fragments from French New Criticism and a running commentary on them, Laurent LeSage, for example, has seen the French New Criticism as a defense of "textual" reading and a rejection of going beyond the text. The French New Critics, he says, insist that criticism "belongs on the inside — with the work itself and the creative personality that produced it. Biography, history, sociology belong on the outside" (*The French New Criticism*, pp.

10–11). LeSage makes this statement in the teeth of Goldmann, who has based his position on sociology, Mauron, who has based his on psychoanalysis, and Barthes, who has openly invited the use of Marxism, psychoanalysis, and existentialism into the critical practice. Picard's wrath has been directed at the ease with which Barthes has left the text of Racine's plays to indulge in irresponsible and highly subjective reasoning. One can sympathize with LeSage, however, when one considers that while Picard has accused Barthes of leaving the text and opening it up to nonliterary disciplines, Barthes has accused Picard and the old criticism of doing the same thing. Barthes is against what he has called analogical criticism, that is, the reduction of literary facts to some other order of facts, to which it is assumed the literary facts correspond. He is thinking of such familiar procedures as explaining the work by bringing it into alignment with the work of some other writer (influences), or with some item of the author's biography, or with some set of historical circumstances. The issue is further complicated by the fact that, while condemning analogical criticism, Barthes has opened up critical practice to a far-ranging set of disciplines, which we ordinarily consider to be "nonliterary."

Barthes's position is not only a challenge to Picard and the settled habits of French criticism, but also a distinct challenge to some of the habits of American criticism. When one attempts to reduce his position to being for or against the text, one runs into contradictions and one misses the point. Doubrovsky in this study does a remarkable job of digging out the assumptions and developing the implications of Barthes's and Picard's positions, as well as placing their positions in the context of contemporary French criticism. His *The New Criticism in France*, which was written in the heat of the polemics, provides the American reader with the most extensive treatment of the Picard-Barthes quarrel and the most refined analysis of the issues at stake. It is not, one must admit, a cool and dispassionate treatment of the issues. Doubrovsky has a point of view, and the book is an example of the premise he accepts from Barthes that no critical position is "neutral" or "innocent." Yet he has managed to present the basic issues in a provocative and sophisticated manner and to draw out the philosophical implications for critical thought in general. His knowledge of French literature and the French literary and critical scene is extensive and intimate, and he writes with ease and clarity about very complex matters. Although he is frankly on Barthes's side, he has some reservations about Barthes, and his own position raises some very interesting and important matters.

Doubrovsky has seen more clearly than any other commentator — French or American — that the French New Criticism has little to do with the American New Criticism. In fact, he criticizes Barthes for his tendency to gravitate to the kind of "sterile" structuralism that in Barthes's own opinion afflicted the American practice. What Doubrovsky emphasizes again and again is the human factor in criticism. "To define literature," he tells us, "is always, as we have said, to define a conception of man." And "Through the written text or the acted play, through the beauty of the words or the rigor of the construction, *a man is speaking of man to men*." He sees the French New Criticism as a reaction against the error of the American New Critics. Of the latters' position he writes: "Nothing could be more ingenuous than this conception of the work as a sort of machine for producing "effects" in obedience to recipes provided by a "technique" which it is criticism's role to formulate." His few but penetrating remarks about the relation of the French New Criticism to the American New Criticism remind us that, whatever their differences, a dialogue exists which up to now has been unspoken.

II

Barthes, like the American New Critic, is concerned with what is distinctly literary; he thinks of himself as a structuralist, he has an intense concern with poetic language, and his avowed intent is to read the text as it actually is. He is, as were the American New Critics, against the reduction of a literary work to biographical or historical correspondences. What he has to say about the futility of such procedures bears a strong resemblance to what the American New Critics had to say about the use of literary works, to use R. P. Blackmur's phrase, for "ulterior purposes," and the commission, in Cleanth Brooks's term, of "the heresy of paraphrase." He is against, as were Wimsatt and Beardsley, the reading of a work according to the conscious intentions of the author, that is, against "the intentional fallacy," and he believes, as they did, that the work does not copy the world. Its structure supports "multiple meanings" and its ambiguity is "toute pure." He even uses some of the same terms that the American New Critics have used: irony, sign and referent, suspended meaning, plurisignification, and ambiguity.

Yet he has said things that violate the most cherished assumptions of the New Critics. Men like Richards, Brooks, Blackmur, Tate, and Ransom affected powerfully our way of thinking about literature; they trained a generation of critics and teachers of literature, and that generation has trained a generation of graduate students, and if these two generations have agreed on anything, it has been on the sacredness of the text. Even those who opposed the movement or deviated from it in essential respects — critics like Winters, Burke, Crane — were just as firm in their fidelity to the text. There were many movements during the years 1930–1960, but they diverged like spokes from a hub, and what brought them together was a common and unquestioned assumption that critical discourse was a commentary about, and measured by, an objective text. They were careful to state that this commentary did not "paraphrase" the text, nor did it state the meaning in some categorical and definitive way. Blackmur's "A Critic's Job of Work" is still a masterful example of how strongly they felt about the task of criticism as a tentative, complex, and self-interrogating craft. The critic for Blackmur, like the author of a creative work, asked questions more than he answered them. Kenneth Burke, for whom Blackmur expressed admiration more than once, was a good example of the critic who raised more hares that he pursued. Despite all this, Burke, Blackmur, Brooks, Wimsatt, Crane, Winters, supporters and antagonists of New Criticism, never questioned that criticism was an act of approximating in language a work that had objective status, and that its intelligibility and worth were measured by that objectivity. The critic was looked upon as a scientist — despite the New Critical opposing of literary and scientific language — who weighed and measured an object that was ambiguous and complex. This is

6

why Stanley Edgar Hyman's frank espousal of scientific methods for criticism in *The Armed Vision* (1948) may stand as a logical tendency of American New Critical assumptions.

Every critical virtue, then, for the American New Critic had something to do with sticking to the text, and every vice with straying from the text. But for Barthes, sticking to the text is no virtue; it is an act of self-deception and even of downright dishonesty. It is so because there is no objective text; there is only the critical statement. Since no critical position is "neutral" or "innocent," each conceals an ideology. For him "the major sin in criticism is not to have an ideology but to keep quiet about it." All criticism is necessarily subjective, and the belief that the critic is elucidating an object independent of his prejudices and personality is an illusion: "How can anyone believe that a given work is an *object* independent of the psyche and personal history of the critic studying it, with rights to which he enjoys a sort of extra-territorial status?" ("Criticism as Language," *Times Literary Supplement*, 27 September 1963). Yet critics did and do believe that they are doing just that, and American New Criticism believed with a passion in the ideals of impersonal and dispassionate elucidation of an object fixed firmly and independently in the text. Some of the New Critics were aware that it was not always possible to keep oneself out of the critical process, but such subjective adulteration was something to overcome and not to encourage. Barthes, on the other hand, goes so far as to identify the critical process with subjectivity. If history can be looked on as the repository of objects and events firmly beyond our subjective tampering, then Barthes cries out sacrilegiously that history and subjectivity are the same thing.

Because there is no object apart from the consciousness that constitutes the object, the work has no prior sense that the critic discovers and explains. Rather he creates the sense, imposes, if you will, the meaning on a *vide* (vacuum or emptiness), which is Barthes's characterization of a literary work. There is no *Racine en soi*, a single Racine who waits to be discovered by some complete criticism. Racine exists in the readings of Racine, and apart from the readings there is no Racine. There is, of course, an objective text in the sense of print on a page and objective meaning in the normative and public meanings of the words. But such a conventional reading of the text is a special reading of Racine, one of many, and a bad reading at that because it is a Racine reduced to the platitudes and banalities of the age. The patient reconstruction of the meanings of the words of past works and the social and political circumstances that the words denote is a reconstruction of dead meanings; to reduce the meaning of Racine or Shakespeare to such historical reconstruction is to reduce them to the fossilizations of the past. Even more, such reconstruction, usually put forth as objective and impersonal, is just as much a choice and just as subjective and special as a critical interpretation that openly avows its special ideological position. Barthes did not deny the right of Picard to practice his reasoned and patient criticism, but he did deny that it was the only criticism exempt from ideology and subjectivity. It is because every critical position is a choice and no criticism is neutral that Barthes is able to invite the so-called ulterior disciplines to participate in the critical act. He denies positivism or neopositivism a claim to universality, and asks for a total criticism in the assemblage and complementariness of subjective criticisms. He says, "Racine lends himself to several languages: psychoanalytic, existential, tragic, psychological (others can be invented, others will be invented); none is innocent. But to acknowledge this incapacity *to tell the truth* about Racine is precisely to acknowledge, at last, the special status of literature. It lies in a paradox: literature is that ensemble of objects and rules, techniques and works, whose function in the general economy of our society is precisely to institutionalize subjectivity" (*On Racine*, pp. 171–72). Barthes is, then, at one with the American New Critics in wanting to read the literary work *immanently*, but he is very far from them in the way that he believes it can be done. For him, one must leave the work in order to return to it: "In order to have the right to defend an immanent reading of a work, one has to know logic, history, psychoanalysis; in short to return the work to literature, one has precisely to leave it and to appeal to an anthropological culture" (*Critique et vérité*, p. 37).

What is especially fascinating about his critical point of view is how it collapses the antithetical positions of the forties and the fifties in America. The Barthes-Picard feud seemed to be a feud between the historian and the critic, just as the early feuds of American New Criticism were between historians and critics. The New Critics saw the historian of literature as a reducer of literature to environmental facts — to biography, history, and political and social events — and because of this a desecrater of what was purely literary. Barthes too opposes the historian because of his analogical procedures; he and the American New Critics would seem to be in agreement on this point. Yet Barthes sees something in the historians of literature that the New Critics did not see, and what he sees collapses the opposition between them. This is why the American New Critic would be more at home with Picard than with Barthes, and why Picard in a piqued but accurate statement said that French New Criticism had nothing to do with Anglo-American New Criticism. What Barthes sees is that the traditional historian and the American New Critic shared the most fundamental of assumptions, so that their disagreement was on secondary matters and not on primary matters. Both the American New Critics and the historians of literature against whom they argued believed in the existence of an objective text, which could be elucidated by critical process. It was the objective text against which one measured the elucidation whether it was one of close reading or of referential criticism, whether intrinsic or extrinsic criticism. They both believed in the "text in itself," and if they had interpreted Racine, they would have believed with Picard in a *Racine en soi*.

One may explain Barthes's position by saying that it is a radical identification of sign and referent, for the referent is as many things as there are ways of "writing" about the sign. The American New Critic had moved in the direction of identifying the sign and the referent by his opposition to traditional historical readings of literature and his opposition to so-called referential readings of literature. He even talked of the relationship of sign and the referent in a way that seemed to imply that they were one. Brooks's paradoxical formulations of the nature of poetry as "the poem says what the poem says" is an example of such a tendency on their part. Yet the insistence of American New Criticism on the objectivity of the text and the impersonality of

9

the critical process was at odds with its tendency to move toward such an identification. No small part of our interest in contemporary French criticism and particularly of our interest in Barthes comes from the challenge that his radical statement on criticism offers to some of the theoretical problems that New Criticism in America faced in its mature formulations.

III

In a 1958 article entitled "Critics — English and French" (*Encounter* 11, July 1958), Yves Bonnefoy wrote about how little acquaintance and understanding there was between contemporary French and Anglo-American criticism and how much need there existed for such understanding. He finished the article with this wish: "One day perhaps there will be a dialogue between the two criticisms and we shall be able to see what it would be like." Such a dialogue would, I am convinced, be particularly important for American criticism today, which still has not recovered from the dominance that New Critical theory held in the forties and the fifties. American criticism today seems to be marking time, as if waiting for some new theoretical impulse. There is a growing sense that New Critical theories, especially in the way that the so-called extrinsic disciplines were drummed out of the realm of criticism, need revision if not supplanting. The summation of many of New Criticism's tenets and its shortcoming can be seen in the immensely influential *Theory of Literature* of Wellek and Warren, which still enjoys the status of a basic introduction to literary theory and the practice of criticism. The book presents itself as an objective assessment of the ways in which literature can be read; yet it takes very little discernment to see that a clear bias for a special ideological position runs through the entire work. It is a good example of Barthes's view that no criticism is neutral. Wellek and Warren have institutionalized their bias in the distinction between "extrinsic" and "intrinsic" criticism. The distinction, which has become one of the platitudes of our time, is not tenable theoretically. By what criteria can one determine that symbol and myth are intrinsic and psychology and sociology are not? The distinction served only to honor some approaches and to dishonor others, and what was dishonored is returning to claim its due in the critical process. In the general malaise that has afflicted American criticism since the theoretical demise of New Criticism, one thing seems clear: that some way must be found to bring back the so-called extrinsic disciplines into accepted critical practice. New Criticism felt strongly that poetry had to be saved from contamination from "intellectualist" disciplines; there is a sense now that criticism must be reattached to such disciplines and by such reattachment to participation once again in contemporary issues. Only psychoanalytic criticism seems capable today of fresh innovations, and a new generation of psychoanalytic critics — Frederick Crews is an example — seems to be saying something new. Yet it is testimony to the power of New Criticism that the psychoanalytic critic is often at pains to justify himself vis-à-vis New Criticism. Crews's brilliant article "Anaesthetic Criticism" (*New York Review of Books*, 26 February 1970) is an example of this dialectical dependence.

Psychoanalytic criticism is unlikely to provide the theoretical basis for taking us beyond the formalisms of the last generation. It is a special point of view, as are myth criticism, Marxism, and other forms of criticism practiced today. Barthes's position too is unlikely to provide us with the basis we need, for American criticism has its native tradition, distinct from the existential and phenomenological sources that have contributed to Barthes's views. It is unlikely that we will abandon what we learned in a generation of New Critical dominance, and likely that what comes to replace it will include it. Yet it is possible that Barthes's position and the practice of the French New Critics may provide us with a vantage point from which to examine some of our unspoken assumptions. If French New Criticism can provide us with a motive for reexamining our assumptions, it is possible that it too can learn something from a study of American New Criticism, which, whatever it shortcomings in theory, produced much excellent practice and did reeducate a generation of scholars and critics. It would be even better if the conversation Yves Bonnefoy hopes for between French and Anglo-American criticism were extended to include the criticism of other countries. Both French and Anglo-American literary establishments tend to be very enclosed upon their own traditions, and the ultimate concession

11

from either seems to be a slight and often condescending awareness of the traditions of each other. I am thinking of the immense
good that an acquaintance with Russian Formalism would do for
both. Russian Formalism came before American New Criticism,
and its astonishing development in the twenties was unfortunately
curtailed by official government action. It is still little known in
America and France. All three movements have been characterized by a desire to find a place for literature in a rapidly complicating twentieth century; all three were convinced that poetry
needed defending; and all three in a curious way pursued the
same goals, but the pursuits were based on different assumptions,
reasonings, and conclusions. All three movements may be looked
on as a search for the "poeticity" of poetry or the "literariness"
of literature. The latter term was contributed to our lexicon in
1919 by Roman Yakobson in a small book on the Russian poet
Khlebnikov. By 1921, Russian poetics was beginning its own
search for a place for literature in the twentieth century, and
in an uncanny manner it duplicated, though in anticipation, many
of the questions, procedures, and searchings of American New
Criticism in the thirties, forties, and fifties. The comparison of
these two influential and important movements is yet to be written. In a strange and oblique way, these two movements antici-
pated French New Criticism, and in a way the French New Criticism has called into question some of the shared assumptions
of American New Criticism and Russian Formalism.

IV

The aims of both American New Criticism and Russian Formalism were remarkably the same: to define for literature a basis
which would make it independent and self-sufficient. Both movements were defending poetry from similar threats, and both were
reacting to roughly similar traditions. American New Criticism
was reacting to the misuse of poetic language by a tradition of
genetic scholarship and critical impressionism; the Russian Formalists were reacting to a century of vulgar sociologizing and
several decades of symbolizing. What makes the comparison of
these two movements so fascinating is that while both were determined to define what was specifically and uniquely poetic, the

way each went about establishing the literariness of literature and the definitions they ended up with were significantly divergent. If American New Criticism had a beginning that one could pinpoint, then it would be in the publication in 1926 of I. A. Richards's *Science and Poetry*. The title itself was to become emblematic of one of the central oppositions that was to haunt American New Criticism. Science in the sense of all intellectualist disciplines was to represent for I. A. Richards and subsequently for other New Critics the main threat for poetry's continued relevance in the twentieth century. If poetry was about the world in the way that the intellectualist disciplines were a commentary on the world, then poetry could not compete very well with the rapid advance of such disciplines. It was and would be increasingly a kind of amateur or prescientific knowledge.

Richards was to defend poetry by taking it out of competition with such disciplines by showing that it was doing something else. It was a mistake, according to Richards, to look on poetry as making statements about the world and consequently seeing its function as the communication of the content of such statements. Propositions are to be found in poetry, and the form of such propositions was the same as those used in other disciplines. But such propositions were, in Richards's opinion, "pseudo-statements." A proposition properly speaking points to the world and can be verified by reference to the world. The propositions one finds in poetry do not point to the world but rather to the poet who makes the statements. They tell us something about how he "is," not how the world "is." The propositions in science and in practical language are referential; poetic propositions are not. The poem was an experience for Richards, no different in kind, in his words, than catching a trolley, eating breakfast, or going to work. But if it was no different in kind, it was different in refinement and subtlety. A poetic organism was a highly organized system of attitudes (a kind of incipient action), which by an intricate structure kept conflicting interests and attitudes in balance and prevented them from degenerating, by simplification, into practical action. The content or ideas of a poem did not have any independent or objective validity in themselves; they served the emotional interests and attitudes and in so doing were inevitably distorted by such interests. The function of poetry was not to make statements about the world or to express ideas, but to organize in a very subtle and refined way our emotional experiences. Our interests in the practical world of action were often in conflict, and the exigencies of the practical world worked almost always to make our interests and attitudes crude and simple. Good poetry was a kind of antidote to the wasteful conflict of interests and a corrective to the crude and stereotyped emotional responses that characterized our practical life. It permitted us to experience how it felt to be in the presence of highly refined, sutble, complex emotional responses, balanced and harmonized so that one interest did not cancel out another. Logical thought, and the emotions it ordered, operated to exclude one of the conflicting impulses; poetry operated to balance and reconcile them. Logic impoverished emotional life; poetry enriched it. Richards had begun by attempting to cope with a threat to poetry's use in the modern world, and he ended up in reasserting its high purpose. In this sense he was very much in the tradition of defenders of poetry like Shelley and Arnold, who, though concerned about its future, reaffirmed a high and exalted purpose for it.

Too much attention is often given to I. A. Richards's behavioristic psychological learnings and the admittedly ridiculous charts of wiggly nerve endings that are found in the appendix of his early work *The Principles of Literary Criticism*. But if one disregards this aberration, his contribution to the New Criticism was immense, and he can rightly be called the father of the movement. He had a brilliant theoretical mind, and it is possible that the movement would not have ended in theoretical muddles if his restless attention had not been turned to such things as basic English and other problems of communication. Richards had defended poetry against competition with referential disciplines by making it an experience rather than a statement, but he had won only half the battle because, though he had closed the poem to the world, he had opened it to the inner world of poet and reader, and the poem was in danger of being absorbed into some general conception of experience. The work of those who followed him was devoted to making the defense more complete: to cut off poetry not only from the world of meanings outside it but also from the inner world of the poet and reader. The practical consequence of this was to establish poetry's independence by cutting it off from the world, the poet, the reader, other poems, and theoretically even from acts of interpretation.

William Empson, with I. A. Richards's encouragement, was to convert the complex system of emotional and attitudinal signs into a verbal play of conflicting meanings. The poem was no longer a sign of conflicting interests and needs held in delicate balance, as it was for Richards, but a system of conflicting verbal impulses and ambiguities held in delicate balance. The impetus for his interesting experiments in the range of verbal ambiguity was already suggested by an incidental remark of I. A. Richards in *Practical Criticism* (1929). The following quotation from this work could almost stand as an epigraph to Empson's experiments: "No one who uses a dictionary — for other than orthographic purposes — can have escaped the shock of discovering how very far ahead of us our words often are. How subtly they already record distinctions toward which we are still groping. And many young philologists and grammarians must have indulged dreams of bringing some of this wisdom into the ordered system of science. If we could read this reflection of our minds aright, we might learn nearly as much about ourselves as we shall ever wish to know; we should certainly increase enormously our power of handling our knowledge. Many of the distinctions words convey have been arrived at and recorded by methods no single mind could apply, complex methods that are, as yet, not well understood" (*Practical Criticism*, Harvest ed., p. 208). What was unpalatable in Empson's experiments, however, was his disregard for a controlling context. Almost any meaning of the word was presumably relevant to the line of poetry. His multiplications of possible verbal ambiguities added up to an aggregate rather than a whole, to an addition rather than a system or a structure. It was for others to retain his conception of the range of ambiguities that poetic words enjoy, but to contain these ambiguities within a closed poetic context. In the later formulations of the movement, best represented in simplified form in Brooks's *The Well-Wrought Urn* (1949), the poem was looked upon as a closed context, self-sustaining and self-nurturing, a system in which the pressure of the whole and of the different parts on each other acted to bring out a range of meanings and functions and at the same time to control and restrict them.

Between Richards in 1926 and Brooks in 1949 a significant change had taken place. What Richards had established on an emotional and psychological level, Brooks — with the help of others who had come in between — was to translate onto a linguistic level. For Richards a poem was a sign of highly complex emotions, needs, interests, and attitudes organized into a meaningful system in which contradictory impulses were held in balance and which did not discharge themselves into practical action by a self-sustaining structure. Poetry was incipient action, and Burke's conception of symbolic action may have had its source in Richards's reasoning. Richards's system of complex and balanced conflicts had the same characteristics as Brooks's self-sustaining verbal structure. For Richards the highly organized system kept the attitudes from discharging (and simplifying themselves) into practical action; for Brooks the highly organized system of verbal signs and the pressures and counterpressures kept the meanings from discharging (and simplifying themselves) into practical and referential language.

Neither for Richards nor for Brooks was poetry about the world, and for neither did poetry have anything significant to do with ideas. For Richards, ideas were "the servants of our interests," and if you read poetry for its ideas, you were reading poetry badly. By the time New Criticism had reached Brooks's *The Well-Wrought Urn*, it had excluded much more than had Richards: poetry became autonomous and self-sustaining at the price of cutting itself off not only from the world but also from the poet, the reader, other poems, and literary history. In theory at least it was not even possible to speak of the poem without breaking the self-sustaining poetic context. The conception of poetry was in danger of buying purity at the price of emptiness; in theory at least, it was not even possible to speak of the poem without breaking the self-sustaining context. This dilemma is neatly summarized and puzzled over by one of the official philosophers of the movement, Murray Krieger, in the following way: "How can poetry tell us something about our world that we can learn nowhere else when for the contextualist it is not in any obvious sense referential? We have seen how great the cost of making poetry referential would be. If it were referential in the sense in which prose discourse is, then obviously what it would tell us about the world we could learn anywhere else. But if it were not referential, how could it tell us anything? If, like Richards, the contextual theorist assigns the referential to science, how, unlike Richards, can he allow poetry to have meaning?" (*The New Apologists for Poetry*, 1956, p. 192). And, "The contextual theory, then, felt by many modern critics to be utterly indispensable if they are adequately to explain their experience of poetry, would seem to carry with it many weighty burdens. Not the least of these, if one with the courage of Croce is content to follow where his theory leads, is that it denies him the right to engage in the one activity for whose sake he bothers about theorizing: the detailed technical analysis and criticism of specific works. Indeed, such a theory makes it difficult for him to see how he can even experience these works fully. But the only alternative would be to break open the context; and this, we have seen, would be at least as costly since it would end even more obviously in destroying the possibility for an aesthetic experience to be produced by the poem. Once open, the poetic context would be prey to an indiscriminate host of arbitrary meanings derived from other contexts. Poetry could no longer hold itself aloof from paraphrase; and thus, no longer free of the ordinary demands of reference, it would lose the one characteristic that could set it off from other modes of discourse" (ibid, p. 138).

V

The Russian Formalists, on the other hand, who had sought with the same determination for the self-sufficient poetic system and were as determined as the New Critics to defend poetry against its absorption or subordination to other disciplines, did not fall into the contradictions outlined by Krieger. They succeeded, in a manner of speaking, in establishing the autonomy of literature without cutting it off from the world, from other disciplines, or from history. How they were able to do so is, at least in retrospect, extremely illuminating for American critical theory. They began with a significantly different first premise. For the American New Critics the basic premise was the opposition of poetic language to referential language, a premise that pushed the movement toward further and further exclusions. Russian Formalism did not begin with any set of oppositions. One can turn for an early statement of its basic premise to an article that has been called the banner of Russian Formalism, Victor Shklovsky's "Art as Device" (1919). Art, said Shklovsky, is what is felt to be art or what is perceived to be art. The premise implied that art is not art simply because it is called art or because it appears in some conventional artistic form. Literature is not literature because it is printed as literature, because its words appear in stanzaic form, or because a certain quantity of words are published under the format of a novel. The premise also implied — and this was destined to have enormous consequences for the Formalists — that what was once felt as art need not be and indeed was not art if it no longer was felt as art. That is, a good deal of what has appeared in art and which was art at a certain point in history would not necessarily be art at a subsequent period in history. Moreover, what is not felt as art at a particular moment in literary history may be so felt at another point in history. The same work, device, element could and could not be art depending on how it is perceived at a particular and concrete point in literary history.

New Criticism tended to be occupied with defiining the nature of poetry in some permanent and unhistorical way. The best they could do with history was to pay lip service from time to time to a kind of historical scholarship as a necessary precondition of the real "job of work." The Russian Formalist view of literature as something that changes with history and which is not defined once and for all bears some resemblance to Barthes's view of the meaning of literature as something that is not fossilized in a particular historical period but is open to the interpretations of subsequent periods and the incrementations of man's knowledge. There is a bias toward the present in Barthes's position, and although there is a similar bias in the Russian Formalists' position — for the perception of form is always present perception — the definition of art for them is not tied to the general advance of knowledge. Like the American New Critics they were interested not in the meaning of the work but in specifying its aestheticizing elements. Barthes's and Doubrovsky's "total" criticism (in the sense of its connection with the whole of man's consciousness of the world) is lacking both in Russian Formalism and in American New Criticism. These movements were interested in isolating literature from other manifestations of consciousness, not in integrating them.

The proposition "art is what is felt to be art" leaves open the whole problem of the conditions under which art is felt to be art. Shklovsky made a stab at coming to terms with this important problem by putting forth two "devices" that are in some way constitutive of art: the device of "form made difficult" and the device of "defamiliarization." He had correctly perceived that we become conscious of form when our attention to it is prolonged and when we feel its opposition to something else. Poetry is a very uneconomic way of expressing something. The poet multiplies difficulties for himself; he never goes straight to the mark, but insists on indirections and the obstacles of rhyme, rhythm, meter. One of the devices, then, or group of devices by which one feels language and by which form escapes the automatism of perception and feeling is the device of prolonging and making form difficult. The other device that Shklovksy put forth as constitutive of art is that of "making strange" or "defamiliarization." We feel form when it is presented to us in a "new" and different way, when it represents a departure from a habitual manner of presentation. Perception for Shklovsky constantly becomes automatized, and we perceive or feel something when the perception is de-automatized. The function of poetry is to "de-automatize" perception. A separation of poetic language and referential language is implied in the conception of de-automatization. Automatized language is practical referential language, something that is not felt but functions automatically to carry one to the object of perception. The oppositions of practical and poetical language were never permitted to harden into the opposition that characterized New Critical thinking, because the Russian Formalists saw a constant interchange between practical and poetic language.

Although Shklovsky does not draw out these consequences, his somewhat casual and idiosyncratic and quite unsystematic remarks contain already most of the basic propositions that were to be elaborated by later Formalists. What is perhaps the most far-ranging consequence of his remarks is that there are no absolutes in the way that the Formalists will look upon art. Art is defined by no static quality or set of conditions. Everything can be art and not be art. No element — metaphor, special diction, or special device — is in itself artistic. The same device may or may not be art; it all depends on whether it is perceived to be art. But Shklovsky gives us very little clue as to what the conditions or circumstances are under which a work is perceived to be art or not art. The conception of automatization and the devices of form made difficult and the device of "defamiliarization" do not provide the answer. They identify the conditions under which a work is perceived to be one or the other, but they do not explain why the perception occurs.

It is Yakobson who provides us with a clue to what these special conditions of the perception of form are. In his small study of Khlebnikov, *The Latest Russian Poetry* (1919), he tells us that we perceive something to be artistic against the background of the reigning literary tradition, the background of the practical language of the time, and the movement of the literary tradition. Basing a definition on art as felt-form or felt-perception would seem to base the criteria of art on something subjective, but Russian Formalists are at pains to deny this, and Yakobson's three conditions make clear that it is not subjective perception but objective conditions that constitute the difference between art and non-art. Art is conceived of as a relationship between (1) the work and the tradition from which it grows, and (2) the practical linguistic circumstances in which it exists. We feel a work of art against the background of the reigning literary tradition. The same is true of the other two conditions that Yakobson set forth. This means then that we can perceive the form of the new work only as a separation from some set of norms, and in order to do this we have to perceive both the norms and the separation. This further implies that the work itself must include both the norms of the tradition and the deviation from the norms.

In Russian Formalist theory, literary history came to be looked on as a progressive wearing out of "canonized" forms; what was

20

felt to be artistic is condemned by the movement of history to wear itself out and to become inartistic. The new form defined itself by opposition or at least deviation from these reigning forms. But the new, and the artistic, did not arise in a vacuum. It is in a sense composed of the elements of the old; it is in Formalist terminology a "deformation" of the old. But such an appearance of the new includes the old, as any dialectical opposition does. This meant in practical terms literary tradition (a word that they came to reject because it was too vague) was a constitutive element of art as felt-form. It is the relationship or the tension between the two that is felt. Form is felt and hence is art against the background of form that has become inartistic, that is, automatized. The new form was spoken of as a deviation (*otklonenie*) or deformation (*deformirovanie*) of the old form. Neither word was entirely accurate, since neither expresses the most important element in the relationship, which was one of the new including the old and including it in dialectical relationship. This meant that the language and form that are felt to be artistic within a literary work — whether diction, meter, rhythm, or any other element — are artistic because both the new and the old are felt. This also means that the poet has to have a sense of the continuity of literary tradition in order to create art, and that the reader too has to have the same sense of continuity. A writer or reader who is captive of the canonized forms is condemned to repeat them, that is, condemned to repeat the automatized and inartistic forms. And the critic and reader who are captives of the canonized forms will be unable to appreciate a deviation or deformation of the old. Tynianov and others pointed out quite correctly that most vital art movements are first perceived as "errors"; because correctness is conceived of as repetition of canonized forms. A writer who has no sense of tradition, of the continuity of literary change, will be condemned to create what is abstractly new, something eccentric and possibly outlandish, but in any event inartistic because the necessary constitutive elements of art will be missing. His work will not be perceived as artistic because he will create the new without including the old, in relation to which the new can be felt. One is tempted to ask — and to my knowledge none of the Formalists did

21

so — how much tension, deviation, or deformation makes the best art. Too little distance between the old and the new will create conservative art; too much, an eccentric art. It is almost certain that no precise measure of deformation or deviation can be given, without risking unhistorical definition.

The conception of a work of art as appearing in dialectic opposition to old forms led the Russian Formalists to a conception of literary history as a dynamic and self-sufficient system. It was literature that created literature. They carried on an unremitting battle against what they called genetic conceptions of literary history, that is, the conception of nonliterary facts such as the author's life and social and cultural facts causing literary facts. In this respect they agreed with the New Critics. But unlike the New Critics they did not reject history in rejecting genetic history. History of a purely literary nature was at the very heart of their conception of literary fact, since the appearance and disappearance of artistic forms was a historical process. They were able to escape the atomism of individual works cut off from other works by their assumption that individual literary works do not exist in isolation but depend on the context from which they proceed. By rejecting the static qualities that the New Critics vainly attempted to define (paradox, ambiguity, intransitiveness), they were able to integrate the individual work in history and to make its very artisticness depend on history. Although they championed an independent and self-nurturing conception of literary history, they came to see that there existed an interchange between literary facts and such nonliterary facts as social, political, cultural, and economic facts. In this sense they seem to occupy an intermediate position between the strict contextualism of the American New Critics and the total criticism of Barthes. They were able to see a relationship between literature and things other than literature without, however, confounding the two, as the French New Critics have been charged with.

The American New Critics, following upon I. A. Richards's rejection of ideas as unimportant to the artistic process, were never able to come to terms with the obvious fact that ideas — political, sociological, and psychological — do appear in works of literature. They continued to justify the exclusion of

22

Brooks talks at times in a similar way when he speaks of the poem as warping and bending the ordinary usage of the word, but his vocabulary is vague and his remarks are casual and unsystematic.

What constitutes the specific element in the poem is duplicated on a larger scale for the whole poem, which takes on its specific character because of its relation to other poems (what is outside it) and to the literary norms of the time. The reigning literary movement is conceived of as a system too, and it takes on its specific character as a deviation from preceding literary periods. This conception of system determining system may be extended to include the whole literary order of facts, because literature conceived as a whole takes on its specific character in relationship to orders of nonliterary fact. Russian Formalism conceives of all specificity of fact as a series of mutually conditioning systems. Like relativity, there is no absolute point of reference. Everything is relative to everything else.

VI

The resemblances between American New Criticism and Russian Formalism are strong. Both movements attempted to define what is specifically literary, and both conceived of what is specificially literary as something distinct from such things as biography, sociology, philosophy, and general cultural criticism. Both refused to subordinate literary fact to these disciplines. The Russian Formalists avoided the hard oppositions of American New Criticism, conceiving of literary fact as a parallel and discrete order of facts, the specificity of which, however, depended on the conditioning of other orders of facts. There are specific contexts, but no "closed contests" in Russian Formalism.

Barthes, too, shares the view of both movements that the literary work is not explained by analogical conversion to other disciplines. He has argued against the Lansonian and positivistic procedure of explaining the literary work as an expression of the author's life and the historical circumstances surrounding the work. He has not commented on American New Criticism and Russian Formalism except in a few casual remarks, but I am convinced that if he were to comment on both movements in an informed way, he would say something similar to what he said of Picard's position. That is, he would see a strong similarity between American New Criticism and Russian Formalism and the historical and referential disciplines they were opposing. From the vantage point of Barthes's theories, American New Criticism shared in a very subtle way very basic assumptions with the kind of critical activity it so vigorously opposed during the heyday of its critical formulations. American New Criticism was doing some very different things from the historical criticism it opposed, but it was also doing the same thing.

What was this same thing? American New Criticism, for example, based itself largely on opposition to referential interpretations of literary objects, yet from the point of view of Barthes's position, one can say that it was just as referential as the criticism it condemned. Barthes gives us some intimation of this in a recent article in *Tel Quel*, in which he discusses J. Kristeva's conception of *inter-texte*: "The idea of 'inter-text' has first of all a polemical side which serves to combat the law of *context*. This is why. Everyone knows that the context of a message (its material environment) reduces multiple meanings; if you speak of *jumelles*, a word with a double meaning in the French lexicon, the rest of the sentence will have the task of eliminating one of the two possible meanings and to fix definitely the meaning of a 'double lorgnette' or twin sisters. The context restricts the meaning, or, in order to be broader and more precise at the same time, restricts it from significance to communication; 'to take into consideration' the context (in philology, criticism, linguistics) is always a positivist, reductive, legal step, aligned with the evidence of rationalism: context is, in short, an a-symbolic object" ("Réponses," *Tel Quel* 47, Autumn 1971). The quotation is significant for our purposes, because American New Criticism based its "immanent" reading of poetry largely on contextual considerations, and they opposed referential interpretations because of the violence such procedures did to the context of poems. But if one reads Brooks closely, as well as other New Critics, one will see that their procedures operate simultaneously to bring out the richness of verbal meaning and at the same time to restrict such meanings. It is precisely on the point of restriction of poetic mean-

26

ing that Barthes differs strongly with American New Criticism. For the American New Critic, not every meaning of the word was relevant, but only those meanings that the context or the pressure of context brought out. Such referential readings as psychoanalytic and social interpretations were condemned because they violated the specific context of the poem. But if we ask ourselves what exactly the measure of relevance is, that is, what exactly determines the specific context, then we come across a kind of void in the reasoning of the American New Critics. If we search very hard for hints, we are likely to come up with such an explanation: the specific function or meaning of a word in the poem depends on the pressure of the context, that is, on the other words in the poem, and not on some ready-made system or conception outside the work. All well and good. But the pressure of other words in the poem, which are supposed to shape the context and determine the range of relevant meanings of specific words, are themselves dependent on the words they are presumably delimiting. The reasoning is circular, and, in practice, the New Critics escaped this circularity by assuming a context which the poem itself could not possibly give. What they assumed, however, was not one thing: in their practical criticism, they made all kinds of assumptions about man's moral, psychological, and social being, and when they were aware that they were doing so, they justified it by underpinning their theories with recourse to such words as "taste," "sensitivity," and "intelligence," which underlay all good critical practice. These unexplained critical qualities, however, were themselves not universal and abstract qualities — although the New Critics' reference to them would seem to indicate so — but qualities and habits of particular people living at a particular historical time.

The American New Critics practiced what Barthes has called "dishonest" criticism, because they failed to acknowledge that their most basic assumptions were a matter of choice, one among many, and not in the nature of criticism itself. The context did not determine itself; they chose it. In the quotation above, Barthes points out that "contextualism" is a specific approach, which he calls positivist and rationalistic, and not the universal determinant of poetic quality that the American New Critics assumed it to be. They were choosing a sense for poetry that was based on specific ideological assumptions. These assumptions, as I have pointed out, bore striking resemblance to those of the historians of literature whom they were presumably opposing. Like them and the dogmatic ideologists whom they accused of using poetry for ulterior purposes, they assumed that a literary work existed in some objective sense prior to the critical procedures used to explain it, and they believed that the criteria by which good criticism was to be measured against bad criticism were in some way objectively in the work itself. The work for them was in a curious way univocal, even though they took their stand on the ambiguity, paradoxicality, and plurisignification of poetic language against the univocal interpretions of causal and genetic criticism. They believed that the work was "one" thing, although more complex and multiple in sense than the one thing as explained by such procedures as psychological, philosophical, and social criticism. Krieger could not, despite his tortuous reasoning and his obvious sympathy for their theories, solve their dilemma, because they were doing two contradictory things at the same time. They were saying that the poem was not about the world, and that it was about the world. If the poem was really about itself and not about the world, then its meaning could not be controlled and measured by anything outside of the linguistic signs that composed it. It is futile to assert, as Picard has done, that the linguistic signs are fixed in meaning, without admitting at the same time that that fixity is a restriction of meaning to the norms of the historical period in which it was created. And if the poem is so restricted, then it is not about itself, but is tied to a specific cultural and historical set of circumstances. That is, the poem is about something outside itself in the sense that it corresponds to something outside itself. If the poem is really about itself, that is, if it is not restricted by something outside itself — neither historical period, nor author's life, nor some set of historical antecedents — then there is no way of controlling or determining a relevant context. Barthes is correct in saying that although in practical life multiple senses are controlled by situations, in literature "no practical life exists to tell us what meaning we are supposed to give it" (*Critique et vérité*, p. 54). In "History or Literature" he says, "if the work sig-

28

nifies the world, at what level of the world are we to halt the signification? Contemporary events (the English Restoration for *Athalie*)? The political situation (the Turkish crisis of 1671 for *Mithridate*)? The current of opinion? The 'vision of the world' (Goldman)? And if the work signifies the author, the same uncertainty begins all over again: at what level of the person are we to establish the thing signified? The biographical circumstance? The emotional level? A psychology of age? An archaic psyche (Mauron)? In each case we are choosing a level less in terms of the work than of our preconceived idea of psychology of the world" (*On Racine*, p. 165).

If there is no way of determining the context, one possibility follows — and it is what Barthes opts for: all contexts are equally possible and valid. Whatever human imagination, ingenuity, intelligence can marshal is relevant. No resources of developing human intelligence and knowledge can be excluded as a possible agent of enriching the literary work. Its meaning is not ready-made, but it is to be made. Doubrovsky puts it succinctly: "The work is *still to be*, and *I make it be*." The literary work does not embody truth, but is a situation about which one makes truths. In Barthes's language, criticism is concerned with validity and not truth. He says of criticism: "It has its sanction not in truth but in its own validity and any criticism can be applied to any object" (*Essais critiques*, Paris: Seuil, 1964, p. 270). The American New Critics wanted to say what Barthes has come to say: that the sign and the referent are the same, but you can say that without contradiction only if you get rid of a preexisting object. The New Critics could not accept the referentiality of poetic meaning, but they could not accept the implications of non-referentiality. Barthes could and did. The historical criticism that New Criticism opposed and the genetic criticism that Russian Formalism opposed were historical referential systems: the meanings of literary works were controlled and measured by a specific set of historical facts. But what the New Critic opposed to this kind of referentiality was a vague, unhistorical referentiality, based ultimately on concealed assumptions about human nature.

Barthes, on the other hand, frankly accepted the unhistorical character of a work of literature. It is, as he says, an "unrealism" because there is no reality that sustains and controls it. It is not something definitely finished and hence tied to history and to the specific personality and the time that created it. Rather it is for him a *vide*, having no definite and determinable meaning, but something that can be traversed by various meanings. It is not a meaning to be discovered, but a vacuum into which meaning can be poured. One can say, without being too far wrong, that literature is for him what criticism says it is, and it takes form in the critical statement or "writing." This means that it is as many things as there are languages to describe it. There is involved in his position a rather radical identification of criticism with the creative act. Criticism creates the creative work. This may sound preposterous, especially in view of our habits of keeping a fairly rigid separation between the critical and creative act. For the American New Critic, good criticism was elucidation and not creation; the good critic effaced himself before the work. He kept his dreams, emotions, imagination, and subjective being separate from his dissecting intellect. He held unswervingly to the tradition of the humble critic and the superb creator. Barthes says of this tradition that it is a worn-out myth, and that "the writer and the critic meet under the same difficult condition, face to face with the same object: language" (*Critique et vérité*, p. 47). If *Phèdre* or *Hamlet* are not what the critics have said they are, then their significance exists somehow outside the human consciousness that has tried to understand them.

Whatever the difficulties in accepting Barthes's assumptions, and there are many, his position explains better than does American New Criticism, conventional analogical criticism, or Russian Formalism the variety of critical reactions that a great work of literature engenders. Even during the dominance of New Critical theory there was wide disagreement on how to read certain works. If a literary object has a definite form and supports a definitive meaning, then the variety of critical interpretations can be explained only as errors or, at best, approximations of truth. If there is one big truth, and different generations have read works in different ways, then there are many lies. For Barthes there is no problem in the fact that different ages have come up with different interpretations of Racine; such variety is to be expected, since different ages have found different languages and created different meanings. For Barthes, the works of Racine are growing things, as large and complex as human intelligence and writing have been able to make them. Russian Formalism, whatever its virtues, had no way of handling different interpretations of literature in different ages; the conception of automatization seemed to condemn past works to obsolescence. Barthes's position also permits him to accept various critical systems without insisting on the exclusiveness or rightness of any particular one. Even in his argument with Picard he could afford to be charitable and to accept Picard's kind of criticism as valid. He did not attack Picard's right to say what he wanted to about Racine, but he did attack Picard's claim that this was the only right way of reading Racine. What seems vulnerable about Barthes's position is, however, its openness. A work of literature seems to be everything that has been said about it. This would seem to lead one to a position in which there are no criteria by which to choose or decide between good and bad criticism. A subjective criticism would seem to be the logical consequence of the assumptions Barthes has made, and Barthes has confused the issue by frankly accepting subjectivity in criticism as the hallmark of honest criticism, without, however, adequately explaining what he means by subjectivity.

The word "subjective" is likely to evoke a number of meanings, one of which would be that one can indulge in one's idiosyncratic whims and caprices in interpreting a work of literature. Such a meaning would make of criticism a kind of self-indulgence. But Barthes has another meaning in mind: that critical processes involve human choices and that such choices entail certain consequences and responsibilities. If the work cannot impose a constraint on what one says — and it cannot because the work is what we say it is — something else can. Barthes calls this "validity" instead of "truth": one is constrained by the rules of the critical system that one has chosen. Doubrovsky is correct when he says: "Barthes does not say that anyone can say 'anything,' which would be absurd, but that the critic can say what he is saying 'in any way,' which is something quite different." One is not restricted by the meaning that work had in the period in which it was created, nor indeed by the meaning that any age gives it, nor by the meaning that any particular critical system gives it. The work is open to all the knowledge that humanity has created and is creating. This is why such ulterior disciplines as psychology, sociology, and philosophy are and are not valid critical approaches. They are valid in the use one makes of them to create new meanings of a work; they are invalid if the use of such disciplines is directed to fixing the work in one particular system. One can say anything, but one cannot say it irresponsibly. Once the choice of critical language has been made, one must obey the rules of that critical language. One must be logical and relevant, and the point of the critical language must be to create new meaning and not to repeat what is already known.

One could argue that Barthes has opted in his subjective approach for simple another kind of objectivity. The laws of validity and coherence that control the critical system he chooses are as "objective" (in the sense of holding for everyone) as the objectivity of a truth existing before the critical interpretation. He may choose the critical language but he cannot make of the critical language anything he wants it to be. The issue then is not one of saying "anything," as Picard charged, and saying something responsibly, but it is an issue of kinds of responsibility. The difference is important. What Barthes is opting for is a human, ongoing, and unlimited objectivity, and truths created by human choice and intelligence, not truths existing somehow before them. Barthes has in a sense carried forward Sartre's revolt against a priori ideas into literary criticism. Barthes' position is an assertion of human right to create meaning in literature and a rejection of the view that such meaning lies ready-made. This is what the French New Critics and specifically Doubrovsky mean by total criticism: a criticism that includes the consciousness of the human beings that read and write about literature. The object does not exist without the subject. The *je* continues to change the object with its developing consciousness and developing knowledge. We make works of literature; they do not make themselves or us. The meaning that a work of literature has is affected by and is part of the developing consciousness.

This is why Barthes can invite psychoanalysis and Marxist criticism into the critical process. He can also reject them, and there is no contradiction. Marxism and psychoanalysis, practiced as analogical disciplines, are part of the old criticism. A Marxism which conceives of the literary work as a reflection of social and economic forces that are finished and complete and a Marxism which conceives of itself as complete and finished is a Marxism that has no place in French New Criticism. Even more, a Marxism that conceives of itself as "exclusive" criticism and one that has found the truth has no place in French New Criticism. But a Marxism conceived of as a choice of critical systems, which represents in part what may be fresh and advanced in human thinking and which can project a meaning into a work of literature, is a criticism that Barthes would accept. The same can be said of psychoanalysis and other critical languages. A psychoanalytic criticism that conceives of the critical task as finished when some analogue in the literary work can be found for the topographies of Freud's system is a referential criticism. But a psychoanalytic criticism that uses the insights of Freud and others into the human psyche for interrogating the literary work and to multiply the perspectives from which we see it is a psychoanalytic criticism that has a place in French New Criticism.

VII

I suspect that, whatever value American critics find in the French New Critical "structuring consciousness" and its invitation to participation of other disciplines, French New Criticism will not find fertile ground in the United States. We can agree, as Doubrovsky puts forth eloquently, that it is man who unites all the diverse disciplines in reading a critical work, but our scientific reflexes will remain strong or rigid enough to insist that consciousness does not determine entirely the work, but that the work determines partly the consciousness. We have never in our philosophic tradition felt tempted by variations of idealism; consciousness does not determine reality for us. Determinism and behaviorism continue to exercise a strong influence on our thinking. We do feel — as I said at the beginning of this introduction — that some way must be found to break the sterile formalism of the last generation and to include the ulterior disciplines that were relegated to extrinsic relevance; but we will probably do so by broadening the context that the New Critics worked with. Barthes is right that the "context" of American New Criticism was arbitrarily restricted, but that will not prevent us from broadening it without permitting consciousness alone to decide what the context should be.

The faith that the French New Criticism has in the structuring consciousness as the arbiter of literary meaning is a continuation of the faith that contemporary French criticism and thought have had in consciousness generally. And that faith is probably a variation of the French reflex of seeing the mind as the only trustworthy instrument in human life. Our tradition is very different and probably goes back at least to British empiricism and its characterization of the mind as something of a passive vessel. We are a nation that is attached or condemned to scientism and the faith that the mind is an instrument for the analysis of given entities. Russian Formalism, if ever enough texts are adequately translated and if ever enough intelligent commentaries are produced, is likely to exercise a greater influence on American criticism than the French New Criticism. Russian Formalism combines a belief in objective literary processes and yet permits one to include the ulterior disciplines in literary criticism. The conception of parallel conceptual series among which there is a constant interchange was a late development of Russian Formalism, and many of the problems raised were not sufficiently elaborated. Such elaboration might occur in the process of adaptation to American needs. American New Criticism suffered grievously from too restricted a conception of context, and the Russian Formalist conception of parallel conceptual series is a way in which *context* can become *contexts*. Still, whatever direction American criticism goes in in the future, it will not be able to avoid the provocative and challenging assumptions of French New Criticism. It can only enrich itself by confronting them, and this translation of Doubrovsky's book may make the task easier.

BIBLIOGRAPHICAL NOTE

by Edward Wasiolek

INDISPENSABLE for understanding the quarrel between Picard and Barthes are the reading of Barthes's *On Racine*, translated by Richard Howard (New York: Hill and Wang, 1964) and most especially the essay in this work "History or Literature" and Picard's attack on *On Racine* in *New Criticism or New Fraud?* translated by Frank Towne (Seattle: Washington State University Press, 1969). Barthes's answer to Picard is to be found in *Critique et vérité* (Paris: Seuil, 1966), unavailable as yet in English. The best source for Barthes's views on a variety of critical questions is to be found in the collection *Essais critiques* (Paris: Seuil, 1964), also unavailable in English. One of the most recent sources for his views on selected questions and a general, though partisan, evaluation of his significance can be found in volume 47 of *Tel Quel* (Autumn 1971), devoted entirely to him. In English the issues and something of the emotional intensity of the quarrel can be found in the juxtaposition of articles in the 27 September 1963 issue of the *Times Literary Supplement*, Picard's "Magical Criticism"— a mordant attack on French New Criticism — in the *New Statesman* of 15 July 1966, and Barthes's "Science versus Literature" in the *Times Literary Supplement* of 28 September 1967. Two commentaries on the quarrel can also be found in the *Times Literary Supplement*: "Civil War among the Critics," a review of Picard's *New Criticism or New Fraud?* (3 February 1966), and "Crisis in Criticism" (23 June 1966), a fair and generally balanced appraisal of the stands of both men. In America one of the best appraisals of the French New Criticism is to be found in Leo

Bersani's "From Bachelard to Barthes" in the *Partisan Review* 34 (1967): 215–32. General estimates of the movement may also be found in Laurent LeSage's *The French New Criticism: An Introduction and a Sampler* (University Park: Pennsylvania State University Press, 1967), and in John K. Simon's edition of *Modern French Criticism* (Chicago: University of Chicago Press, 1972), where an introductory essay on Barthes is included by Yves Velan. One may also want to consult the following: the essay "Structuralism: From Barthes to Levi-Strauss" in Wallace Fowlie's *The French Critic, 1549–1967* (Carbondale: Southern Illinois University Press, 1968); Hugh M. Davidson, "The Critical Position of Roland Barthes," *Contemporary Literature* 9 (1968): 367–79; Gabriel Josipovici, "Structures of Truth: The Premises of the French New Criticism," *Critical Quarterly* 10 (1968): 72–88; Paul de Man's "The Crisis of Contemporary Criticism," *Arion* 6 (1967): 38–57; and Frank Towne, "The New Criticism in France," *Research Studies* 35 (March 1967).

AMERICAN NEW CRITICISM
Since American New Criticism dominated almost all critical writing in America from 1930 to 1960, any list of recommended readings must be highly selective. The works of the following writers are, however, indispensable in tracing out its development and assessing its accomplishments: Eliot, Richards, Empson, Brooks, Ransom, Blackmur, and Tate. The theoretical vein of the movement may be mined in these selective works: I. A. Richards's *Science and Poetry* (New York: Norton, 1926), *Practical Criticism* (New York: Harcourt Brace, 1929), and *The Principles of Literary Criticism* (New York: Harcourt Brace, 1925); William Empson's *Seven Types of Ambiguity* (New York: New Directions, 1935); Cleanth Brooks's *The Well-Wrought Urn* (New York: Harcourt Brace, 1947); and in the following essays: R. P. Blackmur's "A Critic's Job of Work," in *The Double Agent* (New York: Arrow, 1935); W. K. Wimsatt and Monroe C. Beardsley's "The Intentional Fallacy," in *The Verbal Icon* (Lexington: University of Kentucky Press, 1954); and Robert Penn Warren's "Pure and Impure Poetry," *Kenyon Review* (Spring 1943). Something of the pervasive

influence of the movement can be traced in Rene Wellek and Austin Warren's *Theory of Literature* (New York: Harcourt Brace, 1949); an analysis of the theoretical presuppositions of the movement may be seen in Murray Krieger's *The New Apologists for Poetry* (Minneapolis: University of Minnesota Press, 1956); and the most comprehensive history of the movement is to be found in the German work, Robert Weimann's *New Criticism* (Halle: Max Niemeyer, 1962).

RUSSIAN FORMALISM

Until recently very few Russian formalist texts were available in English. Now two anthologies are available: Lee T. Lemon and M. J. Reis, eds. and trans., *Russian Formalist Criticism* (Lincoln: University of Nebraska Press, 1969) and Ladislav Matejka and Krystyna Pomorska, eds., *Readings in Russian Poetics: Formalist and Structuralist Views* (Cambridge, Mass.: MIT Press, 1971). In addition, the following individual works are available in English: Boris Eikhenbaum, "O. Henry and the Theory of the Short Story," translated with notes and postscript by I. R. Titunik, *Michigan Slavic Contributions* (Ann Arbor: University of Michigan Press, 1968); Boris Eikhenbaum, "The Structure of Gogol's *The Overcoat*," Russian Review 22, no. 4 (October 1963): 377–99; Boris Eikhenbaum, *The Young Tolstoy*, edited by Gary Kern (Ann Arbor: Ardis Press, 1972). Critical commentary in English is still sparse. Victor Erlich's *Russian Formalism: History-Doctrine* (The Hague: Mouton, 1955) is still the most comprehensive historical and analytic introduction that we have to the movement. Other works that may be consulted are the following: A. N. Voznesensky, "Problems of Method in the Study of Literature in Russia," *Slavonic Review* 6 (1927): 168–77; Manfred Kridl, "Russian Formalism," *The American Bookman* 1 (1944): 19–30; William Harkins, "Slavic Formalist Theories in Literary Scholarship," *Word* 7 (August 1951): 177–85; Barbara Korpan, "Literary History as Style: 'The Intrinsic Historicity' of Northrop Frye and Juri Tynianov," *Pacific Coast Philology* 1 (1967); Krystyna Pomorska, *Russian Formalist Theory and Its Poetic Ambiance* (The Hague: Mouton, 1968); Ewa Thompson, *Russian Formalism and Anglo-*

37

American New Criticism (The Hague: Mouton, 1972); Frederic Jameson, *The Prison House of Language* (Princeton: Princeton University Press, 1971); C. J. G. Turner, "Tomashevsky's Literary Theory," *Symposium* 26 (Spring 1972): 67–77; and Barbara Korpan, "Juri Tynjanov and Cleanth Brooks: A Comparative Study in Russian Formalism and Anglo-American New Criticism" (Dissertation, Indiana University, 1970).

The
NEW CRITICISM
IN FRANCE

A POSTFACE BY WAY OF PREFACE

I

THERE has been a great deal of anxiety expressed recently over the state of criticism, and by a curious paradox this austere and academic discipline is now arousing infinitely stronger passions than the fate of the novel or of poetry. One might well feel astonishment, at first glance, that the "Barthes-Picard affair" should have produced such a tremendous stir in a reading public that normally shows no interest whatever in another work about Racine, however good or bad. Indeed, before reading Barthes's last book, *Critique et vérité*, at a time when I was just finishing my own, I had not myself really grasped the extent and the violence of this collective storm of vituperation; for as Barthes himself observes, "the striking thing about the attacks recently made upon the new criticism is their immediately and, as it were, naturally collective nature. One senses something stark and primitive stirring in this reaction. It is as though one were watching some savage rite in a primitive community, aimed at the expulsion of a dangerous member. Hence a strange vocabulary of *execution*. The new critic's opponents dream of *wounding* him, of *blowing him up*, of *beating* and *slaughtering* him, of dragging him before the *judge*, to the *pillory*, to the *scaffold*. Some vital spot has obviously been touched." What is it? Barthes's reply makes it clear: the new critic has broken certain taboos by undermining the settled order of our language. Let us pause for a moment to consider this point.

Barthes is quite right. In a country such as ours, which as we all know is "Cartesian," language and literature must necessarily

41

be the literature and language of "reason." It is only too well known also that our admirable "clarity" is in fact indivisible from our no less admirable "classicism," and that "clarity" and "classicism" together constitute the two prime "French" virtues. Nisard and Maurras both expended great energy reiterating these facts, the first to rebut the romantics, the second to refute the symbolists. And now Picard has brought these venerable truths out of the Holy of Holies once again in order to blast the "new criticism," which he oddly associates in the process with Rimbaud, with Dada, and with surrealism. Nothing could be more longstanding then, that much is clear, than this literary battle, which at its primary level — by which I mean its fundamental level — is a battle about words. We find the adversaries of Barthes and his fellow new critics reiterating the same complaint again and again: they aren't "clear," they employ a "jargon," they won't say things "simply," they "complicate" everything, in particular Racine, who is really so simple. This anxiety is extremely well founded: if we don't keep a watch on our words there's no knowing what they'll get up to. They might end up affecting our ideas. And that is the crux of the drama.

When Hugo thought he was starting a revolution, he began by expressing the wish to "clap a Phrygian cap on the old dictionaries." And in practice the great breakthrough achieved by modern literature, from Rimbaud and Mallarmé to Proust and Breton, let alone Céline or Beckett, was only achieved at the expense of a tremendous assault on the conventional language that we at some time christened "classical," no doubt in order to raise it to the status of a hereditary aristocracy. But to do that to a language is to corrupt it. There are good historical reasons for the constitution of a certain form of language in the seventeenth century; but the wish to preserve an impoverished and stereotyped idiom intact in the twentieth century can derive solely from an idolatrous pseudoreligion. To love one's mother tongue, certainly, nothing could be more admirable; to wish to perpetuate its excellence, nothing more laudable. But when that love is transformed into necrophilia and that excellence becomes confused with mere conventions, then nothing can be more suspect. The "clarity" of a language is not an innate and immutable thing;

it evolves in relation to the norms imposed by developments in the culture that produces it. Its categories, and therefore its words, change. It is just not feasible to prevent changes in men's thought by trying to freeze their vocabulary in the good old days of Littré. The way in which one section of the critics and the bourgeois reading public coddles, coaxes, cotton-wraps this phony "clarity" of a frozen and Malthusian language, as though the French tongue were an ailing old lady to whom the slightest neologism might prove fatal, is purely and simply a reactionary attitude, on the political as well as on the cultural level. What "good" society sees — and admires — in the clichés of its language is its own reflection, the pledge of an eternal hierarchy of truths and values. Richelieu knew what he was doing when he created the Académie: absolute order in a nation must first be imposed upon words if it is ever to be imposed on men's minds. Valéry waxes ecstatic over the ordered beauty of classical style and thought; he lauds the beneficent constraint imposed by their rules, which alone as he sees it can guarantee poetic freedom, and then he ends up admiring Salazar. We all know about that. And it makes it easier to understand the transgression committed by "the progressist Barthes", as one of his detractors significantly refers to him.

But surely, you will say, the revolution in our language, mirroring the profound upheavals in the relations between man and the world in our time, has already happened: in the sciences, in the arts, in literature itself. After all, Taste, Tradition, Order, Clarity, all those battered old myths, those musty slogans, have long since been given the push in the novel, in poetry, in modern plays. There are doubtless people who still feel a nostalgia for Henri Bordeaux, or loyal fans of dear old Marcel Achard, but do they count, other than on a purely numerical level? And you would be perfectly right. So here is the problem: why should people with perfectly good heads on their shoulders, people who greet the work of Robbe-Grillet with evident sympathy, recoil with horror when faced with Barthes, who is merely carrying out in his own domain the selfsame process of reexamination that Robbe-Grillet has already carried out in his? In short, why all this hullabaloo about literary criticism, and why now?

43

Criticism is an inoffensive and distant activity only on the surface. In reality it is the machinery of censorship, the ultimate policing force that a society produces as a means of keeping strict watch on the expression of thought within it and ensuring the preservation of its values. Traditional criticism does its level best to perform this double function to society's satisfaction. Where the past is concerned it keeps the lists up to date and the collection dusted, writes out labels, generally keeps the national heritage in good repair, safe behind glass. As to the present, needless to say, under a democratic regime it does not actually censor, it informs; it keeps the public "up to date," as they say, with what is happening elsewhere: in literature, in the arts, in philosophy. New or in the past, the fundamental protest that any work of art must be, always takes place *elsewhere* than within the realm of criticism. Assimilated, digested by the "clarity" of a savorless and immutable language, even the most revolutionary undertakings of yesterday or today are dismantled, disarmed; their explosive charges are defused. They are kept at a distance. Barthes dared to speak of "sexuality" in Racine's plays, like some madman actually mentioning legs in the presence of Queen Victoria; Picard replies that Racine's theater is "violent, but modest." We breathe again. Nor is his cliché ineffective, because in everday language in France "modesty" is the antonym of "sexuality"; as long as it is repressed, in other words, sexuality *does not exist.* It would be hard to find a more naïve revelation of the glaringly signposted deceit inherent in pre-Freudian language. At the other extreme, Robbe-Grillet is reduced to an obsession with things; Ionesco to oneiric ravings, and Le Clézio to heaven knows what; but all catalogued, neatly inserted into acceptable commonplaces, and therefore henceforward inoffensive. So that now, if you happen to feel like it, you can go ahead and read them yourself. You know what you have to expect. The Absurd, once it has been suitably translated, becomes clarity itself. Because traditional criticism in every sphere — conforming to the essential role laid down for it by society — is simply a vast machine for translating the original into the banal. And to this end it has at its disposal a perfectly devised tool: that sacrosanct "belle langue française" in which the the stakes were down long ago, the dice fixed, and all human relations established for all eternity by Vaugelas and Littré. Criticism does, then, inform the public. But as long as it remains itself uninvolved, as long as it gives back to that public its own language, it protects the public; the reader is vaccinated against the shock of too brutal a collision with the work itself. It is understandable why criticism clings so tenaciously to this precious tool, and a large section of the public with it. "The age of the fundamental is beginning again," one of Malraux's characters said in the midst of the Spanish Civil War. In our affluent age, as long as the old criticism holds its ground, nothing fundamental has even the slightest chance of beginning.

So it is easy enough to see in what way Roland Barthes and the "new criticism" generally are, to use Raymond Picard's revelatory word, "dangerous." They are violating a double taboo. Or, if you prefer, they are storming two Bastilles at a single stroke. On the one hand they have suddenly dared to lay hands on Racine, that last bastion of clarity, the last symbol of classical grandeur; they have dared to blow the dust off that belaureled and decrepit author; they have broken and entered a jealously guarded hunting preserve. And on the other hand they have begun to reexamine the meaning of the critical act itself, to say nothing of denouncing the traditional method of performing it. With the bursting of this double safety lock, with the breaching of this dam, everything else is bound to go down too. They have begun leaping without warning from the seventeenth or the nineteenth century right into the middle of the twentieth. And suddenly we are being asked to question or defend the worth of this language of ours, which we used to handle with such intrepid confidence. It has become impossible henceforth to speak of literature without having probed thoroughly into the language we use; impossible to ask questions about our language without first becoming familiar with the findings of linguistics and psychoanalysis; and impossible to make use of such findings without first integrating them into a total philosophy of man. Ultimately, then, it is the ready-made conception of what man is, as historically constituted and laid down in our everyday language, that is tottering. Common sense, natural truths, psychology — everything is sliding into the abyss. The result, in

45

short, is "madness," which is to say a new reason attempting to establish itself. The collective hysteria, the mob fury crying out for Roland Barthes to be burned, to be pilloried, to be beheaded, is quite simply that phenomenon met with in any age: hatred of the Intellectual who questions the foundation of our intellectual comfort. It is the revolt of the small-time wielders of pen and thought, a cultural Poujadism. They are appalled to discover that in order to write about Racine nowadays it is no longer sufficient just to lay hand on heart and exclaim "Ah, how beautiful, how noble!" That it is no longer sufficient merely to know the rules of seventeenth-century tragedy, and with whom Racine slept and for how long. That the history of literature is no longer merely a series of heartwarming or titillating anecdotes. That in order to understand Racine you must be able to confront a total conception of what man is — our own conception — with another total conception of man — Racine's; and that obligatory though it undoubtedly is to be familiar with seventeenth-century culture, it is no less necessary to be deeply imbued with that of the twentieth. And what in fact characterizes the culture of our day is precisely the profound revolution it has undergone: the image of man can no longer be provided by the traditional humanities and "classical" thought. Innumerable human sciences have now emerged; philosophy, as a consequence of Husserl's work, has changed its face and turned itself bodily toward the elucidation of the concrete, abandoning the philosophy of the great systems. Our culture, while assuming the past in its totality (which is why Barthes concerns himself with Racine), has become anthropological; it is now the locus of a confrontation between the human sciences and the philosophies of existence, between which Merleau-Ponty succeeded in outlining a possible reconciliation and synthesis.

The understanding of literature ought likewise to move forward into the twentieth century. We need express no astonishment that some people are indignant at this suggestion or yell "mad fools," that they outdo one another in twittering "Patience-Modesty-Prudence"; such intellectual conservatism is no more than a pitiable rearguard action. By patience they mean marching on the spot; by modesty, mediocrity; by prudence, paralysis. It

46

is not difficult to imagine the gnashing of teeth that is going on among the already established who intend to turn their high places into fortified dugouts: culture as they know it must now be largely rethought. The teacher is going to have to go back to school himself. In the study of literature, as in the sciences, the need is for a total reorientation, a complete retraining program. But where the genuine modesty of the scientist accepts the need for perpetual rethinking, the feigned modesty of our "humanists" is intended above all as an excuse for their laziness and an apology for their ignorance. And opposing forces, God be praised, exist. A group of young university teachers, all assistants or master-assistants, and members of a variety of faculties, recently demanded that the teaching of individual disciplines should not be turned in on itself, as is the case now, but that it should on the contrary be adapted to contemporary realities: "The more recent disciplines (Sociology, Psychoanalysis, Linguistics, modern Logic, not to mention the Science of Education, a very old discipline still unknown in our universities) should be strengthened, the programs given a face lift . . . , each discipline situated within contemporary perspectives" (*Le Monde* 6–7 March 1966). It could not be better put, and what is called the "new criticism" in France is nothing other than a first step in the application of this program to the field of literature. There are those who would prefer to put the lid firmly back on and screw it down even tighter. But they should take care: their pressure cooker will eventually explode.

II

One thing is clearly apparent: the debate "for or against" the new criticism is *already out of date*, in exactly the same way as arguments "for or against" jazz, abstract art, serial music, or the "new novel." When a new form of thought exists (and modern criticism in its most outstanding manifestations certainly does), is is absurd and futile to contest its existence in the name of outworn intellectual habits. If one is not satisfied with it, then it is of course proper to discuss it, to make improvements in it, even to attack it outright — but from within, by transcending it, not simply by trying to deny its existence. Pollock or Mondriaan are certainly not the last word in the history of painting, and it is perfectly licit to desire a return to representational paintings, but only if those paintings take Pollock's and Mondriaan's experience into account, not if they are mere neo-Courbets. There is always plenty to be learned and everything to be gained by any reexamination buttressed with solid arguments. Formulated with even a minimal understanding of what are new, still tentative researches, Raymond Picard's remonstrances would have been profitable; everything in what he says is not untrue. But his manner of saying it is at once so dogmatic and so superficial that it destroys the cogency of some of his observations and the accuracy of some of his intuitions. Like any attempt at innovation, today's criticism gives rise to numerous objections; it lays itself open to a great deal of criticism itself. A *criticism of criticism* is precisely what we need. But instead of that Picard has instituted a trial, on the grandest scale and with a maximum of pomp and circumstance; his verdict is a blanket affair, he sets himself up as Common Sense in person, as Reason, as the University, and almost as la France, whose reputation Roland Barthes has apparently tarnished abroad by the publication of "more or less defamatory" texts (*Nouvelle critique ou nouvelle imposture*, p. 84). What one would have liked was an acute, a zealous analysis certainly, but a serious one; what one gets is a maximum of facile sarcasms and self-righteous expressions of indignation together with a minimum of arguments. Having little ballast in the way of ideas, Picard naturally approaches the subject lightly. And the result, needless to say, is both titillating and comforting, it has entertained and stirred up a whole pack of prematurely aged literary hounds. But can anyone believe that this provender is going to satisfy the needs of the new generations of students who live firmly in their own times, and who require an understanding of the world in keeping with their own epoch?

A reply had to be made to Raymond Picard's pamphlet, and to the subsequent wave of idiocies for which Picard himself, it is true, cannot be held personally responsible, but which the style of his discussion nevertheless encouraged. What is at stake here matters. And the need for such a reply was all the greater in that the "new critics" have in the event kept strangely mute, allow-ing Barthes alone to take the full brunt of a storm that was intended, as I perceive even more clearly now, to sweep all of them away en bloc. For my own part I put no faith in the value of silent scorn or indifference; nor, on many points, do I share the ideas and attitudes of Roland Barthes. But since he has taken the blows intended for us all, since both challenge and anathema were aimed, through him, at each and every one of the inquiring minds who are attempting to fight their way out of the old ruts, someone had to roll up his shirt sleeves, someone had to get down to the task of replying. But not on the same level. This literary squabble, doomed in advance to be of no more than mere historical interest (for despite this noisy diversionary hullabaloo, modern criticism will undoubtedly hold to its course), had somehow to be raised into a true debate, an exchange of ideas. A literary dispute had to be transformed into an examination of conscience, polemics into reasoned confrontation.

The present work is thus quite simply a long and general questioning of contemporary critical attitudes: such a contestation must either be rigorous, systematic, and universal, or else without interest. "To answer Picard" thus meant also answering myself. It was not a matter merely of counterattacking but also of self-examination, of attempting to provide an echo to that question Sartre once so radically posed — *What is literature?* — by asking myself honestly, and without fear or favor (to the "new critics" any more than to the others): *What is criticism?* The two questions are clearly linked; indeed, they are the same question but approached from two different aspects: that of creation and that of interpretation. To examine the status of criticism was thus the same thing, from another angle, as questioning the status of literature itself. Since Sartre's famous book, much water has flowed under many bridges. We seem to be a long way these days from "engaged writing." But that is an illusion. Attempting to "disengage" literature merely means looking for a way of engaging it in some past time. What has been discovered since Sartre, and can never now be forgotten, is *the profound engagement constituted by any act of writing*. The ferocity with which certain young cubs continue to worry at the old lion is in itself sufficient proof that the questions he posed were the right ones, since they still continue to haunt these young adversaries so vainly attempting to shake them off. Criticism is also a form of writing: in what way, and in what, does it engage us? And what is ultimately at question in its questions?

The bent of this inquiry must by now be clear enough: there is no question whatever of establishing a "present state of criticism," of painting a total picture, of achieving a panoramic view of all the present currents in literary criticism. In a word, my undertaking is epistemological, not historical in nature. If literature is an expression of man in written works, what is the meaning of that expression? What exactly is this "literary meaning" that every critic strives to grasp, and that traditional criticism has attacked the new for violating? And that meaning once established, what means has criticism at its disposal for defining it and, in the scientist's sense, isolating it? What *type of understanding*, what *model of intelligibility* can it legitimately propose for itself? It is these models, these types of understanding that I have successively attempted to examine, using examples that are not intended to be exhaustive but that seem to me particularly representative. Certain names, some of them celebrated, will fail to appear in the roll call; once again, it has not been my intention to compile either a catalogue or a portrait gallery. The result is rather a process of valuation, of "assaying": what is the *value* of the joint conception of literary creation and critical act we are offered by each of the principal schools of contemporary thought? These latter fall into two distinct groups, though the division is not so much a matter of their adherence to "new" or "old" criticism (it is time we put that controversy behind us) as the notion they have of a work of literature. The types of criticism studied in this first volume view a literary work as a particular *object*, and as falling in consequence within the scope of an objective type of elucidation, based upon appropriate techniques: traditional forms of historical, psychological, and aesthetic analysis; or, more recently, with the remarkable development of the human sciences, psychoanalytical, sociological, linguistic, structuralist approaches, etc. Without for a moment denying the decisive contribution made by these various disciplines, is it possible for them, either all together or each one separately, to provide the principle of critical decipherment or, which comes to the same thing, of literary comprehension? My reply is no. I have explained why in detail; and since any criticism is always made from a certain point of view (even those that think of themselves as "objective"), I have explained mine, as clearly and radically as possible, in the portion of this book devoted to what I have called the "critical cogito" and "existential psychoanalysis." In the fundamental confrontation of our day between anthropological culture and philosophical culture I believe that the second alone is able to provide the principle for a unitary comprehension of man, since it subsumes the first, whereas the converse cannot be said. If man is not, ultimately, an object for man but a *subject*, then the literary work is a false object; it is the cipher for a subjective existence which should be interpreted as such, beyond or before the exterior signs, within the perspective of a true philosophy of subjectivity. We shall see these "subjective criticisms" in action in a later volume. But that does not mean we shall be out of the wood, by any means; there will be plenty of difficulties. The controversy still goes on.

A last word on the nature and goal of this controversy. The very essence of the problems implied by this analysis leads us into the realm of philosophical reflection: there is no way of avoiding it if we do not wish to remain on the level of mere gossip and chatter. I have done my very best to be as clear as possible, for I love clarity as much as any man, but clarity must not be confused with truisms when we are faced with questions as complex and difficult as these. Even with this aim of maximum communication ceaselessly present in my mind, there are passages in this book that will appear arduous to some who lack the necessary training. It is a great error to suppose that one can just wander into literature at will. Attempting this autocriticism of criticism has inevitably led me to confront the great currents of contemporary thought: Marxism, structuralism, Freudism, existentialism. On each occasion I have taken up a specific position in my own name, and this engagement of criticism, for which I am here asserting the need, engages no one but myself. I have received orders from no one, and least of all from the "new criticism," which certainly does not exist as a school. But the proverb says that a cat may look at a king: I have taken advantage of that right and looked hard at an activity I have myself practiced in the past, in the conviction that a systematically conducted exploration of such a kind is always profitable to all. And, strange to relate, I have often been obliged to hack my path through virgin jungle. Because although there do of course exist a great many theories and an extensive history of criticism in France (of which Roger Fayolle has recently provided us with a succinct and very timely account), there is no modern body of fundamental research comparable to that which exists in the field of Anglo-American literature. The New Criticism there preceded the French "new criticism" by twenty years. Moreover, it seems incredible that the works of such men as Leo Spitzer, Auerbach, or René Wellek are still awaiting French translations. Insularity often lurks where one might least expect it. Be that as it may, it is within his own cultural context that the French critic ought to seek and find his own paths: What is a "specifically literary" expression or structure? What does "comprehending" or "explaining" a text mean? What is the relation between the writer and his work, between the critic and the writer, between the reader and either the writer or the critic? And what is it to write, to read, to criticize? These are all essential problems that confront literary criticism with questions of deontology as well as methodology, problems that involve theoretical reflection not merely upon literature but even upon the process of teaching it; yet it is remarkable how narrowly and repetitively they have been dealt with up till now, with hardly any attempt to face them squarely, or examine them with any scope or rigor within a framework of contemporary thought.

This book, written in five months, in the heat of a literary battle, cannot claim to exhaust a subject that would require five years of methodical reflection in calm and solitude. The intention is to open a debate — but at the necessary level. That there are gaps, prejudices, and inadequacies in the work is glaringly obvious. Research into the different realms of symbolism — scientific, imaginative, linguistic — and their relationship to each other, is in its infancy. And today we sadly lack a mind of Merleau-Ponty's caliber, one capable of drawing these diverse areas of knowledge together into a unified field of comprehension. In the time at my disposal, and within the limits of my capacities, I have done all I could — not, needless to say, to resolve, but at least to *pose* the problems in a coherent and systematic way. I have tried, at all events, to produce an honest piece of work. And the proof is that there will certainly be some who will find weapons in this work, written in defense of the new criticism, to turn against that criticism. So much the worse for them. My aim was not to announce to the world that everything in the new criticism is perfection, to indulge in mutual congratulations and exchange laudatory paeans. I was concerned with facing up to the very real contradictions that exist and with taking on a responsibility for them, while also demonstrating that despite all its defects the new criticism is nevertheless opening up as yet undiscovered horizons for us, whereas the old criticism, despite all its virtues, is merely turning its eyes in vain toward the past.

I have spared no one's feelings and do not expect my own to be spared: all I ask is that my arguments be met with other arguments, my thought with thought of even greater rigor and precision. A book written to challenge is also written to be challenged in its turn. If this long stocktaking of mine engenders others that conflict with it, then far from complaining I shall congratulate myself on having attained my goal. Each alone; each against the other; and all together: such, in the domain of thought, is the essential condition of progress.

Part One
THE BATTLE BETWEEN OLD AND NEW

1
AIMEZ-VOUS
BARTHES . . . ?

TELL me whom you like and I'll tell you what you are. Posed in comminatory tones, Raymond Picard's question in his recent pamphlet *Nouvelle critique ou nouvelle imposture* (Paris: Pauvert, 1965) is being used at the moment, on the above principle, to tell the goodies from the baddies in what is now by general agreement called the "battle of the new criticism," which has rapidly evolved, in practice, into a battle between the Old and the New. Raymond Picard first attacked Roland Barthes, in the name of France's universities, in the columns of *Le Monde* on 14 March 1964, thereby unleashing the first phase of hostilities, already ferociously arustle with letters and counterletters. But with the publication of this pamphlet a state of total war has been reached. Not a week passes without broadsides from both parties being fired in magazine interviews; bursts of deafening and vengeful indignation disturb the pages of our dailies; in short, each side is trying to blast the other into oblivion. Naturally, when personalities are involved whose talent (or position) is sufficient to lend them a measure of celebrity, it is in the interest of the press to keep affairs of this sort well stirred up: it is good both for sales and for a laugh. Molière was aware long ago of the comic possibilities of pedants' slashing away at one another in barbaric fury, and Ionesco recently mined the same vein in his *Impromptu de l'Alma*. However, it would be an error to interpret all this "sound and fury" as no more than the squabbles of a Trissotin-Picard and a Vadius-Barthes about Racine, cleverly milked and magnified for the greater amusement of the audience and the

greater profit of publishers and printers. We must not let ourselves be fooled: we are in the presence of a considerable cultural
phenomenon in which the quarrels of the individuals concerned
are far transcended by the collective ideological crystallizations
they have brought about. I have already referred to those. For
the moment, let us get straight to the heart of the argument.
What is it all about? Nothing less than the way in which we understand literature. It is easy to see why such an argument, which,
over and above any intellectual affirmations made, also involves
the entire personality, is soon going to stir up men's passions.
Defining literature, both for society and for the individuals constituting it, is an opportunity for self-judgment. Our age, less
stable than previous ones, is familiar with these periodic revalua-
tions, of which Sartre's *Qu'est-ce que la littérature?* (1948) and
Barthes's *Le Degré zéro de l'écriture* (1953) constitute the principal
milestones. But why this new flare-up?

Although it involves the question of understanding what literature is, in this case it is with the particular purpose of deciding
how to teach it. Picard is posing the same question that Sartre
has already posed as a writer and Barthes as a critic, but he is
posing it as a teacher. Hence the particular turn the present dispute has taken and the specific cause of its virulence. This dispute
between teachers is above all a dispute about teaching; that alone
is sufficient indication of its scope, at a moment when teaching
in our society (and in all others) is going through a major crisis,
is in fact being confronted with the duty of resolving — radically
and painfully — the whole problem of its own immediate
methods and culture's ultimate goals. Moreover, the very changes
taking place within the disciplines are a governing factor in their
instructional methods. Thus we find a great deal of fuss going
on at the moment, in the United States, over the recent introduction into secondary schools of the New Math., which involves
making use from the very outset of the latest advances in knowledge, and stands all the old ideas on their heads by starting at
the end instead of the beginning. Is there then a "new criticism"
in the sense in which there is a New Mathematics? That would
be going too far. It would be truer to say that there is a "new
criticism" in the sense that there is a "new novel," a formula that

lies halfway between legitimate recognition of innovation and a pure advertising slogan — to be taken at all events with a grain of salt. What we ought to speak of, as Jean Starobinski has done, is "new directions in critical research," directions that are themselves often contradictory. (See Starobinski's "Les Directions nouvelles de la recherche critique," *Preuves*, June 1965 — an illuminating and accurate piece of work that should be read, and from which I shall take pleasure in quoting.) It would seem, however, despite these disparities, that these new directions possess sufficient cohesion and a broad enough relevance to have influenced a large section of the reading public, and have in consequence obliged the adherents of traditional criticism to react by mounting a crusade against "new criticism" as a whole.

For the crusade was in fact a reaction, or, if you prefer, a counterattack, since, to be honest, it must be said that the first missiles seem to have issued from the Modern camp, immediately precipitating a devastating barrage in return. Raymond Picard accuses the new "school" of "assuming an existence based solely upon opposition," of possessing "a reality more polemical than intellectual" (*Nouvelle critique*, p. 10). And it is true, since Roland Barthes, for example, does distinguish between "university criticism" and "ideological criticism" in no uncertain terms ("Les Deux Critiques," in *Essais critiques*, Paris: Seuil, 1964). But since Picard immediately adds that this university criticism does not exist, that it is merely a figment invented to bolster up a bad argument, we are then at a loss to understand what exactly recent criticism is in fact opposed *to*, or in what way, or even what meaning there can be in an argument that ultimately seems to dismiss both "university criticism" and "new criticism" as equally factitious creations. Let us try to clear this problem up. If by "university criticism" we mean some uniform and invariably applied method, with no room for the slightest diversity or divergence of views, then clearly Picard is quite right, and there is indeed no such thing as a "university criticism." It would be better to leave the notion of "Lansonism" out of it altogether, in the first place because Lanson was and still is a sound scholar,[1] in no way responsible for the excesses of his followers, and second because, until now at least, our universities have never, God be thanked, either proposed or imposed any single doctrine that could be condensed into an "-ism" of any kind. That said, is everything in Barthes's observations false? It is difficult to see how our universities could evade the general rule; how the superstructure of ideology could fail to have a dominant, if not dominating, orientation within a society that is itself so strongly structured. In short, though there exist divergences within the university world, they exist within a certain total convergence or, if you prefer, within a certain tradition. Taken in this way, not as a doctrine but as a state of mind, there does without doubt exist a tradition of literary teaching and critical research within the French universities (a simple statistical examination of the doctorate theses written since the beginning of the century would provide ample proof of that). This tradition, although it comprises very many diverse points of application, is founded first and foremost on a historical knowledge of literature which is in fact termed "literary history." We must be careful not to oversimplify. Literary history is itself multiform; it includes biographical analysis, lexicographical analysis, the study of the genres and sources, and, more recently, detailed examinations of the evolution of literary techniques. Side by side with those who seem to be more interested in the authors than in their works, and in the context rather than the text, there are others, such as Raymond Picard, who justifiably affirm the absolute primacy of the work in relation to the event, and of aesthetic values in relation to historical meaning. No one is about to dispute the validity and the necessity of these researches in their rightful and essential domain. Though necessary, this traditional approach, erudite or at all events empirical in general tendency, has nevertheless shown itself to be insufficient in practice. Not, I must add, by virtue of some mysterious perversity of soul among zealots of novelty at any price, but as the result of developments in contemporary history itself and under the influence of the new problems that the human mind faces today.

Perfectly aligned as it is with the ideological values that dominated the late nineteenth and early twentieth centuries (reason, science, metaphysical and psychological positivism), the traditional criticism, when considered not as a point of departure but as the goal of research, not as a preliminary form of investigation but as an ultimate language, is today nothing more than an outdated form of thought, lost and out of place in the second half of the twentieth century, maintained in existenced solely by inertia, which is as much a property of intellectual structures as of material bodies. Still, it would be false to conclude from this that the "new criticism" is therefore "anti-university," for the very good reason that those now atempting to practice it are themselves members of the university world. Indeed, one of the most striking features of the whole affair is that men like Roland Barthes, Lucien Goldmann, Georges Poulet, Jean Starobinski, or Jean-Pierre Richard, to name only a few, follow the same vocation and profession as Raymond Picard himself. So that if this is in fact a "war between critics," it can be nothing other than a civil war. Far from being a weapon hurled against the University, the new criticism — for we must begin using this rather vague, ambitious, but convenient term without quotation marks — was born of the desire, among certain university teachers, to bring their researches into harmony with their age; hence the hostility of so many of their colleagues. For a strange time lag had in fact appeared between the academicism of our literary teaching methods and the activities of living literature. In the seventeenth century, the preoccupations of the critics and of the dramatists and poets were the same. In the twentieth, on the other hand, it would be difficult to imagine that Mornet was a contemporary of Proust or Joyce. And it is not possible to live perpetually lagging behind one's own times, even inside the protective enclosure of the Sorbonne. So it was within the Sorbonne itself that literature, having been constituted as a mythology with Joyce and Kafka, produced with Bachelard a criticism based on the myth. How then could it be expected that writing itself, conceived of since Mallarmé as a radical controversy of language, would not eventually be subjected, as it was with Blanchot, to a total critical reexamination? How can anyone be surprised that the total revolution in man's knowledge achieved by Freud and the various other branches of psychology have awakened answering echoes in the existential analysis of Sartre, or in the thematic analysis of J. Starobinski or J.-P. Richard? Even someone determined not to budge an inch from the terrain of history itself, indeed the

terrain of purely literary history, must be hard pressed to go
on pretending that Marx does not exist, to go on thinking of
the history of literature as a mysterious succession of works and
authors, connected in the textbooks by the merest chronological
thread like the beads on a rosary, cut off from the contradictions
and real struggles of their age. In short, the new criticism, with
all its obvious divergencies of viewpoint, all its self-evident disparities, is no more than the long delayed emergence of academic
research into the modern world.

One may well feel astonishment therefore, at first glance, that
a man as intelligent and cultured as Raymond Picard should suddenly hurl his anathema at *all* new criticism, treating it as an
all-or-nothing package deal, refusing to make even the slightest
distinctions. For this new criticism, in which Raymond Picard is
just able to make out a few doomed and erring talents, is in reality
Sartre, and Bachelard, and Blanchot, and Poulet — in fact, not
to mince matters, everyone who counts at all, over a period of
thirty years, in the great struggle to renew French thought. Would
one need to scratch very deep to discover that the mortal enemies
of the new criticism frequently have little more affection for the
new novel? And one might wager with advantage that they are
not so crazy about today's poetry or plays either. Impostors? Of
course, in the eyes of all right-thinking people in West and East,
that is what abstract painters and concrete composers always have
been and still are. In short, for certain professional humanists
traditionally one culture behind, the way France tends to be
always one war behind, the Republic is always more magnificent
under the Empire, and Papa's tastes in art and philosophy are
always to be preferred. We know all that. But we also know that
militant misoneism does not pay in the end, and Raymond Picard
must be a man of some courage to give himself over to it so
wholeheartedly, considering the fate that history usually reserves
for the Nisards and Doumics. But, the traditionalists will say, are
we obliged to like what is new if it is not reasonable, or what
is original if it is bad? True enough: we can only pass judgment
case by case. So the observations I have been making are in no
way intended as a reply, only as a prelude. It is now time to
answer the prosecution's imperious question, hurled like some

thunderous aside into the wings: ". . . How far ought the intellectual solidarity, so complacently proclaimed by the adherents of the new criticism, to be taken into account here: do they feel themselves engaged collectively by *Sur Racine*? Do they all recognize themselves in it? One would dearly like to know" (*Nouvelle critique*, pp. 86–87).

2

BARTHES, L'UNIQUE
OBJET DE MON
RESSENTIMENT . . .

IN THE beginning, then, was Barthes. That primacy is of neither a logical nor a chronological but rather, as it were, of a teratological order. Roland Barthes's *Sur Racine* hurls us from the word go — a very Racinian procedure — into the heart of a paroxysm: "You are about to hear the utmost horrors . . ." And Raymond Picard devotes more than half of his pamphlet to enumerating those horrors. A masterpiece stood on its head, Barthes's book is seen as "one of the most significant efforts" to evolve a new criticism (*Nouvelle critique*, p. 12) of which Picard has already (pp. 9 and 10) taken pains to stress the inconsistent and rhapsodic nature. One is inclined to ask, ingenuously, how this *one* work can actually represent a movement which has previously been denied any kind of unity, and just how any evidence that could incriminate Barthes could also be stretched to cover Goldmann or Richard. The second part of the pamphlet brings enlightenment on this point: this unity linking the new critics, undetectable but nevertheless postulated, is a privative unity, the unity formed by the "common errors that define them" (p. 87). The act of confounding the heretic par excellence thus serves at the same blow to unmask every other heresy, since beneath their hypocritical differences of opinion they are all equally renegades from the truth. It is impossible to deny Raymond Picard a certain inquisitorial logic.

Let us look at the prosecution's case in detail. For a start, what form does it take? To which the answer is: exactly the form it would have taken in the seventeenth century. The Sorbonne (in

Raymond Picard's theological sense of that institution) proceeds to extract a certain number of culpable propositions from the work of Jansenius — so sorry, I mean of course Roland Barthes. Here they are: "Nero is the man who embraces"; "tragic action is defined in terms of a relation between sun and shadow"; "Racinian tragedy revolves around the figure of the Father"; the use of an "obsessive, unbridled, cynical sexuality"; the heresy of the *homo racinianus*; the stylistic error of the "eunuchoid environment." These six propositions once extracted, it remains for the defense to wonder only (1) whether they actually occur in Jansenius, and (2) whether they are in fact impious. What we need here is a Pascal in fact. But since there isn't one handy we shall have to make do, alas, with our own modest talents of elucidation.

If subpoena'd by this ecclesiastical court, here is what I would say. I do not deny that Raymond Picard has an absolute right not to like Roland Barthes's style. I myself experience from time to time, while reading Barthes, a certain irritation, and just as Picard is less than fond of Bajazet's "eunuchoid environment" or Racine's "descensional imagination," so I am not particularly enthusiastic over certain eminently Barthian adjectives: "informational," "occurrential," "viriloid," etc. Picard thus has the right, when necessary, to be exasperated and, if he happens to feel like it, throw a conniption fit. One's reaction to a style, like one's reaction to people, is governed by sympathy and antipathy. Roland Barthes himself is the first to point out, in *Le Degré zéro de l'écriture*, the extent to which "style" is a matter of personal, biological temperament. In reply to the prosecutor's indictment — which places great stress on stylistic idiosyncrasies — I can therefore only say that it is impossible for me to "feel myself at one with" those idiosyncrasies, since such a thing would be literally absurd. Barthes's style *is* Barthes, and concerns no one but himself. May I point out, however, that though all precious writing, from Racine to Giraudoux, has its inevitable sillinesses, it is very shortsighted to scrutinize only its excesses and turn a blind eye to its successes. Racine's "Brûlé de plus de feux que je n'en allumai" is admittedly a touch comic. But then there is "Dans l'orient désert quel devint mon ennui . . ." The poetry of the one ransoms the other. And as there are precious poets, so Barthes is a precious critic, one who enjoys projecting his thought in the form of conceits and expressing truths in ironic paradoxes. I find certain of his formulas both remarkable and absolutely clear. As for example: "It is as though the verb to love in Racine is by nature intransitive", or, in Racine's tragic universe, "Ingratitude is the inevitable form of freedom"; or again, "The possible in that universe is never anything but its converse"; and a dozen other observations of the same sort. Then there is the vocabulary. "*Eunuchoid?*" Picard queries. "*Ovoid* means something having the shape of an egg. A *deltoid* is the shape of a delta. So what we have here must be an environment in the shape of a eunuch." At which Picard collapses into well-earned mirth (p. 48). But let us continue this admirable argument a little further. Something "schizoid" is the shape of what? Making fun of Barthes is all well and good, and on this point he does deserve it a little. But attempting to understand *why* this critic, whom many excellent minds, in all respects Picard's peers, look upon as a great stylist, should sometimes fall into certain errors, that would be even better. It is clear enough that Barthes is fascinated by all branches of science, and particularly the human sciences, whose contribution he justifiably holds in high esteem. Hence the permanent temptation he feels to muddy the classical and diamond clarity of his waters with the impurities of scientific terms. The asperities of the style simply reflect the difficulties inherent in a thought that is aspiring to achieve a hard-won synthesis between literature's beauties and science's truth. I do not claim that Barthes is not open to criticism — who is not? But I do claim that in order to criticize his style in any *valuable* way, by which I mean other than simply on the basis of purely personal reactions (because in that case why should Raymond Picard's reactions be any more interesting than those of X or Y?), it is necessary to begin with some attempt to grasp his fundamental intention, and then to put the censured phrases within the context of a general statement.

But in fact, Raymond Picard's essay seems to me to suffer from exactly the same inadequacy on the level of theoretical discussion as it does on that of clinical examination. For instance, we find

66

Picard taking a great deal of trouble to justify Flaubert's invectives against his critics in these terms: *"Instead of entering into the author's intention*, of pointing out to him in what way he had fallen short of his aims, and how he should set about rectifying that failure, he was beset by quibbles about countless details wholly irrelevant to his subject, by people clamoring perpetually for him to do exactly the opposite of what he had intended to do." What strikes me most in this systematic attack of Picard's is precisely the absence of any systematic thought; the total lack of coherence in what is a denunciation of incoherence in another. For not once does the prosecution seem to have asked itself the most elementary question of all, and the most obligatory too — regardless of whether or not, after asking it, the court later decided to convict the prisoner without chance of appeal — namely, the question, What is the general *meaning* underlying Roland Barthes's undertaking? However infuriated he was, Raymond Picard might nevertheless have remembered that Roland Barthes — whom he himself recognizes occasionally as possessing a certain talent — is neither a total imbecile nor a pure exhibitionist, and that the author of *Le Degré zéro de l'écriture*, a man capable of grasping with such accuracy the trends and underlying currents of modern literature, must, in turning his attention toward the classics, have had some fixed design. In order to understand (not necessarily to justify) the details selected for such derision, the only way would be to begin by looking for that design and isolating it. But Picard has not for an instant attempted to make that effort. He picks on a formula here (the man who embraces), a concept there (solarity, paternity), or even, as we have seen, a single word (eunuchoid), and then he picks at them, devotes long commentaries to them, sears them with irony, or blasts them with his fury as the mood happens to take him. Such criticism, scrabbling haphazardly here and there in order to produce a few impious propositions, quibbling at details of style or thought without ever looking for a center, such criticism, garrulous and savagely dismissive at the same time, itself falls headfirst into the double sin of "impressionism" and "dogmatism" for which it seeks to flay Roland Barthes.

In fact, Barthes's study of Racine's plays has a very precise intention: the application to them of a "structuralist" method that will enable us to read them afresh. Any analysis presupposes a certain point of view, a certain language, and it is unpardonable simplemindedness on the part of traditional criticism to believe that it can look objectively at the whole of literary history and take it in with a sort of absolute, eaglelike gaze. The "real Racine," the "Racine-en-soi," is the erroneous fantasy of realist metaphysics lurking beneath so much so-called positive research. Barthes therefore decided (and it was a choice to which he committed himself radically) to study Racine's dramaturgy structurally, in the sense that word assumes in Lévi-Strauss's anthropology, which is to say as "the interplay of purely relational forms," with the aim of grasping their mode of functioning. But since the structures involved here are not sociological but psychic, they had to be described in psychoanalytical terms (Father, Eros, etc.), with the proviso of course — in contradistinction to the aims of Charles Mauron's psychocriticism — that the descriptions are strictly confined to the objective relations of Racine's world as they occur in his plays, without any attempt to link them with the hypothetical processes of the author's own unconscious. And Roland Barthes was justified in attempting this piece of research by the extreme economy of the character types and situations in Racine's theater, as well as by the constant recurrence of those affective obsessions whose dynamics had already been so remarkably analyzed by Charles Mauron.[1] Or if Raymond Picard believes Barthes was not so justified, then he should have given sound theoretical reasons why not, something he does not begin to attempt to do. I am well aware that Raymond Picard disapproves very strongly of the illegitimate use of posthumous psychoanalyses based upon incomplete information, and in that I am wholly in agreement with him; but there is a radical difference between dubious mental autopsies performed on centuries-dead authors and the simple description, in psychoanalytical terms, of the clearly discernible relationships linking the characters they depict in their works. The arguments employed in the first case can have no bearing in the second. And if one wishes to deny all value to psychoanalysis as a language, which seems to me an absurdity, then the responsibility of arguing such a case rests with the prosecution, not with the defense. To judge Barthes justly — or even intelligently — therefore entailed in the first place establishing the meaning of his whole undertaking. Only after that would it have been legitimate to question — and then only with the use of sound arguments — whether or not that undertaking has any validity, and whether or not he has been faithful to it in the event. There is nothing of the sort to be found in Picard's pamphlet, which for that reason never rises above mere diatribe.

That said, are the "criminal" propositions actually to be found in this modern *Augustinus* or not? My answer is that they are and yet are not; for they clearly appear in Barthes's book, but with a meaning which, since no attempt has been made to place them in context, becomes lost. Let us take three examples originally selected by Picard himself: "Eros," the "Sun," and the "Father." He could equally well have picked on the "Chamber," the "Herd," or "Anxiety." Picard's bitter complaint against Barthes here is that he drags in an "obsessive, unbridled, cynical" sexuality anywhere and everywhere (*Nouvelle critique*, p. 30). And it is true that we do often encounter adjectives such as "sexed," "desexed," "phallic," or the notorious "eunuchoid." But the fact is that Roland Barthes has gone to great lengths (excessive lengths in my opinion) to empty this sexuality, which Picard's virtuous indignation construes as unbridled and cynical, of all true sexual content: "It is their situation within the power relationship that directs some into virility and others into femininity, without regard to their biological sex" (*Sur Racine*; Paris: Seuil; p. 25). The error Barthes commits, if it is an error, is to continue to use psychoanalytic language after changing its semantic content in this way. It is not in being too Freudian, it is in not being Freudian enough. But in any case, Raymond Picard's indignation is totally misdirected and derives purely from his own misreading of the text.

The second point is more complex. According to Barthes, "Any Racinian hallucination presupposes — or produces — a mergence of shadow and light" (*Sur Racine*, p. 18). "Everywhere and always the same constellation reforms, that of disquieting sun and beneficent shade" (ibid.). This statement contains nothing revolutionary in itself. Barthes himself observes that the problem of Racine's "eye fetishism" had already been broached by G. May and J. Pommier. And in his study on "Racine and the poetics of the human look [regard]," J. Starobinski had already clearly established the central importance of the luminous hallucination, of the play of light and shade. What Barthes is attempting to do here is to progress from the level of purely psychological signification, where his predecessors had been content to remain, to that of mythic signification. And again we find Raymond Picard at his task, still using the same, now familiar, method — or lack of method. "Everywhere . . ." "Always . . ." He counts carefully on his fingers: ah, but there are two missing. "Alexandre, a solarian, in loving Cléofile loves the prisoner he has made; Pyrrhus, gifted with the power of dazzlement, finds in Andromaque the major shadow, etc." (*Sur Racine*, p. 30). But what about *Bérénice*? What about *Iphigénie*? Picard is triumphant. But a little too soon. After all, it would not be hard for Barthes to point out a similar shade-sun relation between the Roman emperor and the Palestinian queen who entreats: "Alas! more quietness, my lord, and less of dazzlement" (II, 4), or between a captive Eriphile and Achille, who set Lesbos aflame and to whom she is invincibly attracted. It is simply that the relation in these cases moves in the opposite direction, from the woman to the man, or, in Barthian terms, it is the shade that aspires to drink the sun, not the sun that yearns to drown itself in the shade. But even supposing that this particular relation exists in the most patent form in only nine tragedies out of the eleven, its validity is in no way impaired by that; what we must then try to discover is the reason for its absence in those other two. For such an absence can equally be significant, once we have established such a constancy in the rest of the author's work. In order to destroy Barthes's thesis we would have to prove that no significant relation in fact exists between solar and nocturnal in the thematic content of Racine's work; in short, that it is impossible to establish any mythic sense at all in this case.

Twice Raymond Picard sidles up to the real problem without openly facing it. Since he is unable — for the best possible reasons

— to deny a certain obsessive recurrence of the interplay between light and shade in our poet's work, he castigates Barthes's
"solarity" for being a falsely explanatory category, since it varies
in relation to what it is supposed to explain. This objection is
almost on target; but formulated like that it sideslips into absurdity. It is true that Barthes's "solarity" is not genuinely explanatory as a category: because it has been insufficiently worked out,
because it remains constantly allusive, because it does not articulate the structures of personal myth in Racine in any intelligible
way with the constant structures of solar mythologies. Once cut
off from its own dynamic forces, and also for lack of a link attach-
ing it to the other motive forces of the Racinian imagination,
"solarity" becomes a purely descriptive and static category, which
provides, in fact, insufficient illumination. But Picard's objection
is quite different; he complains that this solarity is a moral
attribute in Alexandre, a question of fact in Néron, a particularity
of Greek mythology in Phèdre, etc. A *concept* that varies in this
way in relation to its applications is illogical. But we are not dealing with a concept here, or with logical relations measurable with
the platinum meterstick in the safe at the Breteuil pavilion. One
begins to wonder whether Raymond Picard suspects the existence
of *poetic* thought, or even affective thought, which finds the raw
materials on which the imagination and sensibility can feed in
natural elements. It is painful to have to reiterate such truisms
after all Bachelard's work. That the emotive category of "solarity"
varies in its significance in accordance with the various levels of
activity it denotes (amorous, social, political, even intellectual in
Valéry's *Midi le juste* or Claudel's *Partage de midi*) is obviousness
itself. Metaphoric perception, which lies at the heart of all poetry,
is an authentic perception of the real, though situated on a different plane from practical or scientific perception. It is inadmissible
to reproach an elucidation of poetry for modeling its categories
on its object, or to refuse criticism of the metaphor the right
to be partly metaphoric itself.

The criticism of Roland Barthes does consciously and frequently present itself as a linked series of metaphors, but then
that is true of all criticism, beginning with that of Picard himself,
as when he tells us, for example, that in *Andromaque* "the path

of the event ineluctably fills in the tracer line laid down by fate."
So when Barthes says that Néron is "the man who embraces,"
this does not mean that Néron has to spend his entire time on
stage throwing his arms around his fellow characters. It is sufficient that the phrase should convey, as it does, the way Néron
is constantly reaching out to seize hold of people and things in
order both to draw support from them and also to choke them.
I don't like having to belabor the obvious like this, but it seems
to be the level on which Raymond Picard has chosen to place
the discussion. Barthes was therefore right to follow the development of the solar myth through Racine's plays, observing it at
the different stages and under the different aspects of its expression; his only error was to have done so with insufficient precision
and rigor. That reservation is a long way from filling Raymond
Picard's book, however, and it is soon clear what his trouble really
is. "And besides, even if M. Barthes did succeed in making us
perceive the existence of a solar myth in Racinian tragedy, where
would that get us? What we are being offered is less a philosophic
inquiry than one of those old parlor games that used to go:
Question: What burns? *Answer*: Fire, the sun, my heart, a roast
. . ." (*Nouvelle critique*, p. 23). Reading such idiocies, one's jaw
drops. It makes one think of the silliest elements in a certain
kind of rationalism, fashionable in the eighteenth century, which
believed it could shuck off the whole of "metaphysics" with a few
jokes. Because what Barthes is really being accused of, it turns
out, is not that he failed to push his research far enough — a
quite reasonable accusation — but that he ever undertook it at
all. It is, however, literally an aberration not to know, or to refuse
to accept, in 1965, how much poetic expression, and tragic expression in particular, owes to mythic thought.[2] If Racine's tragic creations, despite their courtly gildings, still move us, it is because
he was able to reach down to the level of the "archaic tufa," as
Roland Barthes so aptly puts it, it is because he was able to touch
the great archetypal fibers that control our emotions. There is
no need here to invoke the name of Bachelard, or Jung, or Mircea
Eliade, or Gilbert Durand. One only needs to have read Aristotle.
How can any catharsis be looked for in a play if the drama is
not a psychodrama, if it does not project, into the interplay of

those legendary figures it evokes, all that is deepest and most primitive in our "terrors" and our "pities"? One is forced to conclude that it was not by pure chance that Racine was so fascinated by certain themes of Greek mythology, as Corneille was by Roman history; nor a simple coincidence that those same Greek myths have also been employed as illustrations in the language of psychoanalysis, and even as models for its researches. Since all poets since the beginning of time have always sensed that the human condition is, in a certain way, the battlefield of a great struggle between Day and Night, Darkness and Light (and, more than any of them, the superlative poet who could write: Et la mort, à mes yeux dérobant la clarté, / Rend au jour, qu'ils souillaient, toute sa pureté," [And death, stealing the light from my eyes, restores to the day, which they were sullying, all its purity . . .]), then to attempt an elucidation of the particular sense that this great cosmic confrontation takes in the Racinian universe is clearly an attempt to lead us into its living center, into the fire from which its inner radiance proceeds. Whether or not Barthes's attempt has been successful remains, needless to say, open to discussion. But to reject the attempt itself as of no significance, when it constitutes a possible means of access to an essential signification, is unpardonable blindness on the part of a critic today.

It is when we come up against a precise detail of this sort, it seems to me, that we are best able to grasp — better than in any amount of theoretical manifestos — the real cause of opposition between the new and the old critical movements, and that we are able to put our finger on the essential reasons for the birth and development of the new movement. The value of the new criticism lies less in its answers, which are always open to contest, than in the questions, the essential and hitherto disregarded questions, that it poses; if there is any real newness, then, it lies entirely in the field of interrogation. All the commentators have noted the importance of heredity and "blood" in Racine's plays; our concern is to evaluate its exact meaning. Roland Barthes sees this blood, "which occupies an eminent position in the Racinian metaphysics," as "an extended substitute for the Father" (Sur Racine, pp. 48–49). But paternity, like sexuality, has a particular meaning for Barthes in this context (which makes

73

it even harder to understand R. Picard's complaint: "One is therefore never sure exactly what meaning to lend to the terms *Father*
[with a capital letter], *Eros, Error, Law*, and *Blood*, which constantly
recur," *Nouvelle critique*, p. 25): "In both cases we are dealing
not with a biological reality but essentially with a form: Blood
is a more diffuse and consequently even more terrible anteriority
than the Father. . . . Blood is therefore literally a Law, which
means a bond and a legality. The only movement open to the
son is to break that bond, not to detach himself from it" (*Sur
Racine*, p. 49). So that far from having "determined to unmask
an unbridled sexuality" as Picard accuses him of doing (*Nouvelle
critique*, p. 34), one may say that Roland Barthes is doing exactly
the opposite: purging carnal relationships until he has lent them
a metaphysical transparency: "The inexpiable struggle of Father
and son is that of God and the man he created" (*Sur Racine*,
p. 49). If Barthes has sinned, then it is through a diametrically
opposite excess from the one of which he has been accused, and
I personally believe that Mauron, by dealing with these parental
relationships more literally, achieved a more accurate and precise
description. The weakness of "structuralist" analysis, to my way
of thinking, is in supposing that it can render the concrete movement of real existence by means of a combination of figures and
operational signs; it is in putting its faith in the illusion that
human reality is in the last resort amenable to some kind of *scientific* comprehension, whereas in fact it is rightly the province of
a *dialectical* comprehension. (This problem will be examined more
fully in parts 2 and 3.) Be that as it may, Roland Barthes certainly
reveals to us, at the heart of the parent-offspring bond, a relationship to authority that he considers a fundamental one, and it
is thus at the level of struggles-for-power that he places the tragic
contradiction in Racine's universe. One may or may not agree
with this interpretation. Personally I believe it to be accurate,
but with considerable reservations as to the details of Barthes's
analysis. Although I arrive at the same conclusion, it is by somewhat different paths, and I am perfectly prepared to accept that
others may judge it to be erroneous.

Raymond Picard does not see things quite the same way however, and once again it is ultimately not the *validity* of Roland

Barthes's interpretations he disputes but their *utility*: "Of what interest is it to observe that in tragedy, as in no matter what human social group, such and such an individual, whether for political, family, or spiritual reasons, possesses power or influence over another?" (*Nouvelle critique*, pp. 39–40). Of what interest? The question is comical indeed, and confirms, if confirmation were needed, the total incomprehension already amply demonstrated with regard to the importance of myth. There can be no tragic action, in the Greek classics as in Shakespeare, in Corneille as in Racine, other than in a world of *greatness*. Tragedy is a sport of kings and princes; and referring to human misfortunes in his preface to *Don Sanche*, Corneille observes, albeit with some regret, that "history disdains to record them unless they have descended upon one of those great heads." It is certainly not by chance that tragic dignity demands, as Corneille again tells us elsewhere, "some great interest of state, or some passion nobler and more virile than love." As George Steiner reminded us more recently, "There is nothing democratic in the tragic vision. The royal and heroic characters that the gods honor with their vengeance exist on a plane higher than ours in the hierarchy" (*The Death of Tragedy*, p. 175). In order for a *fall* to occur (and that according to Aristotle is the essence of tragedy), it is manifestly evident that there must be *height*: the comic character, servant or merchant, could never "fall," since he is by nature already "low." George Steiner has clearly shown that the tragic vision is always bound up with an aristocratic civilization, and that the decline of the latter always entails the death of the former: as soon as the nineteenth century witnessed the rise of bourgeois optimism, as soon as the romantics, faithfully following Rousseau, decided that crime no longer leads to punishment but to redemption, tragedy was finished. And there is certainly no doubt that in the seventeenth century, at any rate, the sense of greatness was inextricably bound up with the monarchic hierarchy. Metaphysics and history coincide in this case; for a man's fall will always be greater in proportion to the degree of his aspiration toward political and ethical "greatness." The "authority relation" and the "power relations" that Barthes speaks of do, therefore, lie at the heart of the tragic universe. A power

crisis underlies the whole anguished progress of Oedipus, proud
king of Thebes; and gives its meaning to the sacrifice of his
daughter Antigone; it is a power crisis that sharpens the agony
of Lear, who is dispossessed of his reason as a result of dispossess-
ing himself of his kingdom. Nor could it be otherwise in Racine.
And not by virtue of some sort of "law of Literary Kinds" with
relevance solely to literary history: such a "law," far from being
a principle of explanation, would have to be explained itself. It
is in the rigor with which he has practiced this necessity that
Racine's genius lies. Whether in Pyrrhus or in Titus, in Agamem-
non or in Mithridate, the emotional crisis has no meaning except
within the context of a moral and political crisis of power, over
self and over others. Racine's supreme art is to show us, in the
character of Néron, the quest for love inextricably bound up with
the will to power: it is to the degree that he is able to appropriate
Junie for himself, with impunity, that Néron effectively liberates
himself from the twofold tutelage of Burrhus and Agrippine,
that he affirms himself as emperor; but just at the moment when
he believes he has grasped true power, his empire escapes him
in erotic alienation. There is no Racinian tragedy that is not fundamentally the spectacle of a "power relation" wrestling desperately with a subversive Eros threatening to undermine a universal
Order.

Such is ultimately the meaning of the "equation" Barthes gives
us:

A has total power over B
A loves B, who does not love A,

which Picard finds so infuriating. The presentation may lack
charm, and I must confess that I agree with Picard in finding
it pointlessly mathematical; criticism is never a form of "algebra,"
despite the secret hopes of the structuralists. But once again,
though one may find objections to the letter of the interpretation,
it is impossible to condemn the spirit behind it, the concern for
truth that ought to guide all research desirous of reaching beyond
mere surfaces. From the primitive "herd" to the court of Louis
XIV, with admittedly important and even essential differences,
which Barthes does not stress sufficiently (this is what I shall term

76

the *political level*, on which *Sur Racine* never moves), it is still true that the essence of tragedy remains centered upon a primal conflect. Whether familial or political, moral or theological, from Father to Prince and from Prince to God, there is a principle of Authority and Order that wishes to yoke Nature to its will, arousing in the latter a contrary desire for rebellion and liberation.[3] Tragedy is the radical frustration of these two impulses, their collision, and their mutual destruction. One may or may not agree with the use to which Roland Barthes puts this "authority relation," one may or may not agree with his definition of it, or with the one I have offered in my turn; on the other hand, to say as Picard does that relations of "power or influence" are of no interest in tragedy, is quite simply to utter a monstrous fatuity.

"Do they feel themselves engaged by *Sur Racine*?" asks Raymond Picard of the "adherents of the new criticism." "Do they recognize themselves in it? One would dearly like to know." In the light of what I have said so far I now feel able to reply. The new criticism is neither a school, nor a club, nor a kind of freemasonry. Those tempted by and those attempting unbeaten paths are not interested in patting one another on the back or holding one another's hands, but simply in confronting and, if needs be, in freely and openly contesting each other's discoveries. Charles Mauron is certainly not overfond of the criticism that stems from Bachelard, and he says so; there is an abyss between the inward probing of Georges Poulet and the objectivism of Lucien Goldmann; Jean Starobinski is very emphatic about the differences between his particular brand of criticism, which is resolutely harnessed to the advances of philosophy, and other kinds of criticism — whether psychoanalytic or Marxist — with scientific pretensions. I myself have just expressed my disagreements and my reservations in the case of many aspects of *Sur Racine*, which, though they are certainly not those of Raymond Picard, are none the less considerable and real. This "intellectual solidarity so complacently claimed," Raymond Picard exclaims. Complacency? We have just seen the contrary. Solidarity? It is clear enough that I consider Roland Barthes alone responsible not only for his style and his thought but for his analyses and their form. He speaks neither for me nor for any other; like all writers he speaks for himself alone, and that is enough. And yet, in a certain sense, yes, I do feel a bond of solidarity with him. When someone starts using methods that put us back three centuries in order to extract "culpable propositions" from another's work, carefully dissociating them from their context; when someone begins quibbling about the letter without making an honest attempt to understand the spirit; when someone chooses to separate statements, sentences, or words from the general meaning that gives them their true signification, so that they become absurd and laughable, like any human expression separated from its intention, then yes, certainly, I do feel a solidarity with Roland Barthes. The very inadequacy of the methods used to attack him are a gauge to me of the solid basis of his own work, which is wholly directed toward the grasping of a global meaning, viewing each element in a vast dramatic universe as part of a whole, and each part as the necessary component in a totality. But that is not all. When someone attacks not the conclusions of this investigation — which are certainly disputable — but its object; when each time it penetrates beyond the more obvious meanings of Racine's work, pointing toward deeper existential and mythic meanings, someone cries: "Pointless! Without interest!" then yes, oh yes indeed, I feel my solidarity with Roland Barthes become absolute. Because in this squabble that the old guard seems determined to pick with the new critics, I can see, sprouting beneath the pomp of academic caps, the donkey ears of obscurantism.

3

ENFIN MALHERBE
VINT . . .

THAT'S enough about Barthes:

> Th' Academy as one pronounces condemnation,
> The rebel Publick still accords him admiration.

And since the strategists tell us that the best form of defense is attack, let us take the war into the enemy's camp for a while. By which I mean, let us go and take a look at what Picard and his friends are up to in the critical field. Which is exactly what one of those friends has in fact invited us to do, since in a rider to his condemnation of the "pretentious" criticism of Roland Barthes he offers us that of Raymond Picard as a model of how it should be done. (Edouard Guitton, in a letter to *Le Monde*, 13 November 1965. We shall return to this letter later.) Very well then, if we accept that all the critical paths recently opened up are actually dead ends, and if the final word on the matter is Raymond Picard's pronouncement that we must "look elsewhere — and above all look more clearly," what are we to be offered instead? I do not know if there is a new criticism, but it is certainly beyond question that there is an old one, and that it has by and large had its day. The impressionist critic takes a work and sniffs at it; he meanders on from sensation to sensation; he tells us what his reactions are; he chatters on; and, depending upon the degree of his talent, he interests us or bores us — either way it is of little consequence. The trendy critic is doomed to delight in the phony and the sham. The academic critic, on the other hand, remains resolutely outside the work

79

he is criticizing: he never allows himself to enter into it, to experience it from the inside; he palpates it, he weighs it in his hand; immured behind his files and indexes he hunts out sources and influences; to evaluate Rousseau's feeling for Nature means first of all acquiring a thorough knowledge of eighteenth-century transportation and modes of travel; the "feeling" itself comes a poor second — if there's any left. And that is no caricature. It is a description of a famous course of lectures. "Intuition" and "Scholarship" of this sort have for the past fifty years now been the two breasts at which traditional criticism has sucked. And though there is little hope that they will ever dry up, it is hard to believe there is much nourishment left in the milk. Then suddenly there came the revelation that there are also the works themselves, that they too have an existence. And the result has been a revolution of the palate, in the course of which some followers of the old criticism have even gone so far as to affirm the *primacy* of the works, and I am delighted to be able to say that Raymond Picard is one of their number. My only regret is that, having declared himself the champion of "aesthetic" and "literary values proper," he should then have devoted his energies almost exclusively to following Racine's "career," with untiring patience, through all its minutest meanders. But let that pass. The important thing here, quite clearly, is not the practice but the theory.

In direct opposition to the subjectivist and paralogical — not to say paranoid — frenzy displayed by Roland Barthes, Raymond Picard sets himself the task of conveying quite simply and modestly (he and his friends, as we shall see, all go in a great deal for modesty) — what? The *truth*. Nothing more and nothing less. And furthermore, please note, the *objective truth*. Here is one passage that deserves anthologizing: "There is a truth about Racine on which everyone can succeed in agreeing. By basing his work in particular on the certainties of language, on the implications provided by psychological coherence, on the imperatives of structure in the tragic genre, the patient and modest worker can succeed in establishing evidence that will, as it were, isolate zones of objectivity; and it is on the basis of these that he will be able — with the utmost caution — to attempt interpretations"

80

(*Nouvelle critique*, p. 69). Such words bring immediate reassurance: we are in familiar territory. For Raymond Picard does not merely mean that before undertaking literary interpretations we need to have arrived at a literal comprehension and established certain indispensable facts, which would be altogether too obvious and — even for him — too modest a point to make. No, he means something more than that, something very much more than that; in fact, he is presenting us with a complete philosophy. Truth defined as "the general agreement of minds," objectivity arrived at by the accumulation of facts until they lead to the emergence of a hypothesis — it is pure Brunschvicg, or Lalande. We can breathe freely again in the pure air of those good old days of Spiritualism and Induction. It is true, of course, that things have changed a little since then. Modern science, having also run mad, no longer expects much from Baconian empiricism; far from constructing concepts from fragments of reality, it has turned visionary, it has started inventing its own world as well as its own signs to describe it. And what about "psychological coherence"? Alas! There are all those people like Freud, and Jung, and Adler, who have popped up to add their complications — I almost said complexes; what with their ambiguities, their ambivalences, the "unconscious," "bad faith," it is no longer very easy to tell precisely what an emotion or a character is. As for "the certainties of language," what language precisely? Racine's? Apart from the lexicographical meanings involved — which we can usually manage to define — its deceptive transparency is in fact a trap, and paradoxically conceals, as we shall see later, a series of multiple meanings, each ambiguous in itself and very hard to pin down. Our own language then? The language of Everyman? In an age when, from Joyce to Beckett, from Ionesco to Pinget, literature itself has taken the form of an absolute protest against that language, how can anyone seriously rely upon its pseudocertainties for the purposes of criticism? And even if it were attempted, could we expect Racine to emerge unscathed from being "understood" with the understanding of Mr. Common Sense? Can we seriously exclaim, with Antoine Adam, quoted by Roland Barthes, that such and such a scene in *Mithridate* "arouses the best in us"? The "best" in us? Less than specific, that "best." But apart from that, who is this "us"? The worthy professor himself? Twentieth-century average middle-class man? Papuans? Unless, of course, it is Eternal Man. Roland Barthes has already pointed out that there is no such thing as "innocent" or "neutral" language. The imposture inherent in the "old" criticism — since charges of imposture have been laid — is that it never stops taking truisms for Platonic Ideas and platitudes for Intelligible Truths. "The majority of critics imagine that a superficial stamp on the brake of their imagination to start off with will ensure greater objectivity: by remaining on the surface of the facts one is respecting them more, so that the timidity, the banality of their hypothesis thereby becomes a guarantee of its validity" (*Sur Racine*, p. 160). It could scarcely be better put. There are no certainties of *language*, only those of the *various* languages from among which, spontaneously or with conscious purpose, we are able to choose. But rather than discussing the thing on a theoretical level, let us examine Raymond Picard's "objective truths" at work.

A single example will make everything clear. Decorously angered by the "sexual" interpretation Barthes gives to the relationship between Hippolyte and Aricie, according to which Aricie "is attempting to smash the secret of Hippolyte's virginity the way one cracks a shell," Picard rectifies this error. The reality is much simpler and much healthier: "Her attitude is clear. She loves Hippolyte, and in order to justify herself she observes that she has every reason to prefer a proud hero who has never succumbed to the weaknesses of love to, say, a philanderer" (*Nouvelle critique*, pp. 31–32). In other words, Aricie's love *comes first*. It is a natural and untreated raw material that simply occurs, rather like a phenomenon of nature. She loves, just like that, because that's the way it is, and without really knowing whom or why. A fine and noble emotion, but quite irrational, as we all know. And only *afterwards*, because human beings are also conscious intellects *as well*, and because they do not just start loving the way the weather can turn to rain, Aricie has to search around for reasons: her love for the chaste Hippolyte becomes *retrospectively*, and in accordance with the amorous code of the age, a "victory" for Aricie. This analysis, apparently considered by its author as a matter of pure common sense, in reality implies a definite ideological position, and a certain metaphysical basis: mental phenomena are *data* occurring in the consciousness without any intrinsic meaning, and upon which artificial meanings are then grafted, a posteriori. But since Brentano we know that all consciousness is intentional; since Freud, that all behavior has meaning; since Marx, that any thought is the interiorization of an objective situation. Racine, I grant, had not read these worthy authors, but he was a genius, which in this case comes to much the same thing, since his particular genius was an intuitive knowledge of man in his concrete reality. One needs only to read through Aricie's long speech confiding in Ismène (*Phèdre*, II, 1) to see how Racine — a less simple mind than his exegetists — has succeeded with extraordinary art in interweaving all the complexity, all the ambiguity that lies at the heart of any emotion. Aricie begins by evoking, in detail and with great emphasis, her *situation*: "I alone escaped from the furies of that war." She recalls the political ban laid upon her by Theseus: it is forbidden to love her. It is within the context of this situation that there occurs the nearest thing to a "natural phenomenon": the *coup de foudre* that convention required to be stressed in a negative mode:

> Non que par les yeux seuls lâchement enchantée
> J'aime en lui sa beauté, sa grâce tant vantée.[1]

Yet physical attraction itself is not without meaning: it is the body speaking. Just as the sudden instinct that drives the Princess of Cleves and M. de Nemours together in Mme de La Fayette's novel "makes sense," as the English so accurately put it, secretes its own internal meaning (Cf. my article, "La Princesse de Clèves: an existential interpretation," in *La Table Ronde*, June 1959), so this pure impulse of the flesh toward Hippolyte is immediately impregnated in Aricie's case with a meaning that is in no way concealed, which she reveals to us in fact with total lucidity:

> Mais de faire fléchir un courage inflexible,
> De porter la douleur dans une âme insensible,
> D'enchaîner un captif de ses fers étonné,
> Contre un joug qui lui plaît vainement mutiné:
> C'est là ce que je veux, c'est là ce qui m'irrite.
> Hercule à désarmer coûtait moins qu'Hippolyte,

Et vaincu plus souvent, et plus tôt surmonté,
Préparait moins de gloire aux yeux qui l'ont dompté.[2]

The very hammering rhythm of the lines conveys the all-devouring emulation, the force of will verging on physical irritation, that are driving Aricie to swoop on Hippolyte almost as though he were a quarry she was hunting. It is this element of violence that Roland Barthes has expressed, on the sexual level, with the metaphor of rape. But the rape of Hippolyte is not sexual; or more accurately, the sexuality is here the carrier of a complex meaning, since all motivations are in any case overdetermined. Aricie's love victory over the legendary hero of chastity (and the fact that he is legendary must not be forgotten) is not merely that of a woman over a man, it is also that of a captive princess over the son of a conqueror king. The amorous confrontation is also a *combat*: it involves "making him yield," "bringing pain," "shackling a captive," "imposing a yoke." The conventional metaphors of love? Yes, by all means. But this conventional language, which it was Racine's genius to be able to use — along with all the other conventions of his time — to his own ends, acquires in a specific situation a precise meaning. This amorous conflict is a *revenge*, which is going to achieve a miraculous transformation in Aricie's condition: from being a humiliated captive ("sad plaything," "remains of a king's blood"), treated by Thésée as a "criminal" (V,3), she is to acquire "fame," to become the superior of Phèdre, her tyrant-mistress in reality ("Phèdre in vain took glory in the sighs of Thésée"), superior even to that hero of heroes Hercules ("Hercules cost less to disarm than Hippolyte"). The victory of these amorous "weapons"— wielded by the only one of his "nephews" to escape death — is to reestablish the dethroned Erechtée in all his glory. Aricie's love, like all behavior, is to be understood from the starting point of its intentions: it is at the same time a fantasy (the magical reversal of a situation, symbolic satisfaction) and the first step in a course of action (throwing off the yoke of Thésée), which, moreover, proves successful, since in the last line of the play she becomes "the daughter." To love Hippolyte, for Aricie, is therefore to love *through* Hippolyte — and if needs be, *against* Hippolyte; it is to forge through him, as with all love, both real and imaginative links with the world, links that simultaneously integrate the instincts of the flesh into an individual destiny and interiorize a historical situation. In short, loving is never a raw fact, an untreated datum, it is always a form of behavior that spontaneously projects possibles, in the Sartrean sense, and that is to be understood on the basis of those possibles. (I part company on this point with Barthes's interpretation, which is in curious coincidence here with that of Picard: "It appears that the verb *aimer* in Racine is by nature intransitive; what is given is a force indifferent to its object, or to go further, an essence of the act even, as though the act consumes all its energies in isolation from any end" [p. 58]. As a good existentialist I cannot possibly subscribe to this totally Freudian vision of a "force indifferent to its object": "displacements of energy," to use the mechanical terminology of psychoanalysis, are always vectorial. So we ought rather to say: all conscious activity is intentional. When it *appears* that "to love" is intransitive, it is in fact no more than that: an appearance.)

We must not be too anxious, then, to correct Barthes's "errors" in order to placate the bridlings of national folkwisdom, or to construe oversimple, not to say simplistic, psychological "proofs" as "objective truths." It is no more desirable in criticism than it is in philosophy to rely, without a preliminary reassessment of them, on the "certainties" of common sense or everyday language, which are often in fact a screen for inadequacies of thought. Which is why the first two points of Raymond Picard's counterprogram, having now long been superseded, are in my view unacceptable. So let us go on to examine the third and most important.

HOW DEEP DOES LITERATURE GO?

THE patient and modest researcher, you will remember, had a third crutch available to aid his cautious progress: the "structural imperatives of the genre." At last we reach the core of the argument. Leaving Racine and Barthes aside for the moment, Raymond Picard switches his attack to the "new critics" in general: they display a total "indifference to literary structures" (*Nouvelle critique*, p. 119); they do not believe in "the specificity of *literature*" (p. 117). These people want to be accepted as "structuralists"; but it is never literary structures that are involved, those they simple abolish or ignore; it is psychological structures, or sociological ones, or metaphysical ones, etc. The sad part is that by dint of interesting themselves exclusively in the "nether regions of the work," in J.-P. Richard's phrase, the "new critics" "are like a man who is attracted to women but who by some stange perversion can only enjoy them when he see them in X-ray" (p. 128). The "profundity" they so often refer to is thus nothing but a trick, a pure metaphor: "The profundity of an expression lies in what it says, in the implications of what it says, and not necessarily in what it is supposedly concealing and revealing at the same time. Why should what is profound be necessarily linked to the obscure and the invisible?" (p. 134) This noble profession of rationalist faith places the argument on its true level. We have been treated to Brunschvicg and Lalande, and now we have Valéry. A step in the right direction certainly. Because the real question, when it comes down to it, is not: *Do you like Barthes*? but *How deep does literature go*? Raymond Picard has now put his cards on the table. I appreciate the fact, and will forthwith show my hand in return. But since the question is such a vast one, too vast for there to be any question of dealing with all its theoretical ramifications in this short essay, I shall limit myself to stressing a number of what I take to be essential points.

For Raymond Picard things are very simple, a happy situation that enables him to keep things neat and clear-cut by professing allegiance to the pure "classical" tradition: "literature, which is to say the willed and lucid activity of a man devoting himself, within the limits of norms and restraints that he has consciously adopted, to a labor of expression" (p. 138). The important thing, therefore, is to reeducate an age that has forgotten them — since Rimbaud and even more so since Dada and surrealism — in "all the classical ideas relating to literature." To fasten as the new criticism does on what is *primal*, to insist upon returning constantly to the *primitive*, is to prefer the "unformed" and the "crude"; it is, in short, "to entrench oneself in the preliterary and to deny literature itself" (p. 137). This stand has the merit of its total honesty; and it also poses, very precisely, the true problem. Let me observe right away that these affirmations, energetic though they may be, are nonetheless gratuitious, by which I mean that they are advanced, or rather battered home, without the slightest attempt at providing proofs. But in fact, this "classicism — whatever Raymond Picard may think — is in no way a self-evident truth with the power to reveal literature's nontemporal essence to the world at large. It is a totally time-bound conception, a method devised in the early years of this century by certain minds, including Paul Valéry,[1] for exalting the supposed virtues of classical literature in order to use them as sticks with which to beat the literary "vices" of their contemporaries. It is in no way an "innocent" position, in the sense that Roland Barthes gives that term, but an ideological stand implying a certain philosophic, moral, and political vision, which Valéry is moreover the first to expound. To define literature is always, as we have said, to define a conception of man. In practice, the "classicism" being invoked here is in the full sense of the word a *reactionary* attitude, one intended to provide a political and aesthetic line of defense against the modern revolutions that are posing a threat

87

to Order, in literature and elsewhere. But I won't harp on that. For the moment, what concerns us is to draw the consequences that affect literary criticism.

The "classical ideas" that Raymond Picard opportunely summons up to hold the balance against contemporary divagations imply, in fact, a veritable *theory of expression*, one that is based on a double postulate: (1) that authentic "literary" signification is situated on the level of the explicit ("what a work says and the implications of what it says"); (2) that what is said in the work coincides exactly with what the author consciously wished to say ("willed and lucid activity"). In short, the literary content signified is wholly exhausted by the work that is directly and transparently signifying it: the words, being carriers of a univocal meaning for both writer and reader, communicate directly the intelligible choice that is precisely what constitutes literary writing. In consequence, there will exist a triple agreement making possible the establishment of a *true* and *objective* criticism: agreement between what the work says and what it intends to say; agreement between what the author intends to say and what his work says; agreement between what I think the work says and what it does in fact say (with the proviso, of course, that my reading of it must be informed and intelligent). All this being so, the tasks proper to criticism are clearly indicated: it must point out the clear significations contained in the work, and group them when the implications are complex; it must, in the exactest sense, *clarify* the work (explication of texts). It must also strive to recapture the processes by which the author performed his expressive task (genesis of works). (This conclusion is not explicitly drawn by R. Picard, but in good logic it ought to have been. It is the logic governing traditional "biographical" criticism: for every clear signification an evident genesis [sources, influences, etc.]. We shall examine later the dead end to which this attitude leads.) Criticism will arrive at a certain number of manifest conclusions, common ground on which all minds will be able to meet and thereby escape from their subjective compartmentalization (the objective truth of criticism). Under color of rallying us to the self-evident truths of common sense, these "classical ideas" put forward by Raymond

88

Picard present themselves in fact as an *optimistic semantics* whose postulates we would do well to examine more closely.

All classicism presupposes, at the outset, a vow of poverty. In the seventeenth century, classical literature was constituted by a voluntary penury of vocabulary (discarding of vulgar, technical, and picturesque words), by a rejection of the teeming multiplicity of the baroque, which gave such richness to the century's first decades, and by an extreme stylization of the genres, whose essence Boileau devoted himself to codifying after the event. Similarly, but in a quite different historical context, Raymond Picard's deliberate sequestration of criticism within the domain of clear significations is accomplished by a refusal to pay any attention to the "crude," to the "primitive." Criticism, for him, is the study of finished products; and the literary end product, the finished work, is a diamond that glitters with the ultimate clarity. Clarity of conception in the first place ("That which is well conceived . . ." Boileau knew best!), intellectual clarity, since what we need to know is "what the work says." But also aesthetic luminosity: the work is not, for Raymond Picard, merely a message to be deciphered (in fact he castigates the new criticism roundly for perpetually treating the work as an enigma or a conundrum); the work is before all else the successful working out of an aesthetic problem. Its *why* is indistinguishable from its *how*. It is by accepting the mediation of "norms" and "restraints" — which he either finds around him or imposes on himself — that the writer is enabled to work on his raw material and turn it into a piece of workmanship that is an artwork. "You gave me mud, and I made gold . . ." In this sense, every artist is a goldsmith, and the craft of the goldsmith consists, in the field of literature, in the assembly and adjustment of "literary structures," which new critics treat so slightingly but which serious critics, on the contrary, will make the principal object of their attention. In restricting criticism's permissible field of inquiry to the domain of conceptual and aesthetic significations alone, Raymond Picard is in fact doing just what Barthes so nicely termed "giving a stamp on the brake" of his imagination: "For any signifier there are always several possible significates: signs are eternally ambiguous, decipherment always a choice" (*Sur Racine*, p. 160). Among the multiplicity of possible significations (historical, sociological, metaphysical, etc.) recognized even by Raymond Picard himself as appertaining to the work of art, he thus refuses validity — as a good disciple of Lanson, who said he hoped "that he had never either liked or blamed anything for any reasons not of a literary order — to all except those he defines as "literary." So what now remains to be decided is whether this decree is a legitimate one or even, quite simply, possible.

Qui te l'a dit, Who told you to? Hermione magnificently demands of Oreste, whose error lies in having confused what she *said* and what she *meant* when she clamored for Pyrrhus's death. Can the critic be as ingenuous as Oreste without also being as culpable and perhaps as insane as he was?[2] For what Oreste discovers to his great chagrin, and what criticism always runs up against right at the start, is quite simply the fundamental ambiguity of language. And this ambiguity is threefold. It exists on three levels: that of the *writing*, that of the *text*, and that of the *writer*. The postulate made by Raymond Picard and his friends is that what a work "means" is exactly the same thing as what it "says," so that the conscious utterance at which the author has arrived alone constitutes the meaning of the text. But in fact it is the opposite that is true. In Bernard Pingaud's excellent phrase: "What a writer means is always distinct from what he says." That is the fundamental postulate of all the "new critics," however widely they may diverge on other issues. What we need to do therefore is to establish the foundations for this affirmation on the threefold set of levels defined by the ambiguity inherent in all literary expression.

Modern thinking on language, beginning with that of Husserl, shows that it presents us with two aspects: it *states* and it *reveals*. Every utterance is the bearer of a *signification* and the depository of a *meaning*, and these two things are situated on radically different levels. On the level of statement, language is communication and instrumentality. To begin with, it presents itself, in the Saussurian sense, as a system of signs, that is, impersonal conventions, permitting the coming together of a significate and a signifier

90

in the act of signification, on the basis of an operative system of operations whose functioning is described by linguistics. It is this aspect of language that is also given prominence, on the philosophical plane, in Husserl's attempt, in his *Logical Researches*, to establish an "eidetics" making it possible to pin down the structures a priori, to determine the forms of signification indispensable to the constitution of all empirical language. But, though signification is a linguistic act, it is also an action aimed at the world; language is not only a formal system, it is also a moving on toward the thing signified, a transcendence. When I say: "It's ten o'clock," that statement has an objective signification linking signs (words) together in accordance with the conventions of the English language but at the same time revealing a state of the world that in some other language would be indicated in accordance with different conventions. To say: "It's ten o'clock," if I am asked the time in the street, is an immediately decipherable reply, and one that can be written off, once understood, as referring to a state of things. But anything that "is said" is always said by "someone." Alongside what is said there is always what that someone means, there is the assertion, by and through language, of a human presence, and a relationship between human beings. To say: "It's ten o'clock" to a group of waiting companions may mean: "Let's go." The sign here is a signal, in which the explicit refers to the implicit by means of a simple and univocal relation. Everything changes, however, when speech permits the Self to surface and becomes, in some degree, personal modulation. If I am waiting for a woman, whom I desire and fear at the same time, and if I observe, noting that she has not arrived, "It's ten o'clock," then that observation, which *states* a wholly clear fact, is *expressing* a wholly equivocal reality: relief, regret, both at once, or perhaps neither, perhaps a slightly disillusioned detachment (she had promised)? I know what I am saying; who knows what it means? When I say those words, as our use of the reflexive pronoun so clearly conveys, I am expressing *myself*. In Saussure's terminology I am impregnating *language* with *speech* (*parole*), which is in fact the ambiguity lying within consciousness itself. Since consciousness is precisely noncoincidence with self, a perpetual time lag and transcendence into an aim, its language is never susceptible of a univocal translation. In order for what one says to coincide exactly with what one means, it would be necessary to remain always within the realm of scientific language (a logical system of signs governed by strictly invariable functions) or that of technical language (meticulously controlled operations on the world). Sartre has quite recently summed up the basis of this ambiguity inherent in all nonscientific language: "I make use of words that have a history of their own, as well as a relation to language as a whole, a relation that is certainly not simple, and which is not strictly that of a universal symbolics either; words that moreover have a historic relation to myself, and one that is equally particular" ("The Writer and His Language," *Revue d'Esthétique*, 1966). If, in Heidegger's phrase, "I am what I say," then I am always in fact beyond what I say, which is why Freud was able to view language as the total "investment" of a life. And Merleau-Ponty has summed up the matter most succinctly of all in his admirable formula: "What we *mean* is not out there in front of us, separate from all utterance, like a pure signification. It is merely the excess of what we are living over what has already been said" (*Signes*, p. 104).

And if that is true of our everyday sort of talk, it is even more true when applied to literary expression. If concrete human life is already in excess of the significations of the language into which it projects itself, then literature, in this respect, is *the maximum excess of speech*, the greatest possible surplus of the significate over the signifier, the infinite overflowing of the obvious statement by the tacit expression. As Sartre reminds us, "The greatest riches of the psychic life are *silent*" ("Qu'est-ce que la littérature?" *Situations II*, p. 201). Literature is made up of as many silences as it is words; what it *says* achieves its full meaning through what it *does not say*: and that is precisely what it *means*. And Raymond Picard is certainly in no position to summon "classicism" to his aid on this point, since classical literature is par excellence the literature of litotes, the literature which, in Gide's phrase, says least in order to say most. Classical art is precisely the art of *reticence*; its celebrated "clarity"— with which traditionalists of every stripe incessantly beat us over the head — is the opposite of an immediate transparency:

> But to render light
> Implies of shade one lightless half.

Are our critics determined to be more Valéryist than Valéry? They are the victims of their own total misunderstanding in hoping to make the seventeenth century into a nature reserve of limpid significations and keeping the seven hells of ambiguity for "modern" authors alone.[3] It is in this unclosable gap between the possible significations and the total meaning of all language that literature resides, and classical literature even more so than any other. Let us demonstrate this with a particular example, one we have already touched on earlier.

If a friend helpfully decides to weed my garden and pulls up a choice plant, and I then ask him: "Who told you to?" that is a banality. But when Hermione cries to Oreste: "Who told you to?" then we are dealing with literature — and great literature too. Why? First because the question cannot be divorced from the Racinian speech in which it occurs; its impact on us is that of the panting climax of a rhythmic series:

> Pourquoi l'assassiner? Qu'a-t-il fait? A quel titre?
> Qui te l'a dit?

This speech presents itself from the outset as a certain verbal modulation or "music" (let us say, for simplicity's sake, that we are dealing with poetic apprehension). But it is immediately obvious that the poetic meaning is paralleled by a psychological meaning, on which it is based: the rhythmic succession is the progression of a frenzied state in which Hermione "forgets", conveniently and in ascending order, Pyrrhus's guilt ("Pourguoi l'assassiner?"— "Why murder him?"), the mission previously assigned to Oreste ("A quel titre?" — "By what right?"), and lastly — and above all — her own responsibility in the deed "Qui te l'a dit?"— "Who told you to?"). Then scarcely have these meanings been established when they converge upon a third: the beauty of the lines and the subtlety of the psychological progress are not ends in themselves; they contribute to a *dramatic* effect, they provide the energy for a final exclamation that explodes as a *coup de théâtre*. But then, in its turn, this *coup de théâtre* turns out to be no such thing: as Raymond Picard himself makes admirably clear, "the play has therefore already been played out before the curtain goes up . . . . The surprise of *Qui te l'a dit?* has been long since prepared for" (Racine, *Oeuvres complètes*, Pléiade edition, vol 1, p. 237). This false surprise, if it is to be appreciated to the full, therefore refers us back to a certain set of laws that is nothing other than Racine's total dramatic system. These various significations, dovetailing into one another, define what Raymond Picard would term the "literary structures" and also the "aesthetic value" of this passage, on the assumption, of course, that *the aesthetic meaning will exhaust the totality of the literary meaning*. We have established "what the work says and the implications of what it says"; any attempt to seek further or to plunge deeper is not merely futile but also dangerous, since, as Raymond Picard tells us, poking about in literature's "nether regions" leads to "a denial of literature." This is precisely the "stamp on the brake" we mentioned earlier. But one can say of this arbitrary decree delivered by a certain kind of criticism what Heidegger said about the dictatorship of everyday language: "It decides in advance what is comprehensible, and what, being incomprehensible, must be rejected" (Letter on Humanism).

In reality, literature overflows this restrictive conception of literary structure on every side. There is no way of preventing meanings from drawing other meanings to them, from proliferating: Raymond Picard's criticism is a Malthusianism struggling in vain to combat a semantic explosion. It is impossible, for a start, to restrict oneself to the formulas of traditional "psychology" if one wishes to grasp Hermione's behavior in an adequate fashion. Picard himself indicates this very clearly in his own commentary on this *Qui te l'a dit?*: "And how could it be otherwise? The tragic hero allows himself to be governed by the passionate and frenzied actions of the beloved. His steps are guided by the aberrancies of the other" (Racine, *Oeuvres complètes*, vol. 1, p. 236). It is impossible to prevent "psychological" signification leading to a dialectic of interhuman relations. And equally impossible to limit oneself to just noting the existence of that dialectic, or assigning it to the simple laws of a "genus" ("the tragic hero allows himself to be governed . . ."). It is not *the* tragic hero but Hermione, *a* tragic heroine, who must experience her relation to the Beloved in accordance with the data of her particular feminine condition (king's daughter, political pawn, etc.), which are radically different from those of the masculine condition. What is needed, therefore, is not the formulation of a vague general law, but the description, in all its complexity, of a particular alienation. For that, we clearly need at our disposal a certain instrument that cannot be that of aesthetic analysis, and even less of mere "literary chitchat." But even before being a precise and perverse relation to another (radical dispossession of the self for the sake of the Other), the *Qui te l'a dit?* is in the first place a distorted relation to the self: it presupposes that particular form of blindness constituted by lying to oneself, the possibility for a consciousness to delude itself as well as to alienate itself. This possibility, yawning before that famous "lucidity" of Racine's heroes like an abyss into which they plunge to destruction, requires for its comprehension the availability of certain theoretical schemas specifically designed to give an account of it — not so that we can then go on to indulge in a vast and vague "interpretation" of Racine's plays, but simply in order for us to grasp in action the nature and meaning of the passion-derived impulses that hurl these "great cats" in their "cage" at one another's throats (in Giraudoux's words). To this end, we shall seek the help of, for example, the concepts of classical Freudian psychoanalysis, or of Sartre's existential psychoanalysis, since it is also true that we see psychological significations "transformed" before our very eyes into existential significations.

Are we to stop there? Impossible. Human existence, in its turn, cannot be understood except in relation to Being; existential signification leads on inevitably to a metaphysical signification. Again it is Picard, whose concrete analyses are considerably superior to his theories, who makes this admirably clear: as soon as the hero "grasps that he no longer controls his own self," as soon as he "renounces his freedom," "the world is filled with gods, and the reign of fatal powers begins" (ibid., p. 233). Well put; the appearance of the gods in Racine is simply the converse of man's abdication. The gods, whose eyes and malice pursue mortals below, are the phantoms of the mortals' bad faith or self-delusion, and the damnation the gods pronounce is the condemnation that bad faith inflicts on itself. But this fits in exactly with what Roland Barthes said: "In Racine, there is one relation only: that between God and the individual" (p. 55). When Hermione cries: "Qui te l'a dit?" the whole question ultimately is to know *who is who*. What the "psychological" surface of the emotion conceals is a willed crisis of identity, into which Hermione hurls herself in order to save herself. Because the *qui* in her question, if we look deep enough, is no longer a Self, it is no longer *anyone*: it is "Vénus toute entière à sa proie attachée," it is the God that stirs within us and comes to fill that void presented by the human soul with its fatal visitation. It becomes steadily more manifest, as we move chronologically through Racine's plays, finally reaching Joad's divine frenzy, that the mouths of the characters are orifices into which the gods breathe the words. "Qui te l'a dit?" is in this sense therefore the central question, the sole question of Racinian tragedy, of which Hermione's anguished expression constitutes the first, still confused stage, and to which Racine's entire life's work will gradually strive to reply.

Are we home and dry? No. No sooner do we think ourselves comfortable in the shady heart of a theology than we emerge into a sociological clearing, where Lucien Goldmann has been lying in wait for us. "A work of art is at the same time an individual production and a social fact," Sartre said (*Situations IV*, p. 33). A "vision of the world," Goldmann replies, whether rightly or wrongly, is *in the first place* a collective vision, appertaining to a time, a class, a group before being that of an individual. Whatever the truth in this matter, the examination of "literary structures" certainly presents a significant relation with the sociological structures of the age, and of Racine's Jansenist group in particular. This theology of paradox, this hero at once wholly determined and wholly responsible, expresses in a certain sense, beneath the sumptuous disguise of fable, the impossible situation of the professional upper-class man, wholly crushed by the development of a centralist monarchy, yet wholly loyal to the monarch; he too is a tragic hero, precisely because of the lucidity of his gaze, unveiling and demasking the Divinity that he also serves. (We are reminded of Pascal's admirable reflections on kings and royalty, prudently cut from the Port-Royal edition.)

The human condition experienced as a cruel and untranscendable contradiction, that is the heart of tragedy (cf. the last two pages of chapter 2). Referred onward from immediate aesthetic significations to an existential signification, and from that existential signification to a metaphysical, then a theological, then a sociological or, more broadly speaking, historical signification, we are now brought back, at the end, to another *aesthetic* signification (and here I am in agreement with Raymond Picard), but a broader, richer, deeper, aesthetic signification: that of the particular tragic essence that underlies Racinian tragedy. But it is impossible here to fall back as Picard does on literary history, and to invoke the laws of a "tragic genre" that was already fixed in the days of Sophocles and Euripides (Introduction to *Phèdre*, in Racine, *Oeuvres complètes*, vol. 1, p. 748). As we have already said, far from making comprehension easier here, literary history itself demands to be understood. Even if we push the problem of tragedy back through time until we are safely beached on the shores of Greece, history or sociology are still nevertheless bound to yield pride of place, in the last analysis, to philosophic reflection. The meaning of Racinian tragedy lies nowhere else but in Racine: you won't find it in Greece, or in Jansénius: it resides precisely in the unique way in which the individual Jean Racine has absorbed and resorbed, till they have become part of his own substance, the diverse or even contradictory data of his culture and his life.

In short, that simple exclamation of Hermione's has ineluctably presented us with a whole multitude of meanings all mutually requiring each other's collaboration, and of which none is by definition sufficient, since all of them refer us on, if they are to be fully grasped, to all of the others. So that given this semantic multivalence, it is futile to claim that we can reveal a so-called "literary meaning" to which we can then give preeminence. The "purely literary," like the Abbé Brémond's "pure poetry," is a myth that just does not stand up to examination. I do not for a moment deny that "literary structures" and "aesthetic values," in the sense Raymond Picard gives to those terms, do exist; nor do I deny their interest or their importance, which I judge, on the contrary, to be central. A strictly aesthetic level of analysis such as I attempted to define at the outset, amenable to particular and invaluable forms of study, does exist. I am thinking of Jacques Schérer's *Dramaturgie classique en France*, without which it would be impossible to comprehend Racinian tragedy as a form of art, as *staged* expression. To comprehend Racine necessarily entails comprehending that he elected to express himself by use of the stage, and not in the novel, and that this choice lends a direction of its own to the essential meaning of his creation. Racinian style, versification, and writing should undoubtedly be made the object of meticulous and searching inquiries. In short, we must have a criticism directed at the fundamental modes of expression. It nevertheless remains true that literary significations are not reducible to aesthetic significations alone, to mere values of conscious euphemia, in which Raymond Picard seems to regard the whole of literature as residing. There is a whole *moralistic* tradition of French criticism, moreover, existing since the classical age, that was clearly aware of the fact that "to please" is inseparable from "to instruct"; and from Sainte-Beuve to P.-H. Simon one senses instinctively that aesthetic judgment includes an ethical affirmation. Literature's psychic, existential, metaphysical, historical, and ethical significations are not, as Raymond Picard believes, "elsewhere" in relation to the work; they do not merely link it to a *"something else* of which it is the more or less symbolic expression" (*Nouvelle critique*, p. 114). They form the living tissue of literature; and a text is nothing else, in fact, but a certain *texture*.

Images of verticality are deceptive here: there is not some kind of foundation, provided by "preliterary" footings, and then on top, miraculously sprouting from somewhere or other, a palace of "literary structures." Although, self-evidently, the artist's craftmanship must always be added to the inspiration (which is still primary, as Valéry reminds us), and although the work is always also workmanship, or in other words a process of formation imposed on raw material, this does not therefore mean that its meaning is going to lie purely on the surface, or that the form is dissociable, even intellectually, from the material embodying it. Form, in any case, is material radiating its own meaning. In the field that concerns us, since the raw material involved is language, the construction process is one of *imbrication*, not of arrangement in tiers. There is no "above" or "below," and the metaphors used by certain present-day critics are likely to mislead on this point; one no more *ascends* to the general meaning of a work than one *plunges* into its nether regions. Although "profundity" still remains a valid category (and even the only one truly capable of defining litierature), it is on condition that its meaning is properly understood: it is neither a linked sequence of clear and evident implications, on Raymond Picard's Cartesian model, nor a descent, psychoanalytic torch in hand, down into the yawning gulfs of unconscious darkness. Profundity is a *possible* virtue of ambiguity, one that can exist only if the ambiguity is not merely a reflection of muddy thinking but a product of the overdetermination of meaning — which is a manifestation of the richness of human existence itself.[4] The meaning is without doubt wholly in the words, but it is not wholly given to us at one and the same time: it can only be made to yield itself up successively, from a certain series of changing viewpoints; it is fragmented according to the direction of our attention. A tragedy by Racine, when one is under the spell of the verse, is a poem; if one follows the action, it is a drama. This dramatic poem, when linked by intellectual processes to its author, expresses a man's life. But a man and his values must entail a relation to God and to other men; beneath the surface, like watermarks, there lie a religion, a politics, a society. Hence the plurality of possible criticisms, corresponding to the plurality of real significations. Racine's plays are all that, and all at the same time; but we can only see in them what we are focusing on at any given moment. The profundity of a work must therefore be understood in a *perceptual* sense, as one speaks of the depth of a visual field, in which the multiplication of viewpoints can never exhaust the material to be perceived, or achieve the flat and total vision that would display its object in simultaneous entirety. So that there are indeed "levels" of signification, defined by the level of perceptual acuity; there are indeed "depths" of meaning, but not strata. The true critical gaze is by no means the radiographic vision that Picard envisages as passing through its object and with which he reproaches his opponents. Nor, to reiterate the comparison, are the new critics a band of perverts who only enjoy seeing women illumined by

X-rays. I would be more inclined to say that they refuse to join the ranks of the libertines, swelled by the traditionalist critics, for whom a woman is merely a bag of skin, more or less delectably clothed or unclothed, whose surface appearance constitutes her whole charm. For the new critics, on the contrary, a body is more than a body, and what their attentive gaze brings into focus — *on* that body — is a soul, which is to say the entire complex of human significations embodied by that flesh. In the same way, the profound literary work — or beautiful literary work, since the terms are here synonymous — is defined as the totality, or alternatively the concrete convergence and confluence, of all those indefinitely multiplied and extended significations that mutually cry out for one another, as we have said, and of which none, on principle, is sufficient in itself, since each refers us on, if we are to grasp it fully, to all the others. Although the value of a literary work is indeed, in the last as in the first resort, of an aesthetic order, this is only true as long as we do not take "beauty" to be a layer of polish, skillfully applied over a more or less dirty fingernail, which criticism must be careful not to scratch. Beauty is nothing other than the plenitude of an inexhaustible semantic wealth; and the genius of a writer is his ability to imprison the principle of its infinite radiance in the written word.

The reductio ad absurdum proof of this truth, moreover, lies in traditional critical practice. Having failed to grasp that pleasurable aesthetic stimulation does not indicate the presence of a surface, but rather constitutes a depth, the traditional critics, determined at all costs to be literary, are most of the time just *literal*. It is not a coincidence that, having arbitrarily brought signification to an abrupt halt at its most immediate level, the old criticism then proceeds to settle down in self-satisfied seclusion and address itself to tracking down sources, editing texts, compiling glossaries or bibliographies, and all the thousand and one other scholarly chores that concentrate upon the letter of literature and leave the spirit till later. They would agree, of course, that one ought *also* to talk about the actual works; but "Jam tomorrow" seems to be their motto in actual practice. Or else, if they do momentarily bring themselves to relinquish such preliminary exercises — useful, undoubtedly, but only as a preparation — and decide to talk about the works, or in other words attempt a critique of immanence, they just don't have the means at their disposal. Michelet expounds ideas on history and politics. We have to turn Raymond Picard's question around on him: as Roland Barthes justifiably inquires, "what interest could there be in submitting Michelet to ideological criticism, since Michelet's ideology is perfectly clear?" (*Essais critiques*, p. 271). More precisely, we can, if we wish, discuss and evaluate Michelet's ideas, but the result will be *historical or philosophical reflection, not literary criticism*. "What cry out for scrutiny are the *distortions* that Michelet's language imposed upon the nineteenth-century petit-bourgeois credo, the refraction of that ideology into a poetic of substances" (ibid.). Similarly, where literary criticism is concerned, to study Pascal or Bossuet does not mean to study their ideas and *then*, separately, their styles, since that would merely produce theology on the one hand and stylistics on the other; it means attempting to grasp the individual turn, the distinctive accent that those general ideas take on within the language Pascal and Bossuet use to clothe them; it means trying to discover, from the way they express themselves in their works, the indirect or even oblique ways in which their works express them. Taking the opposite view, if, as Raymond Picard maintains, the role of criticism is to tell us "what the work says," then criticism inevitably becomes a *retelling*. It is limiting itself to repeating, less well, what the author has already put better. To confine criticism, by a false epistemology, to the domain of the significations explicitly developed by the work itself, in other words to the level of consciousness and communication that the work has *already achieved*, is to condemn it to mere inventorying and reiteration of obvious facts; it is to doom it, where interpretation is concerned, to perpetual *paraphrase*. And that is in fact the mudbank upon which the old criticism does run aground. What French student has not been subjected, at a high school desk or in prestigious lecture-halls — not always, of course, but too often — to those notorious "explications of texts" that in fact explain nothing? A list is drawn up of Shakespeare's or Corneille's ideas, the roll of Racine's or Marivaux's "passions" is read out. "What the works say" is duly translated into the platitudes of everyday language, or into the meaningless terms of some superficial historical parallel; and to add a little spice to the translation it is peppered with witty quips and stylistic roulades, sprinkled with a little Attic salt filched from the pantries of other, higher-flying lecturers. With professorial pride, Racine is summed up in telling formulas: "Oreste - who - loves - Hermione - who - loves - Pyrrhus - who - loves - Andro - maque - who - loves - Hector - who - is - dead." Very telling, and yet at the same time it tells us nothing. Because criticism does not consist of brilliantly condensing what Racine, even more brilliantly, has already said; it is not mere clever rehashing, wit on wit. If, in *Andromaque*, there exists a strange, circular relationship that opens ultimately onto a void, then the concern of criticism must be to search for a reason, and that search will involve a comparison of the structure of human relationships in this particular tragedy with other structures in the other plays. Further, we cannot make such a comparison, the terms of which exist in Racine's plays and nowhere else, other than from our own viewpoint and using a language that is proper to ourselves, here in the twentieth century, a language that relates, as far as possible, to a conceptual system both coherent in itself and adequate to its object. But this means that we have radically changed our viewpoint. We have moved on from the old criticism to the new.

I have attempted to show, in the previous pages, why Raymond Picard's "optimistic semantic," which is also that of a long critical tradition, seems to me unacceptable. By virtue of the very dimensions of language itself, what a work "means" invariably extends far beyond what it "says"; what it reveals cannot be reduced to what it states, yet nevertheless constitutes an integral part of its "meaning"[5]: such is the fundamental ambiguity inherent in writing, or, if you prefer, its inescapable "polysemy." This phenomenon is easily recognizable, in accordance with the distinction already established, not only on the level of the writing, but also of *the thing written* and of the *writer*, that is, by considering not just the act of writing but its result: the finished product, the work, and the relation of this product to its producer. I have dealt with this aspect of the problem in my *Corneille et la dialectique du héros* (Paris: Gallimard, 1964) and shall here repeat only certain facts that seem to me essential. A work is always also an *object*.[6] An object of a special type certainly, a cultural, and even more precisely an aesthetic object, one that presents itself as a human presence deposited within certain linguistic material and signifying through that material. Whether natural or aesthetic, however, perception presupposes a similar kind of relation: the object does not give itself up except to a consciousness, but the consciousness does not therefore constitute either the existence or the meaning of what is perceived; it discovers them in what it perceives. Like any object, the work of art reveals a fresh "profile" to each new angle of view, without it ever being possible to achieve a total perception that would exhaust the concrete richness of its reality at one glance.

A certain number of consequences must follow from this ontological situation. The finished work, that is, the work finally closed upon its own organized — or, better still, *organic* — totality, presents us with the same significative profusion, the same polysemy as the act of writing itself. There is a ghost haunting traditional criticism that needs exorcizing once and for all: the belief that somewhere back there, in the seventeenth century, there exists a "real meaning" for the plays of Racine or Corneille, a meaning deposited in the womb of time, an original model that we need merely coax up, like Bergsonian memory, to surface visibility. But, in reality, such a Racine-in-himself no more exists than the thing-in-itself. What exists (and it is the only reality that criticism as such needs to know) is a work, and a multiplicity of perspectives giving onto it: the point of view of Racine on himself, of his contemporaries on Racine, of the modern historian or critic on Racine and his contemporaries. Are we to imagine, among all these various points of view, one particular "master" viewpoint that somehow manages to evade all the spatial and temporal laws of perspective? Such a thing is, in principle, impossible, except for God — who is not a critic. And a second illusion, linked to the first, consists in believing that if only we could identify ourselves with the writer, if only we could recapture his exact processes of thought, if only we could *suddenly be him*, then we would at last know the "meaning" of his work (and it is this particular illusion that gives its impulse to a large portion of literary historical research). In short, criticism owes its existence to an unfortunate lacuna, a gap in our knowledge that exists solely because authors have omitted to provide their works with an accompanying intimate journal, have forgotten to insert the appropriate user's instruction leaflet. According to Raymond Picard's logic, since the meaning of the work lies in the totality of the "clear" significations it presents, and since this clarity is the result of a conscious and willed activity, it is evident that the ultimate meaning of the work must be indistinguishable from the act of its creation or, if you prefer, with its genesis.

I must therefore repeat here, with regard to Racine, what I have already said elsewhere with reference to Corneille (*Corneille*, pp. 11 and passim). It is impossible to expect from the writer, from his "conscious" lucidity and his purposive "craft" (even, quite often, despite the very understandable pretensions of his own pride) the *secret* of his work. For as soon as the author ceases to be coincident with the act of creation, then his viewpoint is no more than one more viewpoint among all the others, invaluable certainly, but with no special privileges. The divine creation is permitted to become independent of God; let us, if possible, be equally modest in the case of literary creation. It is well enough known now, thanks to the labors of modern philosophy and psychology, that intellectualized consciousness never perfectly coincides with the nonintellectualized consciousness from which it springs. And even supposing that by some miracle it could so coincide, the space separating intention from act would remain impassable: the written page is incommensurable, no matter what, with the projected page. Though the writer speaks a language, there is also a language speaking through the writer. The real meanings of the written word exceed in every direction the restricted meanings of the word meant. Or, more precisely, the framework of willed significations supports the fabric of the possible significations, of which some, by definition, must escape the author (cf. chap. 11, n. 1). In short, the writer alone controls his creative utterance; but the "meaning" of his creation escapes him in a twofold sense. First, and a priori, even were he possessed of all the "lucidity" in the world, the writer is incapable of substituting himself for the critic, for the good reason that a subject can never know itself as object — "Subject when speaking, object when I listen to myself," as Brice Parain admirably puts it. This *for-others* dimension of a work, like that of embodiment for the consciousness, is irremediable. And to the laws of "spatial" perspective must be added those of "temporal" perspective. Far from its signifying essence being frozen in an eternal present, the work of art is constantly projecting itself toward an indefinite and open future. It is with good reason that we speak of a "living" work: it is mediocre workmanship alone that in fact remains imprisoned in its own historical and cultural moment. Racine's work can no longer change, but it is continually transformed; it can no longer progress, but it can become further enriched; it is impossible to modify it, but it can, in its relation to fresh minds, its contact with fresh history, be renewed. Mallarmé's "As into itself at last, time changes it . . ." is true solely of mediocrity. We must turn our backs on the sterile dream of "definitive" interpretations, of a Racine ne varietur. The insignificant work has an essence, the masterwork an existence, that is to say an essence perpetually becoming, an essence that remains forever, as long as men exist, that is capable of extension. There is no such thing as a meaning given once and for all, a meaning hidden in the work that we ought to attempt to disinter; criticism is not a special branch of archaeology. There are various and contrary meanings already coexisting the moment the work is born; but then, with time, with history, *other* perspectives appear and cause *other* meanings to appear in the *same* object.

To use Raymond Picard's terminology once again, "what the work says" and "the implications of what it says" do not constitute a signifying totality that could ever — thanks to some patiently practiced method or the lightning flash of an intuition — become at some future time clearly and totally formulable. Like any existent, the literary work is still "to be"; it is defined by the meanings that it *will have* as much as by those it *has* and by those it has *had*. (From this point of view, the history of criticism is simply the history of the meanings that have been *lost* by works.) The work projects, into an indefinite future, perpetual possibles that can never be frozen at any given moment of time. Hence an absolute openness, plurality, and insurmountable ambiguity in the written word. But that is not all: there is one last illusion

105

that needs shattering. Not only, as we have shown, does what a written work means never coincide with what it says explicitly, but, since the written work presupposes the existence of a writer, comprehension of the work is inevitably filtered, in a particular way, at a particular level, through a comprehension of its relation to an author. This new dimension introduces a new complexity, and one which any theory of criticism is bound to take into account. Indeed it is upon this reef that Raymond Picard's "optimistic semantics," already so rudely battered, is finally quite wrecked. The primacy of the work, yes — wholehearted agreement there. But only so long as we mean the same thing by it. For the work is not a phenomenon of nature, a meteorite fallen from some mysterious outer space, Mallarmé's "calm block fallen here from some obscure disaster." The fundamental error here (shared on this point by certain "new critics", I should add; see below, part 3) appears to lie in taking the aesthetic *object* in the last resort to be a *thing*. I hope I may be permitted to quote here what I wrote elsewhere: "In stressing the primacy of the work it has not been my intention, for a single instant, to advocate the formalism in which English criticism frequently has its roots. For me, the meaning does indeed reside in the sensible material of the object; but the object is not closed in upon itself so that an investigation of its structures can never be related to anything other than the miracle of its internal equilibrium. Any aesthetic object is also, in reality, the work of a *human project*. To question the work and the work alone, as I said previously, is therefore to attempt to apprehend, through that work, the call of another mind to our own, suggesting a quest, and offering us, finally, a salvation. Through the written text or the acted play, through the beauty of the words or the rigor of the construction, *a man is speaking of man to men*. The aesthetic object, in this regard, constitutes simply a particular case of interhuman relations, a special mode of confrontation with the Other" (*Corneille*, p. 20). Or again, if we perceive the work as a totality of literary structures, it is on condition that we always remember that we are apprehending through it, in J. Starobinski's phrase, "the expression of a *structuring consciousness*" ("Remarques sur le structuralisme," *Festschrift für Hugo Friedrich*).

106

Yes, but in what way does that relate to Raymond Picard's position? it will be asked. I am coming to that now. "What is most important to me in the literary work," he says, "is not the obscure world of anarchic tensions that it transcends by its very use of coherent language, it is the work itself, what it says and what it contributes in the striving of an expression in search of itself" (*Nouvelle critique*, p. 136). It is worth noting that odd vision of a literature being hammered out, ultimately, "in the third person." Because a work cannot *say* anything: a man *says*, either in or through a work; an expression cannot be *in search of itself*: some *one*, a man, searches for an expression. In short, the objectivity, or if you prefer the "it" of the work, is merely one moment in the expression of an "I." And that being so, it is utterly futile, not to say absurd, to attempt to make some absolute separation between a "coherent language," alone worthy of our interest, it seems, and the "obscure world" that it transcends. Because transcendence always implies conservation. In the domain of art (I am not concerned here with science or technique, both by essence impersonal), the final meaning of the workmanship involved is not detachable, like a flower from its stalk, from the raw material employed — in this case tensions and intentions powering a subjective process. Which is precisely why Valéry quite rightly saw the first line of the poem as a gift from the gods, since the poetic craft cannot be conceived or exercised other than from that starting point, and "in harmony" with it. But there can in fact be no harmony except in relation to an original sound, with which the *entirety of a being* vibrates in sympathy. A poem is therefore not an object in the ordinary sense,[7] but rather an "object-subject," an objective moment into which a subjective existence projects itself, since the structuring consciousness of the poet alone, in the last resort, provides the poem's coherent structures. But the structuring consciousness and the "making" consciousness are not identical: the second is merely a particular and partial manifestation of the first, since the "willed and lucid labors" are simply serving as the developer of a deeper intention that is searching for and achieving expression — albeit always imperfectly, because fragmentarily — through those labors.[8] To make, and by making to make oneself: this law of human existence is

107

valid for the writer too. At no moment is consciousness of self in fact absolute self-knowledge and self-possession. It is because the writer, like all men, falls short of himself that, in order to find himself, he does not just write, but *goes on writing*. This impulse, which underlies all his work, alone gives the finished work its meaning. Thus the artist's labors do not confer meaning on the work, as Raymond Picard believes; on the contrary, they *receive their meaning from it*. Charles Mauron is therefore correct in seeing literary creation as a specific act of "self-analysis," by means of which the Self apprehends and, in a way, transcends the world of its internal urges, without this intuitive consciousness ever being objective knowledge. The coherence of literary language, which Raymond Picard rates so highly, is thus not at all of a rational or intellectual order, something cashable in the form of abstractly universal and impersonal significations, separable at will from the interior world out of which they emerged.

"Aesthetic" communication, as its etymology suggests, is established on the level of "sensitivity," on the level of experience, let us say, rather than that of thought. More precisely, thought here is the *form* taken by the experienced material being expressed. This is very easily demonstrable in the case of the most evidently "aesthetic" writers such as Mallarmé or Racine. (For Racine, see in particular the work of Charles Mauron's *Inconscient dans l'oeuvre de Racine*; for Mallarmé, J.-P. Richard's *L'Univers imaginaire de Mallarmé*. It is therefore impossible to establish a clear boundary between a "literary" and a "preliterary" zone, between "coherent language" and affective intuition or apprehension, since aesthetically it is affectivity that gives the language its coherence. The two things are simply different expressive levels of one and the same reality. Although Raymond Picard is quite right to protest against the abuse of psychoanalysis when it claims, despite its lack of tools, to reconstitute for us in a crudely simplistic manner the hypothetical unconscious of an author who has been dead for centuries, and of whom in any case insufficient is known, he is totally wrong in condemning the use of psychoanalytic concepts in order to comprehend the affective structurations that alone provide an account of the aesthetic structurations and, ultimately, of aesthetic *pleasure* itself. The psychoanalytic approach in conditions I shall go into more fully in chapter 8, section 1, becomes one of criticism's legitimate tools of investigation, though not the only one, once the literary work is no longer viewed as a thing but as a special mode of the apparition of the Other. Aesthetic relations proper are viewed against the general background of relations to others. In this respect, psychoanalytical language can mislead us if it supposes the existence within man of a secret "storehouse" or, as Picard puts it, "an obscure world of anarchic tensions" that is somehow closed in upon itself. A man is a network, a meeting place of concrete relations with the universe and with Others; he only finds himself and defines himself as a result of multiple mediations. The "inner world" is not a sealed-off chamber, and the inside is simply the interiorization of an outside. At a certain level, therefore, criticism is rediscovering in the work one individual's story suspended in History. Which means that ultimately it is merely a convenient fiction to distinguish absolutely between "works," "authors," and "readers," as though they were all monadic entities, solitarily spinning in a stellar void, which must somehow be brought into communication. What is in fact given, at the very outset, is a complex relation, articulated in accordance with a dialectic still to be described. The work is not a museum that one visits in order to enjoy agreeable sensations or exquisite cogitations, which we must then be concerned to inventory and preserve in critical formaldehyde. The work is the locus of a *total* meeting between two beings, one seeking for himself, finding then losing himself in a succession of written works like so many stages in a quest, the other lending the warmth of his own life to the signs set down on the dead page, reviving the inner movement of the existence with which he merges himself and for which, at this moment, he is responsible. This meeting is not possible, it is true, except at a certain degree of aesthetic value or, in other words, according to my definition, a certain degree of profundity and richness in the human significations. In this sense, criticism, like any form of literature, is a wrestling match with the Angel; it is confronted, at every moment, on every page, with that irresolvable and yet multiple totality, one and contradictory, conscious and unconscious: man. There is no expressive coherence other than on the existential level. Aesthetic value can never reside merely in the internal organization and technical literary use of a language, in accordance with the old objective Canons of Beauty. It refers back of necessity to the human reality the language is expressing. José-Maria Hérédia utters magnificently, but he has nothing to say. Baudelaire is often flat and muffled, but he is a great poet. The difference here lies not in the quality of the verbal assembly process but in the quality of soul or, better still, of being.

It is because it would not or could not place itself on the existential level that traditional criticism has proved lacking — not to say poverty-stricken. Lingering to elucidate literal meanings or to let the work melt in the mouth like some prize fruit to be appreciated only by "literary connoisseurs," criticism has quite simply missed out on the essential: literature. I shall show this with two complementary and, in my opinion, instructive examples. We are all only too well aware of a certain infantile disease of criticism that French university teaching is only just beginning to throw off: "Andromaque *is* la Duparc," "Pyrrhus *is* Racine," etc. One might suppose, at first glance, that this is just an innocuous little mania, an amusing pastime for lovers of culture crosswords; but in fact that is not so: it is in reality a terrorist methodology that has for a long time now rendered research impotent in France. This scholarly aberration is attempting to provide an intelligible decipherment by juxtaposing and matching up a fragment of a work and a little slice of life, both equally detached from their context and both therefore rendered literally insignificant. Roland Barthes has already denounced the defectiveness and the futility of this notorious "postulate by analogy"— and for once Raymond Picard is in agreement with him. Nevertheless, not enough questions have been asked as to the origin of such a curious aberration, or as to the reasons why it has for so long prevailed. Blame has justifiably been laid on positivism, since that was the reigning ideology when the foundations of a "scientific" method of investigating literary facts were laid down. But we need to look further than that. And if we do we shall realize that, for this "positive" criticism, *comprehending its object* comes to exactly the same thing as *destroying it*. It is, to say the least, extraordinary that if Andromaque "is" la Duparc, and Racine "is" Pyrrhus or Oreste, no one has ever wondered *in what sense*. Supposing that an analogy of situation does exist, in what way does the real situation throw light on the imagined situation, whose features have already been fixed by legend? In what way does the resemblance that has been detected add to our comprehension? And conversely: ought we not ask ourselves whether the imagined situation does not perhaps throw light on the real situation?— whether Racine, in projecting himself into Oreste, is not providing us with a fantasy-persona that may throw a curious light upon its author? In short, the twofold and all-important problem of the *meaning* of the reality when introduced into an imaginary context, and of the imaginary when introduced into a real context, has never even been posed. Yet this very interplay, this dialectical relation, is nothing other than literature itself! For positivism, on the other hand, no dialectic is even possible: the only conceivable relation is that of *derivation*. If Racine speaks of love, then it is because he is *at that moment* in love, and such and such a detail of his work *reflects* such and such a biographical circumstance. But what if Racine had in fact stopped being in love? Or was merely dreaming of becoming so? What if he was writing out of a rejection, as a compensation? In that case one would be forced to grant consciousness a duration of its own, a rhythm and a movement *different* from those of the world; one would be forced, in short, to accord the mind a *reality*, which is to be comprehended and known as such. And that cannot be done by a philosophy of consciousness-as-epiphenomenon, which inevitably produces a conception of literature-as-reflection. Since literature, in Roland Barthes's perceptive phrase, is "institutionalized subjectivity," it follows that, since there is no subjectivity, there is also no literature. In which case, reading a text means reading *through or beyond* a text; it means attempting to bring into focus, beyond the appearances of the written word, its *true* significations, which are those of the real world. It is in this way, feeding on the corpse of literature itself, that the monster of literary history was constituted and perpetuates itself.[9]

It was inevitable, in the end, that this excess should become generally apparent. And in the effort to correct it we are about to rush into the opposite excess, of which Raymond Picard provides us with an example. In order to protect literature from the devouring talons of historicism, its defenders are going to hoist it up onto the pedestal of aestheticism. The literary work, having been viewed until recently as a transparent film, an unsilvered mirror through which history (preferably of the social, gossipy kind) could be discerned, is now about to be tempered into a solid and compact object, a thing whose processes of construction we must study: "The poet must employ raw material that has certain given properties and that will provide resistance to his efforts: language; and his work is determined by laws, rules, and conventions, some of which are common to all literature, others specific to the genre under consideration, and a third and last group particular to the author himself. Thus an entire technique may be defined that is explicative of the work, and which, in many cases, ought to be capable of accounting for the effect produced upon the connoisseur" (Picard, "Avertissement," *Oeuvres complètes de Racine*, vol. 1, p. xiv). One might almost be reading a manifesto of the American New Critics in the thirties. Nothing could be more misguided (and the criticism of today is fundamentally a reaction against precisely this error) than this "aesthetic fetishism, so hermetically closed in upon itself and claiming to find a total or even sufficient meaning within itself. Nothing could be more ingenuous than this conception of the work as a sort of machine for producing "effects" in obedience to recipes provided by a "technique" which it is criticism's role to formulate. We have already seen that the literary is in no way reducible to the aesthetic, properly understood. Of course it is true that Racine's plays make use of techniques, and on various levels, from the rules of grammar and versification to those of dramaturgy. But these techniques have no virtue in themselves; you may find them expounded theoretically in d'Aubignac and being practiced by any number of minor poets of the time. Further, these techniques constitute all that is most outworn, most outdated in Racine's plays, and if his spell still works it is not because of them but in spite of them. Because what sustains a technique, what gives such a body of percepts a soul is what Proust calls a *vision* — "Style for the writer, just as much as color for the painter, is a question not of technique but of vision" (*Le Temps retrouvé*). It is the Racinian vision that alone supports his plays from end to end, that alone arouses in us the perpetually reborn emotion that lies beneath the historically dated and old-fashioned literary expression. The "particularities" of an author, which is to say the very impulse of his existence, are not a mere addendum, a factor to be added to all the others, the final item on a list: they constitute the flesh, the marrow of his literary expression. As the result of one of those good intentions with which the road to hell is paved, respect for the literary object has transformed it into a *thing*, with which the "connoisseur" (a significant choice of word) has an appreciative consumer relation, so that literary art becomes a kind of culinary art for which criticism is to provide us with the recipes. Which faces us with a curious dichotomy: on the one hand we have an author, Racine the courtier, the opportunist Rastignac of letters, whose "career" Raymond Picard patiently follows through the world; and on the other hand we have his work, which the same Raymond Picard presents to us quite separately, on a plane that never intersects with the first, as the depository of intrinsic and autonomous "aesthetic" and "psychological" significations. An author crawling on the ground, masterpieces falling from heaven: sort it out as best you can. And after that, Picard goes on to laugh heartily at those "ingenuous" readers who "have expressed shock at being unable to detect any connection between the man whose career was being recounted and the tragedies," because Picard had not *attempted* to establish any such connection, for the simple reason that he believes such a connection to be impossible. And he praises as "perspicacious" those who "understood so clearly that my work could, on the contrary, constitute an excellent weapon in the war against biographical criticism." [10] So: a contemptible life on the one hand, works of genius on the other, and no intelligible link between them: literature is indeed a miraculous product. So much positivism, as Roland Barthes has commented, only to end up "regarding the work as a (mysterious) synthesis of (rational) elements." Thus Racine, we must understand, was bound to create because of his creative properties, in the same way as opium makes us sleep because of its soporific properties. In short, we have not gained all that much by exchanging historicism for aestheticism, and by progressing from the Mornet school to that of Picard. For want of a coherent system that will enable us to understand how a work of imagination reverberates in harmony with the profoundest level of a real life (that of the writer and my own), for want, in short, of a philosophy that is able to grasp and embrace relations of existence, criticism tacks from Scylla to Charybdis, perpetually wavers between authors without works and works without authors, and eternally fails to arrive at literature itself.

Part Two
INTRODUCTION TO THE PROBLEMS OF CRITICISM NOW

5

THE SEARCH
FOR UNITY

So what is to be done? Precisely what Raymond Picard refuses to do in his treatment of both Racine's life and his work. I should like to quote two passages that seem to me particularly conclusive. On the life: "I have tried not to judge, not to draw conclusions, not to reduce to some factitious unity a multiplicity of various kinds of behavior that Racine himself was not concerned to bring into harmony; for he can scarcely be said to have introduced into his life the logic and the lucidity that we believe to be evident in his aesthetic creation" (*La Carrière de Jean Racine*, pp. 9–10). And on the work[1]: "All this apparatus is in truth very fragmentary: there was no question of attempting to be exhaustive, or even systematic. What mattered above all was to accumulate — without worrying too much about appearing ingenuous or academic — a quantity of observations, covering as wide a range of fields as possible, in order to indicate the multiplicity of paths that Racinian studies may take" (Racine, *Oeuvres complètes*, vol. 1, p. xiv).[2] In both cases, what is involved is a conscious intention not to go beyond a simple *empirical* apprehension, a critical paper chase: the important thing is to "accumulate" notations, to make a collection "covering as wide a range of fields as possible" of minute facts. The mortal sin here, it is clear, would be any attempt to be "exhaustive" or "systematic," to search for a "factitious unity." What exists is multiplicity: let the details speak. And with a little bit of luck, when all the facts are gathered in, the meaning will come. What you must do is "allow yourself to be submerged by the richness of a work," and then "anyone who wished to deepen his pleasure might perhaps discover in these scattered observations a certain convergence" (ibid., pp. xiv–xv). "Perhaps . . ." In other words, all you can do is hope and pray for the miracle of this "convergence." Whereas the new criticism, on the other hand, refuses to wait for Godot. Its awareness of diversity is no less acute than that of the old criticism, but it also has the certainty that this diversity intersects and converges, on condition, of course, that it is *made to converge*. The light of meaning is not a flame that will spring to life all on its own at the tip of a candle. Bacon was mistaken, and traditional criticism is his last refuge. We know since Descartes that facts speak, but we have to *invent* their language: a *method* is no more nor less than that, but it is everything.

It is no part of my intention, as I have already said, to write a history of the new criticism. One day, no doubt, a thesis will be devoted to it, an investigation that will decide where it begins, where it ends, and whom it includes. This essay is intended to occupy a rather different level, and I am concerned not with enumerating the new criticism's tendencies but rather with indicating the problems around which it revolves. Significant ambiguity, significant overdetermination, significant multivalence: I trust that the analyses in previous chapters will have successfully stressed their importance at all levels. This proliferation is not, however, an anarchy: it is *oriented*. The multiple meanings that any reading elicits, and which merge one into another, do not constitute a wild vortex, a swirling chaos; they are articulated with one another around a central peak; they converge upon a central focus. In other terms, the diverse *significations* refer us on to an ultimate meaning, which is in fact the secret unity given within the concrete totality of the object: "I shall say that an object has a *meaning* when it is the embodiment of a reality which transcends it, but which we cannot apprehend outside it, and whose infinity makes it impossible to express adequately by any system of signs; what is involved is always a totality: the totality of a person, of an environment, of an age, of the human condition" (Sartre, *Situations IV*, p. 30). And, we should add, the totality of a work. It must be said of the work of art, mutatis mutandis, what Merleau-Ponty said of the "thing," whose aspects all implicate one another in an absolute plenitude: "It is impossible to describe the color of the carpet completely without saying that it is a carpet, a wool carpet, and without implying in that color a certain tactile value, a certain weight, a certain resistance to sound. The thing is that kind of being in which the complete definition of an attribute requires that of the subject in its entirety, and in which, in consequence, meaning is indistinguishable from the total appearance" (*Phénoménologie de la perception*, p. 373). Similarly, the meaning of a work will be its "total appearance," which is to say the totality of its appearances. The correct critical perception will be that which attains a "precise grasp," which apprehends the work simultaneously in its *unity* and its *totality*, in the concrete communication of its particular aspects. It will involve comprehending the parts through the whole they form, and the whole not as the product of mere addition but as a synthesis of interconnected parts. Just as true perception tends to bring out, through the systematic coordination of its profiles, the full cohesion of the thing, so, with Lucien Goldmann, we would say that in criticism "the valid meaning is that which makes it possible to discern the whole coherence of the work" (*Le Dieu caché*, p. 22).

Unity, totality, coherence: I believe that to be a motto common to all the new critics or, if you prefer, their common postulate. It has often been said that the new criticism is a "critique of significations." In fact, it is on the contrary a critique of *meaning*, as we have just defined it. On this point, and quite rightly, Raymond Picard quotes Charles Mauron, who sees "Racine's entire lifework as a unique musical score, unfolding the variations of a singular dramatic situation," and also J.-P. Richard, who asserts that "modern criticism merits . . . the epithet *totalitarian*. By which I mean that it aims at repossessing the work . . . in its totality, which is to say in both its unity and its coherence. It is a criticism of *wholes*, not of details" (*Nouvelle critique*, p. 107.) And, as we have already seen, Raymond Picard could also perfectly well have quoted Lucien Goldmann, or Sartre, who finds revealed in the characters of Genet, as in the actions of Baudelaire, "a different modulation of the original theme" (*Saint Genet*, p. 500), or Roland Barthes, for whom criticism should achieve "its nature as simultaneously coherent and total language" (*Essais critiques*, p. 271).

119

And it would be possible to find another ten analogous quotations in ten other critics.[3] And I must point out that this search for significant unity beneath an apparently irreducible diversity, common to all post-Hegelian philosophic thought and to all the human sciences from Freudian psychoanalysis to the structuralism of Lévi-Strauss, corresponds in the field of literary criticism not merely to a theoretical need, but also to a practical requirement.

I hope I may be permitted to leave Racine for a moment and turn to Corneille, whose work I have had occasion to study with particular closeness. And it is in fact the most empirical, the most positivist studies of him, those furthest from any concern with ideological elucidation, which have proved most conclusively that in this vast and varied body of work, spread over fifty years and prompted by an infinite diversity of personal and historical circumstances, all the very evident differences are organized around a profound central kinship. In his "Remarques sur la technique dramatique de Corneille," as well as in another study, "L'Invention chez Corneille," Jean Boorsch, theoretically hostile though he is to what he terms "the obsession with unity," nevertheless ends up by demonstrating the striking and systematic convergence of Corneille's methods of scenic expression (*Yale Romantic Studies*, 1941, p. 101). Analyzing "the recurrence of characters in Corneille's comedies," Jacques Schérer concludes: "He creates characters of such reality that they take him over, and he clearly has an overall vision of his work. The synthetic nature of his comic plays could also be proved by two other pieces of research. One such study would investigate the analogies between the situations and the themes of all the comedies. . . . The other would investigate the emotional geography of the Paris in which almost all his comic works are set" (*Mélanges Mornet*, p. 61). Stating the case in an even more clear-cut and general form, a purely statistical investigation into "Corneille's self-imitation"— in other words, the textual borrowings that he constantly makes from himself — leads to the following conclusion: "It seems possible that the deeper levels of Corneille's personality may have predisposed him to a certain formal monotony. He is obsessed by certain situations, certain themes; he has a strong tendency to choose subjects for

120

his plays that are really very close to one another beneath their apparent diversity. A subject is not solely an opportunity for him to compose a fine piece of work, it is a chance to express a Cornelian reality" (F. Rostand, *L'Imitation de soi chez Corneille*, p. 10). It would be hard to define the relationship between the aesthetic and the existential better. Lastly, in an article that appeared after his great work on the subject, Octave Nadal indicates very precisely the nature of the work still remaining to be done: "No one has as yet made a precise enumeration of the key motifs, nor clarified their connections and their internal relationships. Such a study would make clear the dazzling richness and the masterly articulation of all the themes he dealt with from *Mélite* right through to *Suréna*" ("L'Exercise du crime chez Corneille," *Mercure de France*, 1951). Convergence, synthetic nature, central obsession giving form to a personal reality, leitmotifs, articulations: these key terms of the new criticisms are discovered and used quite spontaneously by empirical research — when it is sufficiently serious and searching. This considered determination to achieve a unitary and totalitarian comprehension is not, as one might think when reading Raymond Picard, an isolated aberration peculiar to a few misled and perverse intellectuals; it is not even a product of the broad currents of modern thought now penetrating the field of literary thought: it is, quite simply, a fundamental requirement of criticism itself — once it has reached the age of maturity.

CRITICISM AS
PHENOMENOLOGY

THUS, as Leo Spitzer has said, "the time is past when the critic could read a masterpiece as though indulging in some kind of leisure activity, without feeling any obligation to link the parts to the whole, expressing here his approval, there his disapproval, in accordance with the momentary humor of his eudaemonist sensibility" (*Linguistics and Literary History*, p. 129). *To link the parts of the whole*: that is indeed the fundamental procedure of modern thought, as well as the continuation of an age-old endeavor. And without going back as far as Plato's *Phaedrus*, Spitzer also reminds us that Schleiermacher, in philology, was already saying in his day that "the detail can be understood solely in relation to the whole, and an explication of any detail presupposes knowledge of the totality." Dilthey talked of *Zirkel im Verstehen*, "circular comprehension." And since every circle turns around a center, all circular comprehension, on pain of becoming scattered and vaporized, must be unitary. When Taine assigned criticism the task of "rendering the spectacle of the marvelous necessities that interlink the innumerable, subtly different, tangled threads of each man's being," he was mistaken about the means to be employed, not about the ends. Let us say that modern criticism wishes to be possessed by a total coherence. It will therefore set up as its first task the elucidation, within the object under scrutiny, of *structures*, which is to say of a certain internal arrangement or articulation such that the parts can be comprehended solely through the totality they form, and the details signify solely by means of the whole in which they occur.[1] It should be noted

that these structures, or if you prefer, these coherent and signifying totalities, are in no way the exclusive property of literary
criticism; they are to be found in any area where man is in a
dynamic relationship with the world — perception (structures of
the thing, studied by the gestaltists), activity (behavioral structures, analyzed by Merleau-Ponty), speech (linguistic structures),
art (aesthetic structures). This is not the place to involve ourselves
in a philosophy, or even a metaphysics of structure,[2] but simply
to indicate the methodological consequences that arise in the particular field in which we are working. The study of literary structures comes within the province of what is strictly a *phenomenology*,
which is to say the description of an organization — or better
still, of an organicity — existing within the work. As I tried to
show earlier in the case of a particular example, to understand
Hermione's cry of "Qui te l'a dit?" means, it need hardly be said,
to replace it in its immediate poetic, psychological, and dramatic
context (first hemistich of a line in a certain scene, uttered by
a given character and in a given situation). A meaning is fragmentary to begin with; it signifies by means of its immediate environment, within the scaffolding that enables it to achieve concrete
perceptibility. In the theater, to take a particular example, the
meaning of a tragedy will yield itself up only gradually, step by
step, emotion by emotion: we say quite accurately that a play
"captivates" us. But the duration experienced by a spectator's fascinated consciousness is not the same as that experienced by the
reflexive consciousness:[3] time for the critic, reading at leisure,
able to move here and there through the work in any direction,
is not the univocal time of the spectator riveted to the performance. Hermione's cry, when read, is not the same as the cry
heard: it demands new contexts; more remote but no less imperative frames of signification appear. We perceive no longer just
a fragment of one scene, or a single scene, but the entire tragedy,
of which the cry marks an essential stage, and the relation of
that tragedy to a whole made up by all the other tragedies, to
Racine's entire life's work viewed as a body of dramaturgy, as
the development of a unique and ceaselessly deepened vision of
man. It is on this point that the new criticism radically parts company with the old. The latter will doubtless allow that a work

forms a whole, but that whole — in obedience to the logic of empiricist comprehension — still remains *in isolation* (cf. chap. 5, n. 1). For the new criticism, on the contrary, the individual work is, in accordance with Péguy's phrase, "a member of a closeknit family"; the whole it forms becomes in its turn a part of the totality constituted by an author's works taken all together, and does not acquire its true, which is to say ultimate, meaning until replaced within that whole.

This literary phenomenology — or elucidation of the structures of the work and of their mode of articulation — presupposes that there is a meaning immanent in the work that we have to discover. In contrast to the discontinuous and disjointed approach of the traditional criticism, modern — or simply serious — criticism must start by being *une lecture systématique* (a system of reading) in the sense in which *lire* (to read) is always also *lier* (to bind).[4]

In gestaltist language one could say that meaning is a figure or configuration that varies according to the background against which it is placed. For it is true that any structure offers itself to us from a certain exclusive viewpoint. The *objective* elements of its composition (which are undoubtedly present in what is perceived) can yield themselves only to a *subjective* viewpoint (since all perception presupposes a perceiving consciousness). In terms of literature, this means that the same work can therefore be dissected in different ways in order to reveal different structures, depending upon the relation of the observer to the object of his observation, or rather, in this case, of the participant to the object of his participation. Which is where the drama begins. This relation, which in the realm of science would constitute the scientist's "personal equation," becomes in the case of literature the critic's *total engagement*, which involves him on every level, intellectual and affective alike. As Roland Barthes quite rightly says: "Any reading of Racine, however impersonal it strives to make itself, is a projection test." How could it be otherwise? If all criticism entails using a system of references, then that system in its turn implies a choice, which Barthes describes, to Raymond Picard's great indignation, as the critic's "fatal wager." And yet that is exactly what is involved: a "wager" in the sense that Pascal used the word, since after all any ideological position of any sort presupposes

124

and also manifests a personal project; and a "fatal" wager insofar as the first decision weighs ineluctably on all the rest of the investigation. I can already hear voices raised in indignation: we reject this wager and this fatality of yours, we shall content ourselves with outlining "zones of objectivity," with gathering tangible and clear "facts," thanks to which we shall put forward our "prudent hypotheses." We are already familiar with such language: it is that of Raymond Picard. Vain protests. Our answer to this critical Malherbe is Pascal's own: it is impossible not to "wager," you are already in the game — and making a poor showing. Your "certainties of language" and your "psychological coherence" only conceal, as we have seen, uncertainty and incoherence. There is no "neutral" or "innocent" language, no excuse, no refuge. To reject any system of reading is simply to make lack of system into a system, that of facility; to reject all ideology is likewise an ideology, that of the ostrich. When you self-righteously decry Roland Barthes's paranoiac frenzies and offer in its place the "moderation" proper to a "measured" criticism ("measuring out the degree of affirmation that has been decided upon"), this criticism by calibrated doses in no way provides a manifest primary stratum of evidence, independent of any system: you are making a wager. You are putting your money, as it were, on the postulates of an empiricist positivism, a system that believes it is possible to arrive at a meaning by the juxtaposition of fragmentary significations, just as it was believed, in the nineteenth century, that it was possible to provide oneself with an object by adding together isolated sensations; you are wagering that convergence will eventually occur, more or less, all on its own: in both cases there is convergence at the end only if there has been convergence at the outset. When Roland Barthes says that "things do not signify more or less, they either signify or they do not," we must begin, in order to understand him, by actually reading him.[5] This "startling doctrine," as you call it, does not in any way require the critic to "compensate for the gratuity of his assertions by their audacity and depth"; it is simply saying — and how is it possible to disagree? — that any given detail possesses signification solely by virtue of a preliminary and implicit intention that *decides in advance* what signification is, as a function of its postulates. And "positive" criticism decides in this respect just as much as any other kind: to say that the *fact* of Racine's being in love with la Duparc when he wrote *Andromaque*, for example, *explains* this or that in the play must presuppose a system of precise references that relates the author's life to his work in accordance with a certain schema; taken on its own, that "fact" has literally *no meaning*. And if, following Picard and rejecting Mornet, we take the view that biography and literature are two quite separate orders of reality, approachable, at all events, only by different paths, then that too is a decision, a choice, a "fatal wager." So we might as well all be honest about it, as Roland Barthes asks, play the game according to the rules, and openly declare our particular "system of reading."

But one can understand the immediate and timorous retreat of a certain kind of academic criticism, caught *flagrante delicto* indulging in "subjectivism" when it imagined itself to be strolling calmly among Platonic Ideas and Objective Truths, Who, me? The critic looks around in embarrassment for an intellectual figleaf. He feels fingers pointing at him, as though he has been caught in the act of exhibiting himself. Just when he is talking so "objectively" about the work, suddenly he is told that he is using his subjectivity. A vicious circle. The critic pulls himself together, as we have seen; he hits back, he begins to laugh. But the laughter is a mask for his unease: if Racine means something other than what he says and Barthes is saying something other than what he thinks he is saying, can Pingaud be sure of interpreting Barthes correctly? A wild goose chase through a maze. I cannot resist quoting here a nicely turned passage from Sartre, one that might have been custom-written for the purpose: "It is claimed that the novelist depicts himself in his characters and the critic in his criticisms; so if Blanchot is speaking to us about Mallarmé it will be said that he is telling us more about himself than about the author he is dealing with. . . . Now follow that through: Blanchot has seen nothing in Mallarmé but Blanchot; very well: then you are seeing nothing in Blanchot but you. In that case, how can you know whether Blanchot is talking about Mallarmé or about himself? It is the vicious circle of all skepticism, so let us leave such outdated parlor games where they belong. Of course — one feels ashamed to repeat such truisms, but our philosophical dilettantes are so stupid and so vain that one has little choice — of course Blanchot's viewpoint is personal to him. And similarly, whatever the instruments he uses, ultimately it is with *his own* eyes that the experimenter observes the results of his experiment. But although objectivity is thereby, to a certain extent, distorted, it is just as certainly *revealed*. Blanchot's emotional makeup, his individual cast of mind, and his particular sensibility incline him to make such and such a conjecture rather than another; but it is Mallarmé alone who will verify Blanchot's conjecture. A critic's mental habits and affectivity act as "developers," prepare the way for intuition. The conjecture, whether true or false, is a deciphering tool. If true, it is filled out by the facts; if false, it is erased in favor of the fresh paths to which it points" (*Saint Genet*, p. 517). Which means that the critic's subjectivity is irremediable. As with perception, the process of objective revelation remains a personal contact. The subject has no access to the world except through *his own* viewpoint, specifically situated in space and time, conditioned by a geographical and historical commitment that he discards only with his life.

It must also be noted, however, that an acceptance of the critic's subjectivity and, more precisely, of his liberty, by no means resolves the problem: it merely poses it. In the passage just quoted, Sartre very clearly points out that although Blanchot's internal dispositions "prepared the way for intuition," such intuition, if it is to be valid, must be "filled out by the facts." In other terms, the critic's subjectivity, fully recognized and assumed, puts the *truth* of his criticism on trial. For Sartre, ever Cartesian in the matter of intuition, there would seem to be a sort of "evident truth" specific to criticism, which, needless to say, would provide an elegant solution to the problem. But there is no evidence for such an evident truth, and skepticism is not so easily defeated. The spectacle of the disagreements that so constantly and totally divide our critics, old and new alike, conduces to a less optimistic view. In the case of Racine, while the traditional criticism continues to oscillate between the "pagan" and the "Jansenist" interpretations of his work, so the Marxist vision of a Goldmann and the psychoanalytic codebreaking of a Mauron fail to converge at any point; and even within the confines of the psychoanalytic approach, the results of Barthes's work differ completely from those of Mauron's. Where then are we to find the evidence that will say what is true and what false? Of what kind must it be? The ironies of certain old-guard commentators on the confusion of the "Pingaud-on-Barthes-on-Racine" progression are absurd when viewed as an attempt to sidestep a crucial problem; but they are useful in that they pose it. Ultimately, in fact, the indisputable superiority of the new criticism over the old is that it has given up crying ingenuously with Sainte-Beuve: "True art, only what is true," in order to face the problem of truth squarely and integrate it consciously into its research.

Literary phenomenology, as I defined it earlier, must inevitably collide in practice with the phenomenologist's untranscendable subjectivity. Unlike the scientist, whose "personal equation" can be allowed for and superseded by objective relations, the critic's "personal equation" is permanently with him. "It is upon contact with my questioning that structures manifest themselves and become perceptible, in a text long since fixed upon the page of the book. The various types of reading all select and isolate *preferential* structures. It is not a matter of indifference whether we question a text as historians, as sociologists, as psychologists, as stylisticians, or as connoisseurs of pure beauty. Because the effect of each one of those approaches is to change the configuration of the *whole*, to summon a new context into being, to define new frontiers, within which another law of coherence will hold sway" ("Remarques sur le structuralisme"). That passage, by Starobinski, exactly defines the nub of this problem. The ambiguity of literary writing, the multivalence upon which it is founded, immediately give rise to *several possible organizations of the same organism*. The structuralist critic will draw attention to a certain number of frameworks immanent in the work: affective, imaginative, symbolic, ideological, etc. Although the new criticism is defined essentially by its search for "coherence," it is unfortunately true that the type of coherence itself changes with the type of signification selected: as soon as we pass from theory to practice the school of unity becomes disunited.

In order to grasp this more clearly let us return to Racine, a battlefield so long favored by French critics, littered already with three centuries of critical dead. The choice that decides the nature and level of the signification to be sought is also, and simultaneously, a decision as to the meaning of the work and of all literature. Shall we decree, with Raymond Picard, that the literary reality is of a purely aesthetic order? Very well; let us examine the consequences of that. Racine's whole creation then appears before all else as the utilization of a technique, whose value will be measured by its success in producing certain "effects" on reader or spectator. The reality, the coherence proper to this dramaturgy will therefore be defined in relation to certain "rules, laws, and conventions," with Racine's own personality intervening in the role of a differential index within a preestablished framework. Behind Raymond Picard's "technical" choice there is discernible the radical option of an intellectualistic metaphysic. The "value" of a technical result (aesthetic value) lies not in the quality of a raw material (Racinian existence), but in the way it is used (willed and intelligent construction, detachable from the constructor and therefore, by definition, valid when considered separately from him, through its effect on Others). By scrubbing the "literary" clean of the "preliterary," by detaching the work from a biography, man is purged of the accidental and the crude, he is elevated to the nontemporal kingdom of pure Mind. Giving preeminence to "technique" becomes, for literary research, a way of edging furtively a little nearer to Reason, of finding a modern substitute for the abstract Universal of rationalism, for the transcendent I. The choice of an aesthetic coherence understood in this way superimposes upon Racine a certain vision of the would — the critic's. But literature is the concrete Universal, man; not in the clarity of his intellect but in the opacity and animality of his passions. So that in direct contrast to Raymond Picard (whose methodological opposition to psychoanalysis reveals, as is always the case, a metaphysical opposition), the psychoanalytical approach to literature puts forward a quite different view of man: to look for the coherence specific to Racine's theater in the constancy of certain emotional relationships (father-son, brother-sister, etc.) and in their configuration, in order to go on and construe the Racinian dramaturgy as an interplay of forces

(Mauron) or a combination of figures (Barthes), is to decide that the genuine meaning of men's actions, as well as their works, never lies in a purposeful process that is both conscious and transparent to itself, but in the always ambiguous relation of the willed impulses and the emotional stimuli that underlie them. And to think, as Lukács and Lucien Goldmann do, that the true significations are of neither an aesthetic nor a psychological but a sociological order, is not merely to propose just one more possible method among methods: it implies a judgment that the authentic subject of cultural creation is not the individual but the group; it means being led to define, in the heart of subjectivity, an intrasubjective reality that is alone capable of providing the high degree of coherence constitutive of the work of art.

And where does Racine fit into all this? We have Picard's Racine, Mauron's Racine, Barthes's Racine, Goldmann's Racine, just as we have in the past had the Racines of Giraudoux and Thierry Maulnier, Mornet and Lemaître, just as we shall one day, in the twenty-first century, have the Racines of X or Y. All these Racines bear precious little resemblance to one another, and it would be foolish to be surprised by the fact, when you remember that the "Racine-in-himself," the "real Racine," and the "archetypal Racine" are after all pure figments. So should we let ourselves slide into an ironical relativism, a smiling or bitter skepticism? That would be just as absurd. As we have already seen, Picard, Mauron, Barthes, and Goldmann, by fully assuming a *subjective* choice, are all revealing, in Racine, an *objective* reality. That is not the problem though. The difficulty is not: to each his truth, therefore there can be no truth. It is rather: *how are we to link together these individual, real, and contrary truths?* Because the aesthetic, psychological, and sociological significations that are uncovered for us are indeed there in Racine's work, but they do not intersect one another, any more than the divergent viewpoints, the contradictory choices that have served to reveal them. If we could add the viewpoints up like figures and juxtapose the methods in order to arrive at a total truth, then everything would be simple; if we could superimpose a number of partially coherent structures, isolated at different levels of signification, thus arriving at a global structure and a complete coherence, then we could entrust a "super-

130

criticism" with this labor of integration. Unfortunately, however, such a super-criticism no more exists than does a super-vision able to include every possible viewpoint and perceive the six sides of a cube all at once. The same ill-starred law holds good for both natural and aesthetic perception: that which reveals must at the same time conceal. Which is why criticism (old or new), like surrealism, is made up first and foremost of *exclusivities*: Picard, with a stroke of his pen, disposes of Mauron, Goldmann, and Jasinski; Goldmann dismisses Mauron and Barthes. A perpetual circular pogrom. Far from there being any possible agreement, there is an intellectual imperialism at work within each viewpoint. When a critic is apparently paying tribute to all the others, then one should be on one's guard: like an ogre, he is doing it in order to devour them in the end. And yet, within the literary work itself, a convergence of all the levels of human signification does exist — a convergence which, according to my view, actually constitutes literature. The misfortune of criticism is that in the attempt to bring this convergence out from an implicit to an explicit state, it explodes it. The ambiguous does not allow itself to be poured without loss into the mold of a concept: once petrified, it shatters into fragments. And criticism is left standing there, its structures left in its hands, unable ever to collect them together into an undiscoverable "structure of structures." The laws of the tragic genre, Racine's teeming unconscious, the contradictory stresses within the *noblesse de robe*— all these provide us, in certain respects, with a certain grip on these plays: but how are we to make the transition from one particular order of signification to another and radically different one? How are we to bridge the gap between them with some intelligible link? And how are we to grant arbitrary favor to just one of them? Picard tells us: Racine is before all else theater, and the theater, in his day, is a certain reality; you can never find Racine elsewhere than on that stage. Mauron replies: the theater does not exist in a vacuum; the work has an author, and the author projects into his work all that exists in his own depths. At which Goldmannn retorts: yes, Racine has an Oedipus complex, but then so do you and I; the meaning of a particular work does not lie in a universal complex. You must look for that precise meaning, for the work's true coherence, outside the individual,

131

in the structure of his group. They are all wrong, to the same degree that they are all right; because Racine is all that *together*: when he writes, it is *with*-his-Oedipus-complex-*in*-a-professional-upper-class-or-court-environment-*for*-the-theater, indiscriminately; and his "genius" is nothing other than the total convergence of his being in his work. It is this convergence, realized in practice by art, that critical thought attempts to recapture and review. Criticism confronting literature is like the frog confronting the ox; it puffs up its explanations like the frog its body, in the hope of rivaling its model. We know how the fable ends. Is this misfortune, this drama of criticism we mentioned earlier, going to explode into tragedy?

Part Three
CRITICISM AND THE HUMAN SCIENCES

TRUTH OR VALIDITY?

HAVING set out to grasp the work in its unity and its totality, the new criticism has revealed *a number* of unities and *a number* of totalities or, if we wish to use Sartre's terminology, a "detotalized totality." In other words, we do not have *a* new criticism but a number of irreducible and contradictory new criticisms (or criticisms period), all sprung from a shared intention. Roland Barthes's great merit is that he was the first to become acutely aware of this problem, and to have suggested guidelines for a coherent solution to it. For before him, all critics, old or new, despite the contradictory paths they chose, seem to have shared a single ambition: to speak *truly* or to speak *the truth* about Racine. We are now sufficiently familiar with traditional criticism's pretentions to "objectivity." If we glance through the theoretical manifestoes of Mauron or Goldmann, we find that, despite the opposition between them, both are concerned solely with "scientific truth." Even Sartre, as we have seen, invokes "factual evidence" that is supposed to fill out the critic's intuition and decide, as in Descartes, what exactly is true and what false. Unhappily, however, all these guardians of the truth are at daggers drawn, and on this point skepticism is easier to decry than to refute. The ingenious proposition that Roland Barthes has come up with is that the only way of extricating ourselves from an impossible situation is to turn it inside out, and that the only practical method of overcoming skepticism is *to institutionalize it.*

Barthes's great discovery is that in the field of criticism truth, like God, does not exist. "Criticism is something other than speaking accurately in the name of 'true' principles" (*Essais critiques*, p. 254). Critical comprehension is not of an alethic order; its governing principle does not lie within the category of truth. "The world exists and the writer speaks, that is literature. The object of criticism is very different; it is not the 'world,' it is a discourse, the discourse of another human being: criticism is a discourse on a discourse; it is a *secondary language*, or a *metalanguage* (as the logicians say), whose action is directed onto a primary language (or *language-object*)" (ibid. p. 255). The consequence of this parallel between critical and logical activity is immediately apparent: "If criticism is merely a metalanguage, that means that its task is not to discover 'truths' at all, but only 'validities.' In itself, a language is not true or false, it is either valid or it is not — valid in the sense of constituting a coherent system of signs" (ibid.). This being so, it becomes easier to understand why "confronted with his object, the critic therefore enjoys an absolute freedom" (ibid. p. 270); his reading must be systematic, but there exists a multitude of possible systems, and logic here is "*n*-dimensional." The critic's freedom will thus consist in "deliberately advertising that fatal wager which has decided him to speak of Racine in one particular way and not in any other" (*Sur Racine*, p. 166). Since, as we have amply observed, it is possible to bring to bear on the original Racinian language a contradictory variety of critical languages (aesthetic, metaphysical, psychoanalytical, sociological, etc.), which no superlanguage can ever draw together into a unity, we must go on to the end and draw the inescapable conclusion: as soon as it is accepted that the ratifying criterion of criticism is "not truth but its own validity," then "any kind of criticism whatever may be brought to bear upon any object whatever" (*Essais critiques*, p. 270).

That seems to be Barthes's central and most audacious proposition. Though it is essential that we understand clearly what he is saying, and avoid the error that Picard immediately rushes into (*Nouvelle critique*, p. 66) when he triumphantly translates all this to mean: therefore anyone can say *anything at all*! Which of course would be a scandal of scandals. Picard's simple-mindedness here reminds me of the argument used by certain doughty opponents of atheism: if God does not exist, then everything is permissible;

you can kill your father and mother, rape your sisters and your cousins. Barthes does not say that anyone can say "anything," which would be absurd, but that the critic can say what he is saying "in any way," which is something quite different. The critic is free to select the language — or, if you prefer, the level of signification — upon which he will elect to take his stand; but that choice once made, he is committed to a rigid system of constraints and requirements: "This freedom in principle is . . . subject to two conditions, and those conditions, internal though they are, are precisely those that enable the critic to achieve intelligibility within his own account: on the one hand the critical language chosen must be homogenous, structurally coherent, and, on the other, it must succeed in saturating the entire object of his discourse" (*Essais critiques*, p. 270). Which makes it clear what I meant when I wrote that Barthes's solution was to overcome skepticism by "institutionalising" it. For skepticism cannot be defined, in practice, other than in relation to a search for what is true; and we say of truth, quite rightly (excluding the domain of religious faith), that it is "objective," which implies agreement with an object. The reversal that Barthes has achieved is clear. Eliminate the *external* relationship of a conceptual system with its object; replace it with the rigor of *internal* conditions of coherence; for adequation substitute the strict concatenation of ideas, and for truth, validity: you have pulled the carpet from under the skeptic's feet. His "hideous smile" hovers on his lips in vain: with a wave of your algebraic wand the minus sign becomes a plus sign. The irreducible multiplicity of critical languages is no longer an affliction, something we must just go on hoping to be cured of; it is the expression of freedom itself, and therefore of good health. The proliferation is not the symptom of a cancer; it is a measure of fertility. By this genuine tour de force, skepticism has been overcome without being transcended, since after all the fragmentation itself is untranscendable, and there is no unity and totality except in the plural.

This solution, at once open and subtle, has the merit of being elegant as well as that of encompassing the entire problem with total acuity. But I did not, for my part, find it convincing, and for this reason: Barthes presents the "conditions" that restrict the critic's freedom as being "internal" ("these conditions, internal though they are . . ."). Although that is true of the first, coherence, it is not quite true of the second, saturation. The possible "saturation" of the literary work by the critical language presupposes, in one way or another, an adequation relationship. Barthes recognizes this himself when he makes it clear that the choice of any given approach is not arbitrary, that it depends upon the "requirements" and "resistances" specific to the text. "It is therefore a source of fecundity," he writes, "that criticism should search in its object for the pertinence that will best enable it to achieve its nature as a simultaneously coherent and total language" (*Essais critiques*, pp. 270–71). It would be impossible to state more explicitly that, if the process of critical decipherment is governed *by its relation to an object*, to the point that "pertinence" becomes the foundation stone of "coherence," then the autonomy, the autarchy of the critical "metalanguage" must go up in smoke. Because that metalanguage can no longer constitute a closed entity, claiming justification solely from its own internal validity, since that validity is now merely the interiorization of an objective relation. That relation, which *then* enables the critical description to be coherent, may be real or imaginary, true (coherent in practice) or false (coherence impossible). The notion of validity, when probed, contains that of truth. As soon as language implies a transcendence toward the world, it can no longer be judged solely by its effective functioning within a closed system; it must be judged by the efficacity of its application.

In the primary phase of Barthes's thought there remains an insoluble residue of pragmatic truth, on which the dream of a metalanguage runs aground. Any kind of criticism whatever cannot therefore be brought to bear on any object whatever. Everything must be begun again from the beginning. Since criticism is no more than a secondary language, which depends for its existence upon a primary language — literature — we must question ourselves afresh on the subject of literature if we are to reach a better definition of criticism. And it will be remembered that, in a first approximation, Barthes saw literature as being ultimately a certain experienced relationship with the world: "The world exists, the writer speaks, that is literature." After that, despite the distinction made between literature as a language bearing upon the world and criticism as a language bearing upon language, it was impossible to prevent criticism — though indirectly, through the intermediary of literature — from also bearing upon the world. In order to rid criticism of the impurity of such alienating references, in order to allow it to live at last in autarchy, literature itself must previously be scoured free of any too direct referral to the real; the language of its transcendence — Barthes would say of its "transitivity"— must be pruned away. I myself therefore perceive a certain evolution, a certain accommodation of Barthes's thought concerning the ultimate status of literature. Literature, he indicates, has continued wrongly to be taken for a "signifier" whose interest lies in its relation to a "significate" (psychological, sociological, ideological, historical, etc.). Even the "thematic" criticism of people like Poulet, Richard, or Starobinski, when it outlines networks of signifying forms, "recognizes the work as possessing an implicit significate, which is, broadly speaking, the author's existential project" (*Essais critiques*, p. 268). But literature is not "expression," or a "product," or an "index": any conception of literature is erroneous that commits criticism to situating itself on the illusory plane of a "truth" that is to consist of establishing the exact relation of a sign to a signification. Next we come to what I shall call, probably with some oversimplification, the second phase of Barthes's thought, the progress of which I believe it is possible to discern in the curve of his own critical works: "Literature is indeed no more than a *language*, which is to say a system of signs: its being resides not in its message but in that 'system.' And for that very reason, the critic is required to reconstitute not the message of the work but solely its system, just as the linguist is required not to decipher the meaning of a sentence but solely to establish the formal structure that makes it possible for that meaning to be transmitted" (ibid., p. 257). Where Barthes was previously fascinated by logic, now he is fascinated by linguistics: this is not, in reality, a change, but a radicalization of his thought. Criticism can no longer be, in any sense, however "modern" it is, an analysis of contents (which it still was in his own *Michelet*). It can only be the listing of forms and their organization, of signifying structures and their functioning: this

139

means, in the case of Racine, the study of a certain "interplay of figures," the constitution of a Racinian "combinative logic" that will then provide an account of the particular combination found in any given play. Hence the very striking method of presentation found in his *Sur Racine*. "This first study comprises two parts. It may be said in structural terms that the first is of a systematic order (it analyses figures and functions), and that the second is of a syntagmatic order (it reworks and extends the systematic elements) on the level of each work" (p. 9. n. 3). The justification for this method is that put forward by Barthes for the structuralist approach in general: "The object is recomposed *in order* to make the functions clearly apparent" (*Essais critiques*, p. 216). So we can see taking shape, in Barthes's own work, what might be called the transition from criticism of significations to structuralist criticism.

Here again, though, we must be careful not to oversimplify and make Barthes say something he does not mean. The writer remains a man in confrontation with the world, and what he writes still in some way maintains a relation with the world. There is no question of purely and simply slicing through the moorings, so that the balloon of literature can waft peacefully up into the stratosphere. But we ought here to make a distinction between two radically different ways of "speaking the world," two languages — that of the "writer" (*écrivant*) and that of the "writer-artist" (*écrivain*). The first of these languages, in Barthes's terminology, is "transitive": its aim is "an immediate transformation of reality" (ibid., p. 265). What is involved here is a "practical utterance" (moral, technical, political, etc.) that is intended to transmit evidence, instruct, explain. The second language, that of the writer-artist, is "intransitive": its link with the world, which is always *distant* — even if it presents itself in the deceptive form of an "explanation" or a "doctrine"— is in reality nothing but an uninterrupted and eternally ambiguous interrogation: "Each time the description is not *closed*, each time the writing is sufficiently ambiguous for the meaning to escape, each time the writer-artist writes *as though the world signifies*, though without saying what, then the writing releases a question, it shakes what exists, though without ever preforming what does not exist yet, it breathes fresh life into the world: in short, literature does not help us to walk, but it enables us to breathe. Its status is therefore a restricted one"(ibid., p. 264). This being so, it is easy enough to grasp what constitutes the absolute opposition between the "writer" (or intellectual) and the "writer-artist" (or poet): the one is performing a function, the other an activity. "The writer-artist is the man who *crafts* his utterance (even when that utterance is inspired) and is functionally absorbed in that craftwork. The writer-artist's activity comprises two types of norms: technical norms (of composition, of genre, of writing) and norms of craftsmanship (hard work, patience, correctness, perfection)" (ibid., p. 148). In short, curious though it may seem, Barthes is here in close agreement with Picard, to such an extent that the latter, it seems to me, might be perfectly willing to countersign that passage. What stands between them, fundamentally, is a question of style (an approach colored by the human sciences versus the traditional approach) rather than one of thought (in both cases the literary work is defined as an object, the product of a craft governed by rules and endowed with validity by its successful functioning at the aesthetic level). It is not the least paradoxical element in this literary quarrel that Raymond Picard and Roland Barthes should be, without their realizing it, in agreement on the *aim*, if not on the methods, of criticism. When Barthes writes that "it is the attention directed at the organization of the signifying elements that provides the basis for a genuine critique of signification, much more than the discovery of the significate and of the relation between it and its signifier (ibid., p. 268), he is merely saying in his own language what Picard is also struggling to tell us in his when he castigates the new critics for regarding texts "as a collection of signs whose signification is elsewhere," with the result that "having been extended, explicated, and justified in areas external to itself, the work no longer resides within the work. It has become exterior to itself, and consists in relations that transcend it" (*Nouvelle critique*, pp. 113–14). It is somewhat hard to understand why, out of all these "new critics" he so loathes, Raymond Picard should have singled out the most amenable of all — the only one who dreams of a "peaceful coexistence" among critics[1]— to bear the brunt of his fury. Unless his hatred was also an elective affinity, unless it is because Roland Barthes resembles him too closely, like a brilliant brother gone to the bad, and therefore appeared to him in some way as a devilish alter ego. For what could be closer to Picard's point of view, in fact, than this latest definition of criticism offered by Barthes? "It seeks to reveal the functioning process of a certain apparatus, by testing the connections of the components, but also by leaving them free *to work* . . ." (*Essais critiques*, p. 271). Not that a radical and essential difference does not nevertheless exist between Barthes and Picard: the latter addresses himself exclusively to "clear" significations, thus missing the fundamental phenomenon of literary expression, whereas the former, and rightly, posits that the aesthetic meaning is always an ambiguous meaning, a "frustrated" meaning — so that the truths of the first are, in the end, superficial, while the errors of the second bear good fruit. But in both cases, on the hermeneutical plane, criticism itself, anxious not to lose itself in a quest for signifying elements residing "elsewhere," is defined and justified as a formal study of literary structures, even though that formalism is understood in differing ways. In both cases, criticism refuses to be brought to bear upon the particular relation of the work to its author and the real world; it gives preeminence to literary "alienation," attenuating as far as it can the link between art and existence, even though it is unable to cut that umbilical cord altogether. And lastly, in both cases — and it can hardly be by chance — we find the same pious wish for an ultimate convergence that gradually, at some final point, or, if you wish when history stops, will eventually make the various kinds of signification one, just as the pieces of a jigsaw puzzle are eventually all neatly interlocked, thus achieving the integration of the various criticisms into a single, greater criticism (cf., for Picard, the first part of chapter 5; for Barthes, note 1 of the present chapter).

At this point, of course, intellectual honesty forces me to repeat, in the case of Barthes, the very objections previously put forward to Picard's position, since both agree on this important point. This desire for a "final convergence," for "peaceful coexistence," is not innocent: insofar as this desire is, in Barthes's own words, "a dream," it is apprehended by the desirer as unavailing: instead of attempting to attain his object by purposeful activity he is simply hoping for it to emerge, ready-made, from the continuing activity of History itself. Although Barthes is the first to have invented the solution of institutional pluralism, he is the last to be satisfied with it, and deep within, tenacious as ever, he still preserves the nostalgia for a lost Unity. Ultimately, this "plurality of critical languages" is not a solution but just a lesser evil, to be borne with until it can be abolished by its absorption into a "classification of classifications" and a "criticism of criticisms." So how am I to be convinced by a relativism or perspectivism that does not satisfy Barthes himself? Am I to do no more than dream of this ultimate convergence of critical languages, instead of making it the major theme of my enterprise? If, as in Picard's case, this convergence is something merely hoped for, that is because the means are lacking to achieve it: all that can be done is simply to wait for a gradual and passive synthesis of the various points of view to occur of its own accord, since the power is lacking to transcend them by means of an active synthesis, which is to say *dialectically*. Here, I think, we have reached the heart of the problem. I know that Barthes too invokes a dialectic, and stresses that "critical activity helps dialectically both to decipher and to constitute" this "general form that would be the intelligible form itself that our age gives to things." But I do not see how, from his point of view, any dialectic at all can be possible. The mode of thought from which he wishes to derive criticism's model of intelligibility, that is, logic or linguistics, is by definition an *analytic* mode of thought. Both these great formal systems, as Barthes is the first to warn us, are simply constructing a vast tautology:[2] and there is no way in which a tautology can be made to yield a dialectic, since the latter is a process that by its very nature in fact presupposes the annihilation of identity and its transition into alterity. Tautological thought can only turn indefinitely in elegant and precise circles. The critical metalanguage that according to Barthes consists in "covering" the work under examination, and not in "discovering" it (*Essais critiques*, p. 256), is incapable of ever becoming one with its object: it is doomed to be its perpetual understudy, to merely *reflect* the contradictions that it is by its nature incapable of *resolving*. The error, as I see it, in Barthes

143

as well as in Picard (and it explains the curious resemblances between their otherwise utterly conflicting methods of procedure), is in taking the literary work to be an *object*, and then, as a direct result, in trying to model comprehension of it on the modes of objective thought.

But the work, it must be repeated, is a false object, an object-subject, the objective bearer of the subjective intention that alone enables us to grasp the work's specific meaning and articulation. There are no "cogs" or "components", there are no "connections" that must be made to "work": I must repeat to Barthes what I have already said to Picard (see above, near the end of chapter 4). The technical apparatus is no more than the vehicle of a vision. The "organization of signifying elements," to use Barthes's terms, the "literary structures," to use Picard's, are in no way autonomous realities; the signifier can never be separated from the significate, or the literary from the existential. In short, *art is never a craft*. Jean Rousset, one of the critics who have most concerned themselves with literary forms and structures, is also the one who most clearly warns us against a reifying interpretation: "We must therefore resist the temptation to conceive of creation in terms of mechanics or craftsmanship; creation is not mere fabrication. Far from being a passage from inside to outside, from subject to object, we should see it as a constantly internal procedure, one that has recourse to materials and to techniques, to the means provided by language and to natural forms, only so that it may interiorize them" (*Forme et signification*, vi). And that is why the critic is never to be thought of as confronting a work, as a scientist confronts an object, in the position of an observer; he is interrogating the work in its role as the apparition of an Other, and his relation to it is that of a participant; in Heidegger's terminology, the relation of critic and work is never a "being-to . . ." but a "being-with . . ." Barthes knows this better than anyone, since it is he who has best expressed the critic's *total* commitment to the critical adventure: we must return here to the first stage of Barthes's thinking, before the "structuralist" temptation, and before the "syntagmatic consciousness," [3] back to that sense in which he himself distinguishes between *two* Robbe-Grillets, one *chosiste* ("thing-ist" by analogy with human-ist, who "purges things of the unwarranted meaning that men ceaselessly imbue them with," the other a "humanist," for whom the sign refers to a signification that will remain to be deciphered, and by means of which things "though without thereby becoming symbols again, . . . recover a mediating function toward 'something else.' " The active association between Robbe-Grillet and Barthes is, moreover, extremely illuminating: having decided to accept literature — and to understand it — as a "system of signs," Barthes is quite naturally drawn to those writers who seem to introduce the greatest gap between signifier and significate: Brecht with his "alienation effect" in the theater, Robbe-Grillet with his "objectivity" in the novel. The entire art of the latter "lies in endowing an object with a 'being-there' and stripping it of a 'being-something' "; "he ruthlessly disconnects the visual from the rest of the (emotional and intellectual) grid"; he deprives things of "any possibility of metaphor" (*Essais critiques*, pp. 199, 201, passim).[4] Robbe-Grillet's work becomes, for Barthes, that *flat* literature which by defying all symbolic or poetic interpretation cries out for a genuine criticism of its forms or signifying structures for their own sake. But in fact, this "objectivity" of Robbe-Grillet's, which the novelist appears at first to have accepted (it is one of the most curious cases of a writer's being almost hypnotized by a critic — a kind of self-revelation via a third party), has subsequently been disputed by no one more violently than by Robbe-Grillet himself: his "objective" writing and technique are merely, he says, another way of rendering the subjectivity that the novel now aims to explore creatively, no longer imitatively, as in the classical novel. Robbe-Grillet's deliberate "frustration" of meaning (which Barthes was quite right in noting, and which here constitutes the originality of the technique) thus has, in its turn, *a meaning*: Bruce Morrissette has since been successful in establishing it on the psychoanalytic level, (*Les Romans de Robbe-Grillet*; Paris: Ed. de Minuit), and Lucien Goldmann on the sociological level (*Pour une sociologie du roman*; Paris: Gallimard). The world, as it appears in Robbe-Grillet, is simply a way for a consciousness to escape from itself; the pure "object" is nothing but the other side of a human Bad Faith that wishes to be "without qualities"; its "nonsignificance" signifies: it speaks of an anguish and tells a story, the anguish and the story of the individual depersonalized by an advanced industrial society, just as the luxuriating details of Balzac's world spoke of bourgeois delight in the dawn of the age of Possession. Frustration of meaning, yes; but on condition that it is accepted as a positive and not a negative index, that we see it as conveying an abundance, not a dearth.

So although Barthes is entirely justified in emphasizing the untranscendably ambiguous status of all literature, we must remember that there are two kinds of ambiguity, as Merleau-Ponty pointed out: a bad kind and a good kind. In the present instance, I shall repeat once again, the ambiguity that is constitutive of literary expression is not that which tends toward a sort of *degré zéro* of signification, but that which implies an oversignification; not that which presupposes the absence or eradication of contents, but that which is founded upon their inexhaustible density. In other words, although I am wholly in agreement with Barthes that criticism cannot claim to "decipher" the meaning of a work, it is not because the meaning is not there; it is on the contrary because it is present in excess of any possible interpretation, just as the ambiguity and the reality of the world reside wholly in the irreducible excess of what is to be perceived over the act of perception. In literature, ambiguity is nothing other than this *surplus* presented by the finished work in relation to the intention that brought it into being, and the value of the success achieved is exactly commensurate with that density. Even so, we must distinguish different degrees or phases of literary ambiguity in accordance with the various types of intention. Barthes's decision to confine *all* literature to a "frustrated" meaning is not, to use his own terminology again, innocent: it betrays a taste, or in other words a personal choice, which is making one *moment* of literary history (Kafka, Robbe-Grillet) into the *essence* of literature.

Any overprecise, overdirect relation to reality — in other words, any affirmation made too crudely — would reduce the writer-artist to the category of mere writer: the writer-artist must never be "dogmatic" or "engaged." And with that the cat is out of the bag, for Barthes, on this point, is the Antisartre, or to be more accurate, a Sartre who has extended to the whole of literature that right of exterritoriality that in *Qu'est-ce que la litté-*

rature was reserved for poetry alone. Sartre said: poetry is loser-take-all. Barthes amplifies: literature is always "the question minus the answer." The phrase is a good one, but I cannot subscribe to it. Literature seems to me, on the contrary, to be the sum of the possible answers to the real questions that one man— and through him an age, a civilization, and ultimately humanity — is asking himself. If we are to exclude the replies to such questions, does that mean we have to expel from the realm of letters such writers as Dante or Voltaire, Corneille or Hugo, Claudel or Brecht, all men, if any ever were, of "transitive" and "practical" utterance? And if not, then by what ingenious means are we to detach their utterances from the certainly not "frustrated," indeed the triumphant meaning that they fully intended to give it? Are we to deprive ourselves from now on of Bossuet's *Oraisons*, of Pascal's *Provinciales*, because they are works of edification or polemical weapons? It is true, of course, that we must maintain the view, against all Jdanovians past and present, that literature can never be merely a form of propaganda. And if the interest of the *Provinciales* resided wholly in its defence of Jansenists against Jesuits, and if its apologetic intention absorbed the totality of significations contained within the work, then it would have ceased to be read long before now. We will gladly concede to Barthes that literature is always defined — even when it is activist in intention — by a certain distancing, a certain availability, which prevent the clarity of the intention from being dissipated into the void of a transparent signification. There is always a little "play," a certain amount of "excess" in literary expression; in this respect the writer-artist, in contrast to the writer, is always the one who "overdoes it." That said, ambiguity can coexist with clarity, provided it is an extension of it, can be "mystery in the clear light of day" as well as heralding its own presence openly and explicitly; it is there in Molière's *Le Misanthrope* just as much as in Kafka's *The Castle*. The very condition that defines the absolute threshold of literature is also the condition that enables it to engage itself: there can be, and indeed is, from the epic to the sermon and on to the political polemic, a "dogmatic" literature written by writer-artists, not by mere writers, which is in fact literature exactly insofar as the abundance of the writing, like that of authentic speech, invariably exceeds the signifying intention that motivates it. There need be no question, therefore, of doing what Barthes would like to do — of detaching the questioning, which to him is the only essential, from the contingent replies it provides for itself. To take Claudel without his Christianity, or Brecht without communism, is not restricting oneself to literature; it is restricting oneself to a void. What must be grasped is that at a certain degree of lucidity and faith every human reply concerns every human being. Such and such a Christian or communist work retains its total value, for someone such as myself who is neither a communist nor a Christian, provided the author has managed to give his reply sufficient intensity to transform it into a matter that will touch and haunt me. Conversely, as we have seen, the suspension of meaning also signifies: the absence of reply to Vigny's Christ, or Kafka's Surveyor, is also a way, for the world, of replying. In the dialectic of questioning it is impossible to separate question and answer like two opposing poles. At a certain moment every reply is a question, every question a reply. It is impossible to give preeminence without arbitrary choice to either a Literature of the Question or a Literature of Answers. Literature is always a question through a reply, a reply through a question. And this is the nature of consciousness itself: that it is always "meaning-giving," that "nonmeaning" is strictly unthinkable, and yet that meaning can never be "held."

These reflections on the status of literature, undertaken in pursuit of Barthes, and where necessary in opposition to him, will enable me to define more precisely the status of criticism. Because it is one and the same operation that seeks to exclude *reality* from the domain of literature and *truth* from the domain of criticism. If literary language is no more than a system of signs, whose being resides not in a message of any kind but solely in its formal structure, and whose value, in consequence, similarly resides not in a relation of whatever kind to the concrete but solely in its successful internal functioning, then criticism — a secondary language bearing entirely upon that primary literary language — must inevitably be governed by those same criteria, since the critic, after all," is also a part of literature" (*Sur Racine*, p. 166). A work is not true or false: it is valid or it is not. Very well, then the same must be said of criticism. But in fact the "unrealistic" status of literature, to use Barthes's term, which is indistinguishable from its "linguistic" status, rests upon an intransitive and truncated conception of language: the fact of language is quite definitely not exhausted by its linguistic being, or its signification by its functional operations. To think so is to confuse what Merleau-Ponty in a vital distinction terms "the word present" and "the word past," the primal act by which I speak and the products accumulated by the act of speaking in history; in a word, it is to confuse language as we have been using that word till now (*langage*) with language in the sense of "the French language" (*langue*).[5] And although language in the latter sense means language stored away in dictionaries and reconstituted by grammars, in short, language in a dead state — the description of which is the province of linguistics — yet that dead kind of language can become living language again when it is revived by the impulse of an individual existence that becomes one with it and *carries it outward*, toward the world and toward others, as a simultaneous means of being and doing, as *praxis*. It is this transcendent dimension of language, which we have already observed at the level of empirical and everyday speech (see chapter 4), which is amplified and magnified still further by literary writing. If literature, according to Barthes's own definition, is interrogation, then like all interrogation it must be interrogation *of* something or *of* someone: it must involve transcendence of the world and of another person. Which is why Sartre quite rightly classes the phenomenon of language as simply a particular case of our relationship with the Other (*Situations I*, p. 237), and Merleau-Ponty, even more precisely, as "an eminent example of corporeal intentionality" (*Signes*, p. 111). In this sense, as with every corporeal act, "every act of literary or philosophic expression contributes to the fulfillment of our wish to regain possession of the world that was expressed with the very apparition of language, which is to say, a finite system of signs claiming to be capable in principle of capturing any entity that might present itself" (ibid., p. 119). It could not be more clearly put: this system of signs that language unquestionably is, has not come into the world with the sole purpose of chasing round and round in circles like a squirrel in a cage, simply for the delectation of observing linguists; it constitutes a human undertaking, and a human effort to grasp the world that opens up the vast field of truths to man's action and thought. For it is also one and the same act, by means of an operation diametrically opposite in direction to that of Barthes, that articulates language in accordance with a transcendence and gives it truth as its purpose. If language generally is essentially a striving toward a practical and symbolic repossession of being, then the same thing is even more true of literary language, which is not a sublanguage but a superlanguage, one in which man is no longer expressing such and such a specialized aspect of his activity but the total meaning of his existence.

This is the heart of the dispute, and though I have no wish to burden this essay with philosophic discussion that lies outside its scope, I feel it is essentail to go into this one point. The status of literature — and consequently that of criticism — is directly linked to the status we grant to language. Barthes's "formalism" in the field of literary criticism is founded upon a philosophy of language that he has himself expressed very clearly: "We are thus brought back to the ineluctably nonrealistic status of literature, which cannot 'evoke' reality other than by means of a relay system — language, this relay system itself standing in an institutional, not a natural, relation to reality" (*Essais critiques*, p. 264). In another passage Barthes elucidates his thinking even further: not only does literature have a nonrealistic status but, "very far from being an analogical copy of the real, *literature is on the contrary our very consciousness of the nonrealistic status of language*: the 'truest' literature is that which knows itself to be most nonreal" (ibid. p. 164). He gives two reasons for this status as nonreality: first, language is discontinuous; it "savagely shreds this continuum that is before me"; and second, the meaning of words "arises less perhaps from their relation to the object they signify than from their relation to other words, at once close to them and different" (ibid.). This means that the relations of signification are thought of as being constituted *within language itself*, and as "valid" insofar as they are coherent, but not as "true" in that they refer outward to a reality external to the utterance.

150

This "institutional" theory of language, which would condemn it to a total lack of any relation to nature, to being instead pure correlation, seems to me erroneous. First of all, the real is not at all the ineffable "continuum" Barthes speaks of; the very discontinuity of language must betray that. Perception provides us with a structured world of "figures" appearing against a "background," which in turn becomes the "figure against another "background," in accordance with an articulating process clearly established by gestaltist studies. As Heidegger made plain in *Sein und Zeit*, the articulation of language is itself articulated, in a certain way, upon the articulation of the world: there is an ontological relation of language to the real. It is therefore upon the basis of their relation to the object they signify that words enter into relations with each other. As Sartre pointed out in a recent article (and on this point it may be said that an alliance exists between the later Husserl, the early Heidegger, Sartre, and Merleau-Ponty, against the structural positivists), ". . . there is something about the object that signifies language, that assigns to it the role of being itself language, that requires language and defines the words; and at the same time there is something in the signification, i.e. in language, that continually refers back to the signifying object and qualifies it historically, in its being; so that language . . . appears to me as that which denotes me insofar as I am making an effort to denote the object" ("L'écrivain et sa langue").

It follows from this that language possesses a double power of *presentification*, a power at once objective and subjective, a double link of statement and expression with the real, through whose agency, when I speak the world, I also cause myself to be spoken by the world. No one is more conscious of this *truth* in language than the poet (and it is no coincidence that Barthes's method, as G. Genette has noted, is the inverse of the poet's). Yves Bonnefoy describes the process in this way: "Here is how, as I believe, poetry is begun. If I say 'fire'. . . then what that word evokes for me, poetically, is not merely fire in its nature as fire — all that the concept of fire is able to contain of fire: it is the *presence* of fire within the horizon of my life, and not of course as a thing, analyzable and usable . . . but as an active god, endowed with

151

powers," a god such as Bachelard was later to describe. Later
on in this fine piece, Bonnefoy provides a foundation, beyond
linguistic and conceptual fragmentation, for the ontological truth-
fulness of language: "Since a language is, as such, a structure,
it is able, in its very givenness, before any formula has exteriorized
its object, to make itself a *cipher*, an encodement of the unity
that any structure carries within itself, and thus to return
upstream with me, in that instant in which everything is decided,
toward the unity of the real. A language — and this is why the
term *logos*, the Word, has been used — seems to promise beyond
its conceptual aspects the same unity that being does beyond the
aspects of it that have fragmented what comes to our senses. . . . The word, a fragmented reflection of unity, will then
offer me, not the reabsorption of reality into meaning, but, on
the contrary, that of meaning into my participation in the real"
("La poésie et le principe d'identité").

As opposed to the conceptual communication of the mere writer, who strips the sign of all the excess weight he can (in this
respect the model remains scientific communication, in which language tries to make the gap as wide as possible between the signifier, such as a mathematical sign, and the perceptible significate:
hence Barthes's fascination for what he terms, in the mathematical sense, the "elegance" of language), literary writing begins with
what one might call the *naturalization of language*, a weighting
down of language that constitutes it as *being itself nature in an
analogical relation with Nature*. Again, Sartre expresses this admirably: "A prose writer, or a writer-artist, when he talks about a
table, writes a number of words about that table, but he writes
them, ultimately, in such a way — in accordance with his own
purely subjective idea — that this verbal aggregation is a kind
of reproduction or even production of the table, so that the table
itself is somehow swallowed down into the words. There you see
a table; but if I am to express that table in writing I shall have
to give something in the very structure of the words that would
correspond to the wood, here pockmarked, there split, heavy,
etc., none of which is at all necessary in the case of pure communication" ("L'Ecrivain et sa langue"). In short, the writer-artist is
"someone who despite everything brings the object described into the words"

(ibid.) What makes Claudel, for example, such an extraordinary poet, is that in his work, when he is at his best, the language has *become real*. Needless to say, it remains an infinitely complex problem, and one that entails a whole phenomenology of the relations between the perceptible and the imaginary, to comprehend how this "presentification" or "materialization" of the world in language is possible: it is sufficient, for our present purpose, that they should nevertheless exist in literature as realities, and that they in fact constitute the definition of literature.

It is certainly true, as Barthes says, that the writer-artist is "the man who crafts his utterance," but to set up one's workshop in the realm of language does not necessarily mean one must imprison oneself there. And even if one wanted to it would be impossible: one can no more withdraw *into* language than *into* consciousness: it is a void that summons the world into existence within it from every side. Neither word nor image are autonomous realities: they are intentional acts defined as a certain relation to the concrete. The Flaubertian dream of the book "that would be sufficient unto itself," so dear to certain "new novelists," is no more than a myth of the modern consciousness and also, as we have already said, a form of its alienation. The book is an analogue through which the writer-artist ineluctably directs himself at the world, even if only to deny it or to escape from it. Just as speaking is not a gratuitous act, so writing is not an intransitive verb: we write something for someone; we do not write for writing's sake. It is of course possible "to write for oneself" in the same way that it is possible to talk to oneself, and there is a pathology of the written word just as there is a pathology of the consciousness. There is a well-known condition, which psychologists call autism, in which the consciousness tends to become wholly shut in upon itself. And there exists today a literature that we might similarly term autistic, in that it aims to be its own universe, to create its own world outside the world. This illusion, which we find expressed by Robbe-Grillet (in *Pour un nouvean roman*) and of which Barthes is without any doubt the most brilliant and subtle theoretician, has turned out, in practice, to be fruitful: the road to the heaven of literature is as much paved with erroneous theories as the road to hell proverbially

153

is with good intentions. But contrary to what Robbe-Grillet claims, the writer-artist always has *something to say*; and although what he has to say is indivisible from the *way* in which he says it (that fact is indeed what distinguishes literature from the ideological essay or the philosophical exposition), the way of saying refers back, in its turn, to the original impulse and the project in which it is playing its part — in other words, to the particular links that all language has with the real world and other men, at the heart of history. Robbe-Grillet's greatness as a writer-artist is precisely that he gives the lie to Robbe-Grillet the critic: this universe that he believes himself to be creating from scratch, and bringing into being by means of the pure *fiat* of his own Logos, is ours; he is telling our story. Language, once again, is having its ultimate meaning transmitted back to it by the real, and the only authentic literature is a *true* literature. To write, therefore, is not to cut oneself off from the world in an attempt to imprison oneself inside language; it is, on the contrary, to attempt to imprison the world in language; it is to *utter the world*, in the full sense in which we say the law is *uttered*. This being so, we should reverse Barthes's own excellent formulation: "The writer-artist is a man who radically absorbs the *why* of the world into the *how* of writing." For on the contrary, the writer-artist is a man who radically absorbs the "how" of writing into the "why" of the world, a man who makes the very act of writing into his ultimate discovery of the real,[6] from which he expects salvation or damnation. Writing, for the writer-artist, is not to act "as though the world signifies"; it is to express, by more or less complex means and in accordance with variable techniques, *what the world does signify*.

8

VARIATIONS
ON THE THEME

So now we have the "criticism of significations" fully restored to its rights, or better still, to its duties. If, in Merleau-Ponty's words, we must admit, "as a fundamental fact of expression, an excess of the significate over the signifier — an excess which it is the precise virtue of the signifier to render possible" ("Sur la phénoménologie du langage," *Signes*, p. 112), then it is not only licit but imperative to draw out and reveal the whole of the significate, in all its richness and depth. In less technical terms, if the meaning of a literary work is defined by the relations, whether simple or complex, direct or indirect, that it maintains with the real — by the bonds, whether loose or tightly knit, subtle or patent, with which it is linked to the real — then it is necessary to elucidate the exact nature of those relations and those links, in short, to comprehend the *vision of the world* that the work constitutes. This is not, as Picard and Barthes would like to think, for their different reasons, a quest for signifying "elsewheres," a fixed determination to look for the work anywhere at all with the sole exception of where it is. There is no more an "interior" of a work than there is of a consciousness; there is no "inside" that can be set up in opposition to an "outside." The work is nothing other than the particular network of infinite significations that we can bring into focus *on* the material object presented by a printed text, just as consciousness is nothing other than the impulse that is leaping out to meet its own possibles through the density of the world. The imaginary universe of the work is not a substantial entity, a reality *cause sui*; in short, and once again, it does not fall perfectly formed out of the heaven of Ideas.

It mediatizes — via a whole series of complex and hierarchized relays forming the *organicity* proper to the work — the concrete existence of one man. It is in no way to deny or betray the specificity of the imaginary to reveal, in its weave, the obvious or hidden threads that link it to a historical being-in-the-world: it is, on the contrary, to make it yield up the totality of its meaning. In the relation of imaginary to real, the real is the primary, as is being in its relation to nothingness. The image is constituted against the background of the reality it denies, whether its intention is to perceive the absent as present (I represent Peter to myself because he is not here) or the present as absent (that cloud over there is a castle, a ship). If imaging consciousness and perceptive consciousness are not two distinct entities but two antithetical ways open to a single consciousness for taking a sighting on the world, two possible ways of behaving toward the real, then it is by its real *situation* in the world that the imaginary life of the consciousness is to be comprehended: by means of the fictive universe it creates it is giving itself in the form of a hollow "mold" what the concrete universe refuses it in the form of solid "relief." Hence the fact that the act of imagining always possesses the affective value of a symbolic satisfaction. Indeed, it this affective structure of the image that determines the coherence of its representative elements: what psychological research into the imaginative field has established on the theoretical plane, we have already foreshadowed, empirically, in our analysis of the literary work, which is, in the strongest sense of the word, a *work of the imagination*.

We are now in a position to examine in greater detail the stages of critical procedure. During a first phase, criticism is phenomenological description, which tends to reify its object: at this stage it makes apparent the various structures that constitute the work, that present themselves as the product of certain expressive techniques applied to certain raw material. A tragedy by Racine is a certain language, the use of which, regulated in accordance with well-defined modalities, comes into the province of linguistic, stylistic, and aesthetic analyses. But this language is not the written language of the anonymous narrator telling a story in the third person; it is a language that is spoken, on a stage, by characters that are also living people: actors. Hence there are necessarily certain characteristic dramatic structures that govern this global reality constituted by a Racine play, and to which particular kinds of study are applicable. However, these various structures, which define the work's expressivity insofar as it is specifically "theatrical," cannot under any circumstances provide an account of the phenomenon of the expressivity itself, which is to say, the *total communication* that is established between the intention that inhabits the work and the attention that is focused on listening to it. What is apprehended then, *through* the skillful concatenation of those literary structures and by means of them alone, is the modulation of a certain *affective theme*, which governs the work's organization and which will be, in Racine for example, the specific and penetrating quality of his "tragic art." The theme, modern criticism's key concept, is nothing other than the affective coloration of all human experience at the level where the fundamental relations of existence are called into play, which is to say the particular way in which each man views his relation to the world, to others, and to God. The theme is therefore that choice of being that lies at the center of any "vision of the world": its affirmation and development constitute both the basis and the scaffolding of any literary work, or, one might say, its architectonics. So the criticism of literary significations becomes quite naturally a criticism of experienced relations in the world as any written work manifests them, implicity or explicitly, in its content and in its form. At a second stage of comprehension, "structuralist" criticism thus becomes "thematic" criticism. To avoid confusion, Starobinski quite rightly makes a distinction between thematic criticism in this sense and the "diachronic" history of themes, ideas, and symbols (Don Juan, Faust, the Devil, the idea of happiness, the representation of madness, etc), all of which is simply "literary history given a connecting thread." I myself believe that this form of literary history is particularly fruitful, even indispensable, for thematic research as I have just defined it: it enables us to follow in detail, at the collective level, the development and variations that history imposes on the great affective archetypes.

157

1. PSYCHOANALYSIS OF THE THEME

At the moment when description of the structures of the work-object gives way to attempted comprehension of the work-subject's themes, the investigatory method that most naturally presents itself to criticism is that of psychoanalysis. We have already encountered, during our discussion of "literary meaning" in chapter 4, the possibilities it offers and the savage resistances it provokes. Nevertheless, recourse to Freudian hermeneutics seems at this point to go without saying. Lanson never claimed that the researches of historical scholarship could exhaust the field of interpretation: beside the facts, there was taste; beside history, psychological intuition. Moreover, was not Sainte-Beuve the first to demand a psychology of authors? It is simply that we can no longer accept today as "psychology" that spontaneous and simplistic "knowledge of the human heart" so dear to the social lecturers of yesteryear, and still to be found animating drawing-room conversations, not to say, on occasion, university lectures. What psychoanalysis provides in our day is precisely the solid basis in a study of the human psyche that the great critics of the past cried out for. More precisely still, if the literary work is a work of imagination, as our analysis has just shown to be the case, is psychoanalysis not, by definition, a deciphering of the imaginative process? If the work draws its coherence from a certain affective theme, is psychoanalysis not, before all else, a comprehension of affectivity? And if the theme, as we have defined it, is a way of living one's fundamental relation to the world and others — the relation that genetically constitutes a work of art — is not the very vocation of psychoanalysis to provide an account of the way in which a man lives his existence, thematically, as a particular relation to those Others — the Parents — who dominate our lives, and to the perceptible qualities of things, sensed in their immediate signification? There is thus no necessity to justify the fact that critical research and psychoanalytical investigation intersect: their failure to do so would have been inexplicable.

However, the first results of psychoanalytically inspired criticism were, it must be conceded, disappointing. Since literary critics were either ignorant or dismissive about psychoanalysis, it

158

was the psychoanalysts who by force of circumstance turned critic. The first products of this development (writings by Freud, Rank, Brill, Jones, Baudouin, Marie Bonaparte, Laforgue) are still too clinical: for such practitioners a writer was above all a patient, and a fascinating work mainly a document for the study of a fascinating illness. I certainly do not wish to deny that these first commentaries were often penetrating studies, or that they threw new light on works hitherto never approached by any but traditional methods. The most important contribution to the enrichment of literary criticism in this respect did not, however, occur in the field of French studies. In his *Hamlet and Oedipus*, the first version of which dates back to 1900, Ernest Jones signposts with remarkable clear-sightedness the paths open to a serious and, as it were, respectful psychoanalytical investigation of literature. The three parts of his study define, in sum, the three possible and necessary approaches for any such inquiry: first there is the problem of establishing the human relations to the work within the play, the relations linking Hamlet to his mother, to his father, to his uncle, to Ophelia; then, that of comparing the affective structures thus isolated with the affective structure of Shakespeare's own personality insofar as history enables us to reconstruct it, so that the first series of structures may be intelligibly inserted within the second; and last, if we wish to achieve a complete interpretation, there is the problem of replacing *Hamlet* within the mythological context that lends it universality, of working back to the great archetypal tradition of the collective imagination to which Shakespeare's relates, and of noting precisely those revealing distortions that the playwright has inflicted upon it. Of the three phases of investigation thus defined, Anglo-American criticism, at least as exemplified in its most celebrated efforts, seems to have concerned itself mostly with the third. The influences of Frazer's anthropological researches and his *Golden Bough*, and of the historical research work of the Cambridge School into Greek mythology, have combined quite naturally with the Jungian tendency in psychoanalysis to direct the attention of criticism toward a study of the broad mythic forms of the imaginative life that lie at the heart of poetic expression. In France, it is the first two phases of the inquiry that seem to have held most interest for critics;[1] they define the field of Charles Mauron's "psychocriticism," which constitutes the most original and systematic attempt in France to provide a solid psychoanalytic foundation for an authentic literary criticism.

Literary psychoanalysis can never be merely the direct application of clinical psychoanalysis to literature. Charles Mauron's great merit lies in his having fully grasped this fact and gone on to draw the methodological consequences it entailed. The essential task of criticism is to throw light on literary works, to enrich and broaden our contact with them. The work remains an absolute beginning and an ultimate end. Racine, for the critic (not, please note, for the historian or the sociologist), is Racine's plays, and although a full understanding of them necessarily moves along the line of a certain relation they have with their author, the writer is always secondary, the work primary. There are works without any known author; without known works there is never an author. The temptation to which clinical psychoanalysis succumbs is that of regarding written works as symptoms or indices of a conflict which is actually located in the writer's life, *not in the work.* This kind of criticism becomes prone, in a more refined form, to the same latent defect that we denounced earlier among the zealots of historical scholarship. And what we said there holds good here. The text's own reality is dissipated. Andromaque "was" la Duparc, and Oreste "was" Racine; and now, Hamlet is threatened with "being" Shakespeare's Oedipus complex. The relation of derivation remains the same; the complexity alone is different, insofar as it presupposes a certain number of concealed relays and a code to decipher them with. Mauron, on the contrary, begins with a comprehension and an evaluation of the texts as texts, and of literature as literature, not as an aggregation of clinical symptoms. Psychocriticism is therefore, before all else, a method of textual elucidation, a reading technique: by superimposing various passages in the manner of photographic transparencies, we can discover constant associations, networks of images; in a second phase of the research we shall then be able to follow, through the entire work, the modifications of the structures revealed by the first operation. The organization of the "obsessive metaphors" eventually constitutes a "personal myth," in which the unconscious personality of the writer is expressed and which provides an account not only of the work's structures but also of its dynamic. However, since all scientific procedures require controls, the results acquired by this analysis of the work must be checked by a confrontation with the author's life. The meaning established by the literary criticism will be objectively corroborated by the biography. The profound unity constituting the central principle postulated by contemporary literary research is present in the very title of Charles Mauron's book: *The Unconscious in Racine's Work and Life*. "The Lord holds all things in his two vast arms," Vigny once wrote. The Lord, here, is the Unconscious, a single reality that contains the twofold secret of the creator and of his creation.

Mauron's psychocriticism thus presents itself as a "structuralist-genetic" criticism: in its first phase it isolates the structures of a work, which is to say the scaffolding that supports its meaning; in its second phase it provides an account of the emergence of that meaning; the description of the meaning requires its constitution, or, if you wish, comprehension to the second degree becomes explanation. In this way the structuralistic description opens a circuit of intelligibility that is completed by the genetic explanation. Of these two distinct phases, the first — to which I shall refer in my own terminology as *phenomenological* — is of extraordinary richness. Although there is no space here to go into details, the general schema of Racinian affectivity that Mauron reveals (notably on pages 25–26 of *L'Inconscient dans l'oeuvre et dans la vie de Racine*), the originality and precision of his thematic analyses (in particular that of the "look," whose importance he was one of the first to make clear), and the sheer abundance of the suggestions his investigation gives rise to, all combine to make this study the best — which is to say the one most highly charged with significations — that has been devoted to Racine for twenty years. It is now clear that a consistent and rigorous psychoanalytical investigation makes it possible to disclose and define, with a hitherto unheard-of precision, the nature of the affective relations binding Racine's characters together, and also the recurring and tragic pattern that they form. As a descriptive method, psychocriticism is beyond dispute one of the subtlest and most reliable instruments that literary phenomenology has available to it. But is it really capable, as has been claimed, of closing the interpretative circuit it has so admirably opened without the help of means other than its own? Does it enable us, in short, to make the transition from the structure of themes to their genesis, from explication to explanation? I do not believe so.

During a first phase, as we have said, critical description constitutes the literary work as object. During a second stage the object becomes humanized and the themes emerge. But the negation, as in all true transcendence, is also conservation: because the specifically literary structures become polarized around themes in accordance with a new — and to my mind deeper — comprehension, they do not therefore cease to subsist, or to retain their specific reality. (On this point Picard's wariness is legitimate.) In other words, even when they are taken at the essential level of their affective coherence, that is, at the very source and well-spring of the tragic, Racine's writings nevertheless continue to subsist as tragedies for the stage. And unfortunately, insofar as it ceases to describe its object in order to attempt an explanation of it, psychocriticism explodes that object. It does not search deeper into the structures it reveals; it destroys them. For Racine's work consists of various and successive plays, all with autonomous realities: they are acted and read separately. Although Racine's plays do undoubtedly make a whole, it is in the sense that — to use the admirable phrase that Péguy applied to Corneille — his tragedies form a "family closely knit" by the community of their themes. But that does not mean those themes are simply given all at once, in one great avalanche; and though they may form an articulate organization, that organization is not rigid: Racine's theater has a becoming and a duration of its own, an evolution, in short, a *life*. If themes present themselves, it is not all together and pell-mell but in accordance with a precisely ordered chronological and logical development that it is criticism's task to render intelligible. Yet this specific and essential life present in Racine's theater is something that psychocriticism begins by eliminating: "A writer's various works merge together into a single work; situations and characters lose their clear-cut outlines, lose their shape, take on new shapes, like patterns in running water" (*L'Inconscient*, p. 18). In other words, between *La Thébaïde* and *Athalie* nothing happens; and since nothing happens there can be nothing new. The last word written was *already* the first; it brings the wheel full circle, and literature is just that — a vicious circle, at the very best an immense tautology, an eternal rehashing whose individual moments are to be distinguished solely by their greater or lesser degree of expressive clarity. The simple reader thought he was reading Racine's *works*, which formed a whole precisely because they were a developing succession; but it turns out there is only *one* work by Racine, characterized, like infantile perception, by its syncretism.

Nor is that all. Not only did we imagine that Racine wrote a number of works; we also imagined that those works were plays. We even went so far as to go and see them acted, occasionally, in a theater. Because that's what a play is, after all: characters in situations — three trestles, two characters, and a passion, as Lope de Vega put it. The psychoanalyst smiles at our ignorance: no more "clear outlines," no more "situations," no more "characters"; just "the patterns in running water." It's just too bad, folks; that theater of ours was a mirage, in very truth a *dream*. Because Racinian reality, as Mauron describes it for us, is oneiric. We though we were sitting awake and attentive in a theater: we are really fast asleep. What we are experiencing is not the waverings of Pyrrhus, or Phèdre's burning desires; it is Racine's own long, undifferentiated, primordial nightmare. This darkened auditorium is the author's unconscious: "Thus we are led to see, in the hero of a tragedy, the author's ego, and in the characters that surround that hero the ego's temptations or defenses, its desires or its fears" (*L'Inconscient*, p. 21). The reality of the theater has therefore vanished utterly: for theater begins at that precise point when, as George Steiner puts it, "whatever their kinship with the creative sources, the characters of the drama assume the integrality of their own being; they lead their own lives far beyond the death of the poet" (p. 100). The theater is that process of objectivation by means of which the Self projects itself into Others, who from then onward take on an independent existence; for God as for the playwright, that is what *creation* is. And for the actor too, since he lends his body to another, and could never, as we so accurately put it, "incarnate" Bajazet or Phèdre other than by ceasing in some measure to adhere to his own self for a while. The life of characters in a play, the ephemeral but genuine life of the theater, is that gleam of existence maintained for a moment at the crossroads where an author, an audience, and actors meet on a stage. In short, the psychoanalyst's work consists here in undoing all that the poet's labors had achieved: where the author, by successfully transforming his creations into living creatures, his fantasies into existents — Andromaque, Oreste, Hermione, whose destinies continue to be played out from then onward apart from his — has presented us with a world, the psychocritic reveals a mirage; where we had perceived, in the actors' words and actions, concrete relations between real individuals, we now have merely a dialogue between the two lobes of Racine's brain: "The most difficult idea for me to accept in my method was the assimilation of a tragedy into a psychic structure and a psychic process. I was hesitant to see *Andromaque* as the image, if I may so express it, of Racine's brain" (p. 178). So no more Andromaque, or Oreste, or Hermione; instead, an Ego, a Superego, or an Id. The true tragedy is not the one played out between Racine's characters but the one played out *between psychoanalytic concepts*. In short, to borrow the movie-credit format: we present Freud's *Clockwork Andromaque*! — dialogue by Jean Racine.

It is not possible to assess our progress: the structures specific to the literary work — an illusion. Theatrical reality — a mirage. There is nothing left, it would seem, but a psychic process. But even that is another delusion: the psychic functioning is nothing but the image of Racine's brain. Never mind, at least we still have a brain and a Racine. Ah, but we haven't. That too is a trap, the last refuge of our simplemindedness. A brain, yes, but definitely no Racine. Possibly we were under the impression that if the theater is indeed, in the last resort, no more than a void inhabited by the ravings of an individual mind, then there must at least be someone inside it to do the raving, so that if raving it be, at least Racine's work is the ravings of Jean Racine, and the fact of its being his and no one else's is what constitutes its singular reality. And indeed it is the psychocritic himself who

164

tells us so: "The writer's fixations are as singular as his existence, and nothing is more personal than happiness or an obsession" (p. 35). But having said it, he soon has to contradict himself: "Beneath the still personal myth of Racine we perceive the ancient bedrock of the human unconscious" (p. 36). Personality and singularity alike are figments: "The impulses of the libido occur everywhere in accordance with the same laws" (p. 39). When Racine writes *Les Promenades de Port-Royal*, for example, what possible grounds can we have for expecting them to contain a particular signification, one that would throw a particular light on the specific development of his work? "Why should Racine be an exception to this general law of psychology? His sudden love of nature is the result of a libido displacement" (p. 209). Moreover, what possible method could we adopt in order to isolate Racine's originality in any case? "He depicts for us, in sum, an Oedipal, crisis almost normal in its broad outline, with the subsequent emergence of a Superego" (p. 183). You, me, Mauron — what's the difference? But perhaps your simplemindedness is still not about to give up: you may object that neither you, nor I, nor Mauron are great playwrights, and that despite everything we are still left with what must be called, for want of a better term, "Racine's plays." And those particular plays, whose existence still has to be explained, did not write themselves. But you see, they did! For that is psychocriticism's greatest and ultimate triumph: a truly "scientific" explanation of Racine's plays can dispense with Racine altogether. The process must be carried to its ultimate: just as the singularity of the conscious individual merges and dissolves into the impersonality of unconscious psychological laws, so the unconscious itself is finally nothing but an illusion, and psychological laws is just another name for physical laws. Although Racine's writing is the "effect" of a displacement of libido, the libido is in no way a specific behavioral factor that we can attempt to understand in terms of human intention; the psychic in man is nothing more than a "force field," the mental merely a setting in motion of "energy masses" within which "violent tremors" then occur. And that once accepted, everything becomes explicable. Those literary structures, for example, previously revealed by the phenomenological description: they are

165

the product of a parallelogram of forces: "It seems to me that we are now seeing the emergence, and in its broad lines at least the pattern, of the force field we are seeking" (p. 64). Or the emergence of the Father, for example, with *Mithridate*: "It is here that the quantitative factor appears to play a large role. If the masses of aggressive energy were not so considerable, they could dissipate themselves in some way or another" (p. 177). So a number of martial characters must appear in the cast list. In other words, the specific *meaning* of this conscious creation process therefore lies in the accumulation of a certain *quantity* of energy. Which is to say, strictly speaking, that it is without meaning. The act of writing, like any other human action, has ceased to be an intention, comprehensible in terms of its aim, and is now simply an effect, to be explained in terms of its cause. When Racine thinks he is writing, his pen is in reality being pushed along by kinetic energy impulses. When he thinks he is creating a play (for he too must have been very simpleminded), his words are being literally stolen from under his nose by a universal determinism: "When Racine depicts a fundamental psychological law for us in this way, he is certainly quite unaware of the fact. He believes himself to be quite simply working out a plot" (p. 182). So we certainly don't need Racine to write *Bajazet* for us: "M. de Cézy's story already contained all the elements of the Racinian myth. All Racine had to do was allow them to find their own directional pattern" (p. 102). And as for the attempt to discover that significant unity and totality which criticism sets itself the task of revealing (in this case, the unity of a work produced through Racine by random molecular impacts, and the totality of a body of plays whose circumference is certainly clearly defined but whose center is, literally, nowhere), here at last is the true principle behind it: "The underlying force field constrains Racine to the perpetual and monotonous reworking of a single theme, to the varying of which all his art is directed" (p. 95). Poor Racine: the emanation of an impersonal psychological force, which is in its turn the reflection of a state of the universe, he is doomed to keep on eternally churning out his same old tune, rather like the half-wits Samuel Beckett depicts, though with the one exception — and this is the entire margin of freedom conceded to his genius — that he may, with a little luck, be able to introduce one or two modest variations into the refrain that the Unconscious is whispering perpetually through his mouth.

So what went wrong? How, as Mallarmé put it, into vile lead has that pure gold changed? How has this psychocriticism, whose exceptional fruitfulness on the descriptive level I stressed earlier, resulted on the explanatory level in such absurdities? Mauron, like his Racine, is a victim of Freud, not of Freud the innovatory genius, but of Freud the scientist left behind by the times. Because we must in practice make a distinction here. On the one hand there is practical Freudianism, which provides a concrete approach to emotional life and an experiential, day-to-day manipulation of it; the discovery of our true relations with ourselves and others, orienting and articulating our existence; the prodigious intuition of human depths and ambiguity; in short, a new and authentic comprehension of being-in-the-world. Then, on the other hand, devised as a means of providing some account of the psychoanalyst's practical experience, we have psychoanalysis, which is to say a theory worked out, in the late nineteenth century, with the means then available: associationism of distinct psychic entities without internal links; instincts; vibrations, which may be vibrating in the mind or the ether for all we know; reification of the consciousness, itself fragmented into particles named Ego, Superego, Id, without intelligible communication,[2] and whose "states are produced by a psychophysiological causality and determinism that reduces them ultimately to the status of being not even a phenomenon in its own right, but a mere epiphenomenon; in a work, all the bric-a-brac of scientistic materialism still littering turn-of-the-century ideology — all that "humanism" inherently so inhuman or antihuman for which the knowledge of man consists in making him into an object among objects, a thing among things, and aims ultimately at annihilating, by means of its dissolution in the maelstrom of the abstract Universal and "scientific laws," whatever unique and irrecoverable properties have accrued to the human presence in the world by means of objective thought. In this sense there is a psychoanalysis of psychoanalysis itself still to be attempted, as indeed there is of all materialist ideology. By making the conscious a reflection of the unconscious, without any autonomous reality, and by resorbing the unconscious, sooner or later but ineluctably, into some cerebral process, the psychoanalyst rejects the mystery and the responsibility of his own existence, and unloads them onto the universe; the better to escape himself, he *denies himself*, he escapes into materiality, driven by a wish for security that is the equivalent, on the theoretical plane, of the infantile desire to return to the womb. Hence the proliferation (theoretically untenable, since psychoanalysis is defined originally by the decision to comprehend the psychological in terms of the psychological) of terms improperly borrowed from the physical sciences: "quantity" and "transference" of "energy masses," "attraction" and "displacement" of "force fields," and various other "gravitations" or "landslides." This choice of a mechanical vocabulary, this systematic insistence — sometimes carried to absurd lengths — on describing psychic phenomena in physical terms, quite unjustified by scientific experiment or mensuration of any kind, betrays the psychoanalyst's own complex: his pseudo-objective terms are so many "obsessive metaphors" that in their turn reveal his "personal myth." This wish to petrify consciousness is a form of suicide, and the theoretical superstructure of Freudianism denotes the triumph, within the psychoanalyst himself, of the death wish over the life force.[3]

Thus Mauron's psychocriticism shares in equal measure the very same fortunes and misfortunes that beset the orthodox psychoanalysis from which it derives its authority. Just as Freud in practice cured patients, so Mauron analyzes his text with great efficacity: as long as it is simply a question of some concrete experience that succeeds in making explicit a form of human behavior hitherto obscure to itself (in literary terms, as long as it is a matter of critical elucidation expressing the work's underlying affective motifs in thematic terms), the psychoanalytic instrument works wonders and is irreplaceable. But as soon as the *comprehension of psychism* attempts to transform itself into an *explanation of mind*, in other words, as soon as a *scientific* method claims to constitute itself as a *philosophic* system — surreptitiously and improperly, moreover, since it claims to become philosophy and remain science at the same time — then we are simply dealing with a self-deluding ideological position attempting to occupy two incompatible systems of reference simultaneously. Moreover this metamorphosis is not without attendant dangers, for if methodological concepts are allowed to harden improperly into metaphysical concepts, they may eventually warp and falsify the method. It is not my province to demonstrate this process in the field of psychology,[4] but it can easily be observed in the critical field. When Mauron attempts to pass on from explication to explanation, faithfully following Freudian hypostatic development, the errors of the "genetic" construction are reflected back in practice onto the "structuralist" description and end up by distorting it. Although thematic analysis has a function, it can only be that of detecting and restoring the *life of the themes themselves:* their articulation and their intersection, needless to say, but also their origin, their evolution, and their end result. "Gestaltist" metaphors (structures, articulation, pattern, etc.), though certainly useful, tend, as Bergson would say, to give an excessively spatial (and static) image of a reality that necessarily implies duration (and also a dynamic). The human relations expressed by the act of writing, as by any act, intersect, form patterns that dissolve and reform in time; they trace the lines of a becoming. That is what we mean when we say that human reality does not have an "essence" but an "existence," which is to say an essence that constitutes itself in a perpetual becoming. But the psychoanalytic postulate *Wo es war, soll ich werden* presupposes precisely the opposite: it immobilizes man in an objective essence (a sort of mathematical "function" defined by the impersonal laws of the unconscious, in which the only variable lies in the capacity for infantile traumas).

And as soon as it is accepted that a man is given, once and for all, in childhood, the apparent development and the superficial variety of his subsequent behavior are illusory: a life is no more than the modulation of a single theme; and a work likewise. The theory of the "single work" in Mauron, which destroys all specificity in the literary structures, is the counterpart of the "single act" that the Freudian robot forever repeats and relives.[5] Moreover, since duration has been halted and contracted into a single point, these single acts and single works are always *failed* acts and works. Man uses all his ingenuity to vary his behavior, to adapt it to new concrete situations exactly as Racine struggles to modify his art in order to adapt it to new dramatic situations — in vain. The consequences of this for thematic analysis are immediately clear: no sooner has it isolated its object than it annihilates it; for if a theme takes on a meaning it can only be *by means of the successive variations that enrich it*, which is to say by means of its internal dynamic. But the static nature of the themes, which is an inherent part of Mauron's doctrinal position, deprives him of all desire and all means of comprehending the becoming specific to them: "We follow the themes through their metamorphoses. But we do not analyse the variations: they are the passing moment that one savors" (*L'Inconscient*, p. 39). From the moment it has been decreed that "the important thing for us remains to know which structure, and no other, has served as the unavoidable framework and, to express it most fully, as the internal fatality of such and such a work of art" (ibid., p. 17), then psychocriticism's motto inevitably becomes: *Plus ça change, plus c'est la même chose*. Renouncing any attempt to comprehend the meaning of changes that it has declared in advance null and void, psychocritical thematic analysis, in accordance with a radical perversion of its goals, will consist no longer in observing Racinian theater's progress from *La Thébaïde* to *Athalie*, but in ensuring *Athalie's* regression to conform with *La Thébaïde*, in forcing it back, as it were, into the womb that already contained it. This reversal of the method's direction is prejudicial to its results and leads to a very great number of simplified and misleading interpretations. Everything new ends up being cut down to size so that the "facts" will correspond properly with the "law." Although it is impossible here to go into great detail, a certain number of these consequences must be pointed out.

In the first place, since we are bound, even in the "single work" of Racine, to distinguish between — I was about to say plays of unequal value, but let us settle for "reflections of varying *quality*" (a factor that unfortunately resides in the "variations," which are of course incapable of comprehension), that means we have to rely, as far as aesthetic evaluation is concerned, on "the passing moment that one savors." All that "scientific truth," so repeatedly and vociferously heralded, only to find ourselves, at the end of the line, back again nose to nose with Anatole France and Jules Lemaître! Nor, I must add, is the ghost of impressionism the only one to be raised from the dead. Psychocriticism, you will remember, was originally constituted by a refusal to identify literary psychoanalysis with clinical psychoanalysis, since the latter, as such, was incapable of providing a satisfactory decipherment of the work of art. Psychocriticism simply says that the structure of the unconscious and that of the work coincide: "There is nothing specifically neurotic in it" (*L'Inconscient*, p. 181). But it is not so easy to divert psychoanalysis from its primary vocation. Just as, for the ordinary doctor, every man in good health tends to be a man who's sick and doesn't know it yet, so for the doctor of souls every normal individual is a potential neurotic. And it is not much good reassuring us, telling us that Racine's tragedies are really no more, taken as a whole, than the various symptoms of the juvenile crisis by means of which, just as you and I have done, he resolved his Oedipus complex, when *in fact* all the concrete analysis Mauron offers of Racine's plays treats them as the unresolved development of an obsessional neurosis, surviving beyond the oedipal phase. That was of course predictable. From the moment that you condemn the poetic imagination to being an eternal repetition, a monotonous reiteration of fixed themes, which are reproduced again and again with the regularity of natural phenomena and can be "superimposed" like "photographic transparencies" and imprisoned in "networks," then the immobility thus imposed on the imagination is inevitably passed on to the imagined work, and turns creative activity into what is in fact a *paralysis*. Literary writing is therefore no more than a particular kind of that mental paralysis that is so aptly termed a "fixation," and even with the best will in the world one is forced to accept the writer for what he is: a mentally sick man. Sooner or later, therefore, psychocriticism reverts to clinical psychoanalysis and falls into precisely those aberrant ways it began by trying to avoid. And immediately we are faced with all the old specters we had thought exorized: hard on the heels of aesthetic impressionism comes reduction-to-biography.

171

Mauron's "genetic" phase totally annihilates the "structures" that he helped to reveal in his first phase: as in the days of post-Lansonism the genesis of literary meaning is sought outside of literature itself, in the sphere of biographical circumstances. It is the same deciphering system; the code alone has changed. Into the beautiful lucidity of the traditional rules of derivation, Pyrrhus or Oreste = Racine in 1667, the obscurity of various relays is introduced: Pyrrhus becomes Racine's Superego, or Oreste his Id. Basically there is nothing different at all, and the proof of this is that in the oceanic depths of the Racinian unconscious we suddenly find ourselves faced with all the old traditional paraphernalia: Port-Royal and those actresses! "Andromaque may be said to represent the theater, so yearned for despite the accusations of ingratitude, of infidelity, of sacrilege. Phèdre may be said to represent the passion for writing, which having lost the battle now recognizes its guilt" (*L'Inconscient*, p. 184). So there you are: this wonderful "scientific explanation" is to consist ultimately in merely manufacturing for Racine a totally invented unconscious from all the bric-a-brac left lying around by the literary historians, though with the vocabulary changed for the sake of the argument.

I shall take one particular example, that of Jansenism, important enough in all conscience, since Racine's entire drama is ultimately no more, for Mauron, than a vast unconscious scenario in which Port-Royal plays the archetypal Mother and Racine the archetypal Son. Let us observe psychocriticism at work: Jansenism was founded by Saint-Cyran, by his desire to reform the church; but that desire, which expresses a rejection of the reality principle, is a disguised wish for self-punishment. Let us take a close look at Jansenist "theology": "Instead of going back as far as Saint Paul, with the Protestants, or accepting Saint Thomas and the Roman Church, it stops just at Saint Augustine, halfway, and between two stools" (p. 196). Immediately everything becomes crystal clear: this "protestant" attitude within Roman Catholicism is the wish for the impossible, characteristic of the punishment sought by the masochist. Conclusion: "Jansenism, reduced to its essential elements, presents the structure characteristic of an obsessional neurosis" (p. 198). And our scientist goes on to clinch the argument with a piece of expert testimony in corroboration: "This unbalanced streak has naturally struck objective observers. If I were to be criticized for using the word neurosis here, I should quote Bossuet, who speaks of a sickness" (p. 197). The tribute of one "objective observer" to another, because as we all know from La Fontaine, the best judge of lambs is a wolf. And after the judgment of fact we have the value judgment it justifies: "The mediocrity, albeit honorable, of souls thus obsessed" (p. 198), which we are all bound to agree applies perfectly to Pascal, for example, or Racine. Of course you might be tempted to say that if Saint-Cyran rejected both the Paulinian and Thomist poles, and eventually selected the path of Augustine, it was because it seemed to him the *true* one. In other words, his choice was in fact a *theological* one; which would not mean that Saint-Cyran thereby ceased to be a man, and that his choice as such did not form part of the context of his subjective and social existence, but which does imply that, once reached, *the meaning of a choice acquires a truth independent of its genesis*. Whereas, by virtue of an exceptional grace, Freudian psychoanalysis is not reducible to the complexes that Freud certainly had, Saint-Cyran's theology must be so "reduced." We can all see the difference. There is no such thing as intrinsic theological, or artistic, or philosophic meaning: they are all reducible, by definition, to the hidden impulses of the unconscious that masquerade as art, as theology, or as philosophy. Except for one miraculous exception: science, which is not resorbable into the unconscious, and which alone, therefore, has the power of secreting autonomous significations. I do not say that the psychocritical explication is false: I say that it is absurd. False it certainly is not; it is perfectly true that every time a man acts or thinks, he acts and thinks *in his entirety*, with his body, his complexes, his intellect; his total being is involved in his least undertaking. In elaborating his theology, Saint-Cyran will therefore involve his particular complexes, just as El Greco's defects of vision had their effect on his particular style of painting. But one can no more "reduce" the meaning, and in consequence the *value*, of Jansenist theology to the real or supposed complexes that underly it than one can reduce El Greco's painting to nothing more than the expression of an ocular

173

malfunction. This wild and obsessive determination, maintained in the face of all evidence to the contrary, to explain *the higher by the lower* (in this case to eliminate the intrinsic significations of conscious activity in favor of unconscious mechanisms), this *idée fixe*, is only too recognizable. And it has a name: materialism. By now the true target of my attacks in the previous few pages will be apparent: I reject classical psychoanalysis absolutely from the moment when its method ceases to be a fruitful heuristic procedure and becomes a camouflaged naturalistic metaphysic.

One last word: psychoanalysis itself has not been sufficiently psychoanalyzed. Even if its materialism does indicate an "escape neurosis," as any determinist philosophy of consciousness does, it still remains to elucidate the meaning of that flight, which is by no means identical in all materialist approaches. There are in fact a *number* of materialisms, just as there are a *number* of spiritualisms. And the psychoanalyst's complex, which Mauron's psychocriticism, given his unshakeable loyalty to the mother-doctrine, faithfully reflects, is to be found hidden (as is always the case) precisely where it manifests itself most obviously: in this case, beneath its greatest truth. "We know today that all passions arise from the unconscious, which is to say from secretly persisting familial relationships" (p. 200). Agreed. No one doubts it for a moment these days. But traditional psychoanalysis makes both unconscious and familial relationships into *closed systems*, rather after the fashion of Barthes describing linguistic structures. The mind's unconscious life, closed in upon itself, perpetuates in its deeps our age-old habits and dreads: in this sense each man's unconscious reproduces, in the laws by which it functions, that of the whole species. Ontogenesis eternally repeating phylogenesis. And the family too presents a certain type of autarchic relationship, the comprehension of which is self-sufficent, its structures differing in each society like the variables of an identical psychic function. This enclosure within an enclosure has a protective meaning; the unconscious and the family are closed in upon themselves the way a door is closed on a room: in order *to keep history out*. For if you allow history inside that hermetic interiority, into the monadic reality of the mind, then it is good-bye "secret store," good-bye to all those "ocean

174

deeps," those "archetypes," those "symbolic forms" in which human destiny is inscribed for all eternity; it is goodbye to the essence that is wholly governed by immutable and impersonal laws: you will have to perform a quick philosophical about-turn. You will first of all have to throw overboard that past-oriented theory of a perpetually reiterated time, because to say that man has not an essence but an existence, and that his existence is fundamentally historic, is to admit that man has a *becoming*; it means recognizing that if he is defined by the concrete relations he enters into with the world and others, then he is able, by changing those relations, *to change himself*. But in that case everything changes, including even sexuality itself: it is no longer a force field governed by its own internal dynamics, because the "inside" for man is nothing more than the interiorization or signifying organization of an "outside." My "love" for a woman is not an entity or a force mechanically set in motion within my psyche; it is the unifying meaning of an aggregation of complex behavioral patterns that brings into play not only biological desire and its specific laws, but a *situated* desire, which is to say a desire *transformed by its situation* in a given society, at a certain collective and personal moment, from which this (supposedly universal) "emotion" receives its unique affective coloration. There is thus no archeology of love, but a history of love, a sketch for which is possibly to be found in Denis de Rougemont's essay *L'Amour et l'Occident*. My existence, wholly porous and open, ushers the world and history inside me.

That given, the ensuing chain reaction explodes all the rest. If we are foced to change the psychoanalytical theory of time, to say that man is not the past at all but man's future, then that automatically means that human action is not archetypal repetition but free invention. History, the ground of alienation, is also the ground of a possible liberation, or, if you prefer, of a reconstruction of man, of a restructuration of his instincts, of a victory over their "fatality." This moreover, is the meaning of any authentic literary creation: far from being capable of comprehension by a reduction to the "unavoidable framework" conferred upon it by its "internal fatality," to use Mauron's expressions, literature is on the contrary that permanent impulse of breaking free, of

175

transcendence in relation to the inherent contingency and pressure of circumstances, an impulse embodied in the openness and availability of a language whose meaning, as we have seen, continues to be nourished and enriched as it is passed on from man to man, from generation to generation, through successive ages. Literature is the very sign of a certain freedom and a summons to our freedom, made against the background of history and as a possible meaning of history. Sartre was right in defining literature in terms of its permanent power of protest; and it is this essential *negativity* that psychocriticism would like to render ineffective, as though it were defusing a dangerous bomb. All that we are told about the defects of Jansenism, its "ignorance of realities," its wish for the "impossible," its "persecution wish," its "obsessive masochism," could just as well be applied, word for word, to any innovatory attitude whatever, and even more so to any revolutionary attitude. To wish to change the status quo is, by definition, to wish for the impossible, until that impossible has become the reality: I am sure that psychoanalysis would have no trouble in unearthing a persecution mania and a masochist neurosis in Blanqui with all those years in prison. That is the kind of explanation it always has ready-made and at the ready for any radical rejection of "stable conditions": Jesus driving the merchants out of the temple must also have been impelled by his complexes. And Socrates too. It is understandable that Mauron and Bossuet should be in spontaneous agreement over their castigation of Saint-Cyran; Jansenism, as recent studies have shown, did in fact contain a certain ferment of opposition, political as well as purely spiritual, to the regime of the day. The rejection of history here shows its true face: psychoanalysis, like ethics, is in constant danger of becoming a purely conservative ideology. Though the Marxists have been wrong in rejecting it in its entirety — for the dymamics of instinct is *also* present in the dialectic of history, as can be clearly seen in such recent sociological work as that of Vance Packard — they were right in denouncing its ideological foundation. Inspired no doubt by the Cartesian maxim according to which it is better to try changing the order of one's thoughts than that of the world, the vocation of psychoanalysis is to *adapt* the individual to the general order of

176

the society in which he lives, to help him recover a sufficent mastery over his emotions to enable him to *integrate himself* into that order. From this point of view, the rebel is easily perceived as a man who is sick, and the revolutionary as a man to be cured rather than opposed. It is certainly no coincidence that psychoanalysis has flourished so mightily in the United States. But if the mind is not a hermetically sealed retort, if its inner conflicts in fact reflect not merely immemorial archetypes but the external contradictions of history, then the true cure is seen to consist no longer in a form of action aimed exclusively at a change in the self, but in a praxis aimed at transforming the world.

It becomes easier in this light to understand Mauron's peremptory decree and the nature of the interdict that he proclaims from the very outset: "Neither personality nor genius has, in truth, any historical explanation" (*L'Inconscient*, p. 46). Needless to say, he is prepared to accept whatever history is necessary (i.e. a certain amount of historical gossip) to furnish Racine's anonymous and empty unconscious with gleanings from any number of social anecdotes. But true history, which is to say the radical *historicity* of any human existence, the fact that it assumes itself wholly within a given political and social situation, from which it receives the meaning that it can itself then give to its own destiny, this *constituent* history never makes an appearance — and for a very good reason. The political dimension of the Racinian universe no longer exists; whatever subsists of the imperatives of power, the interplay of means and ends in a power situation, which make the universe of Racine's characters, as a result of their situation, a *dynastic* universe (cf. the discussion in the latter part of chapter 2 above), survives only as by-product of a subsidiary activity. Mauron does exactly the same to specifically political signification as to theological signification: renamed "martial instinct" or "aggressive energy," it becomes no more than a disguise adopted by the unconscious, the residue of psychic mechanisms: in order to escape its fatality, the self splits in two to form the loving self and the witness self; "the second of these withdraws from the action: it simultaneously avoids all blame and seeks for another way out, one that will be socially acceptable — war, politics" (p. 179). War and politics — that monarchic context in which every Racinian destiny is played out and overtaken by fate — are thus castrated, shorn of their historical meaning: it is no longer merely the theater, it is History that is a dream. Nothing, even down to the details of military strategy, escapes the all-devouring maw of psychoanalytical explanation, whose "oral" fixation really deserves some kind of denunciation at this point. When troops are attacked from the rear, and run away, then they are acting under the influence of the "parent hostility complex": "We find precisely this kind of panic in troops caught unprepared from the rear (as when Blücher appeared instead of Grouchy) and in the obsessive fear of the traitor" (p. 74). If one put one's faith entirely in psychocriticism one would never suspect that Racine actually lived out his obsessions and wrote his tragedies in the seventeenth century, in short, that his work interiorizes the human condition of his own age. The static "structures" that are revealed to us certainly define a certain internal *space*; but they possess no specific *time* of their own, and belong to no age. The Racine we are offered is strictly atemporal (the "ancient bedrock of the unconscious"), and therefore quite literally *utopian*. Psychocriticism's absolute fidelity to classical psychoanalysis is no doubt a revelation, through Mauron's pen, of Freud's secret dream: like happy nations, happy patients have no History.

2. SOCIOLOGY OF THE THEME

Lucien Goldmann began his research wholly independently, and his work on Racine predates that of Mauron. Yet it is exactly as though, after due reflection on the weaknesses of psychocriticism, on both the methodological and philosophical levels, he had then set out to remedy them.[6] For although psychoanalytical elucidation has an undeniable practical fruitfulness when applied to the comprehension of literary works (despite the theoretical reservations I have been forced to express, Charles Mauron's examination of Racine remains, I repeat, one of the most penetrating and original we have in its descriptive phase), the limits of psychoanalytical explanation prevent it from giving any account of the link that exists between reality and its thematic expression: "This is something sociologists discovered a long while back, when they af-

firmed the *historical and social* character of the objective signification residing in *the emotional and intellectual life of individuals*" (Goldmann, *Pour une sociologie du roman*, Bibliothèque des idées; Paris:
Gallimard, 1964; p. 208; hereafter sited as *SR*). This statement,
which Lucien Goldmann makes with specific reference to the novels of Robbe-Grillet, could well serve as an epigraph for his critical
works as a whole. Not that Charles Mauron was wrong in assigning
the ends he did to criticism: criticism is indeed concerned with
being "a scientific and explanatory study of intellectual and literary facts" (Goldmann, *Le Dieu caché*, Bibliothèque des idées; Paris:
Gallimard, 1955; p. 22; hereafter sited as *DC*). Just as Mauron
talked perpetually about "scientific truth," Goldmann talks perpetually of "science"; in the preface to *Pour une sociologie du roman*,
the words "science" and "scientific" recur no less than six times on
page 11. Mauron was not therefore mistaken in his choice of aim,
but rather, if I may so express it, in his choice of science: he opted
for psychoanalysis when he should have chosen sociology; for
in a comparison of his efforts with those once made by the erst-
while founding father of the positive natural sciences, our
sociologist here presents himself, in all modesty, as the Galileo
of criticism (ibid.). Sociological criticism thus understood is scientific in that it enables us to isolate strict and positive "laws."[7] But
these laws are not of the same kind as the natural laws of the
physico-chemical sciences, which presuppose a causal determinism: "Any wager on a purely legal or causal rationality — exclusive of all finality — is, in the domain of human facts, unrealizable
and contradictory" (*DC*, p. 103). The true method, in the human
sciences, must be dialectical, in the Marxist sense of the term:
as opposed to the "distortions" to which Freudian analyses subject
cultural and historical facts (*SR*, p. 226), and in contrast with the
external or causal conception of the individual's conditioning by
society that is implied in the "rationalist, empiricist, or
phenomenological" positions (*SR*, p. 215),[8] "Marxism seems to
me incomparably further advanced, insofar as it integrates not
only the future as an explicative factor, but also the individual
signification of human facts alongside their collective signification" (*SR*, p. 226). The Marxist method is thus the only complete
method, since it presents itself as constitutive of both a positive sci-

ence and a primary philosophy, that is to say as a science capable both of providing its own foundations and of fully justifying its own status.

The method that Lucien Goldmann proposes for literary criticism, and which he terms "structuralist-genetic," seems to me particularly worthy of attention, since it constitutes the most fully developed and most systematic attempt to achieve a theoretical construct that will provide critical research with strict and objective foundations, and rescue it at last from what Goldmann calls "subjective and ingenious speculations." In this scientific age of ours it is easy to understand the profound interest aroused by a body of thought aimed, before all else, at regaining for science a domain traditionally reserved for the approximations of "literary" investigations — especially when that science is endowed in addition with all the political and moral attractions of Marxism. Even more than Roland Barthes's linguistic or metalogical criticism and Charles Mauron's psychoanalytic criticism, Lucien Goldmann's sociological criticism represents the ultimate spearhead of the effort being made by a whole section of the new criticism to construct scientific models of intelligibility for itself. The attempt — I almost said the temptation — is not new: since Sainte-Beuve and Renan, since Taine and Brunetière, in short since the advent of the positivist ideology that followed, in the second half of the nineteenth century, upon the development of the sciences, literary criticism too has consistently felt the desire to base itself henceforth on solid scientific foundations. But where positivist science failed, positive science must now succeed: disencumbered of the postulates of causal determinism, and armed with the dialectic of Marxist method, today's scientific thought is in a position to understand and explain the specifically human relations involved. Emile Hennequin was already saying, at the end of the nineteenth century, that we must treat the work of art "as a sign." But of what? It is the aim of structuralist-genetic sociology to tell us just that.

Here, as in any positive research work, the empirical facts, once isolated and abstracted, are the necessary point of departure. But their signification only emerges when we form them into certain significative wholes or totalities; it is this integration into a whole that provides the means of "transcending the partial and abstract phenomenon in order to reach its concrete essence" (*DC*, p. 16). Cultural facts thus acquire a signification from their insertion into certain structures, and "the valid meaning is that which makes it possible to discover the total coherence of the work, unless that coherence does not exist" (p. 22). Nothing so far but the usual preliminaries — by now familiar — to any contemporary critical undertaking; the problem, however, is to know *where* to find this "valid" meaning that makes it possible to discover the "total coherence." For Barthes, the principle of that coherence was strictly internal, and inherent to the formal organization of the signifying raw material. For Mauron, the work itself proclaimed and revealed the principle of its own unity, but the key to that unity, in the final analysis, lay in the affective system specific to the author's unconscious personality. Like Mauron, and contrary to Barthes, Goldmann does not believe "that an author's thought and work can be understood by themselves, by remaining on the level of the writings" (*DC*, p. 16). But contrary to Mauron, he maintains that "any individual's life work, taken as a whole, is not already a signifying structure as such" (*DC*, p. 109). Just as Mauron, in order to explain the work, had to insert it into an individual's life, it will now be necessary to insert the individual, in his turn, into the whole formed by the social group of which that individual is only one element. The "operative" concept that links work, individual, and group in an intelligible fashion, and which, for Lucien Goldmann, constitutes the basis of any cultural interpretation, is the "vision of the world": this is "the ensemble of aspirations, feelings, and ideas that unites the members of a group (usually a social class) and sets them in opposition to other groups" (*DC*, p. 26). It is in this way that we should understand the total or almost total coherence that is precisely what defines great works, in contrast to less important works, which are simply works of lesser coherence: it comes from the vision of the world, which is to say from the "maximum possible consciousness of the social group" that writers or philosophers express (*DC*, p. 27). The individual of genius is precisely the one who succeeds in providing this maximum consciousness, or, which comes to the same thing, this extreme coherence with the real, emotional, and intellectual tendencies of a social group; and in his works there must be absolute adequation between the vision of the world as an experienced reality and the universe created by the writer, as well as between the universe the writer creates and the specifically literary means he employs to express it (*DC*, p. 349). A primary procedure, or a first stage in the interpretation, will therefore consist in working from an internal examination of the text toward the vision of the world it expresses — in Pascal or Racine, for example, the "tragic vision."

However, this preliminary stage, which Goldmann calls phenomenological comprehension or study, is literally deprived of all meaning if it does not lead to the following stage, that of genetic explanation or study. Although the individual confers a maximum of consciousness upon the group's tendencies, he does not create them; it is the group which evolves them, even though they may exist within it in a chaotic state, and it is therefore the group that is the locus of cultural creation, and particularly of that which produces a vision of the world. Comprehension and explanation are therefore in practice inseparable; they are two moments of one and the same process: "There is a progression, permanent albeit probably discontinuous, both in the comprehension and in the genetic explanation, that emerges as one succeeds in inserting the relative wholes that one is studying into the greater totalities that include them and of which they are constitutive elements" (*DC*, p. 105). Goldmann was later to clarify still further the nature of the relation that unifies comprehension and explanation, and which is a special mode of imbrication of the one into the other: "The clarification of a signifying structure constitutes a process of *comprehension*, whereas its insertion into a larger structure is, in relation to the first structure, a process of *explanation*. As an example: to clarify the tragic structure of Pascal's *Pensées* and Racine's plays is a process of comprehension; to insert them within the extremist current of Jansenism as a means of elucidating the latter's structure is a process of comprehension with respect to Jansenism but a process of explanation with respect to the writings of Pascal and Racine" (*SR*, p. 223). It is clear, therefore, how every structuralist interpretation has as its necessary complement a genetic explanation; but, inversely, every genetic explanation must be a structuralist interpretation: it consists in the establishing of relations between the structures of the literary or artistic work and the structures of the social group of which those works represent the coherent expression. Unlike previous sociological schools of thought, including a certain rudimentary form of Marxism, which tried to establish identities or resemblances of "content" between the imaginary universe of a work and the social world contemporary with it, the structuralist sociology founded by Lukács comprehends artistic creation as the "creation of a world whose structure is analogous to the essential structure of the social reality within whose matrix the work was written" (*SR*, p. 209). In the final analysis, the "comprehensive-explanatory" method that Lucien Goldmann is offering us is consciously aiming at "effecting temporary groupings of writings on the basis of which one will then go on to search in the intellectual, political, social, and economic life of the time for structured social groupings, in which one will then be able to integrate, as partial elements, the works studied, by establishing intelligible relations between those works and the whole, and, in the most favorable cases, homologies" (*SR*, p. 233).

Thus, in the texts provided by Pascal or Racine, internal study will reveal the broad lines of a tragic vision of the world: this consists in attempting the realization, in this world, of values that are strictly unrealizable within it; the tragic consciousness knows neither degree nor compromise; since it has no knowledge of more or less, it is defined by a simultaneous and untranscendable *yes* and *no*, by its insistence on "all or nothing." Now this structure found in the tragic consciousness, immobilized in the tension of its contradictions (unlike dialectical thought, which overcomes them), corresponds very closely to the structure of the Jansenist groups, which are also trapped within an insoluble contradiction: the *noblesse de robe*, that is, the lower nobility drawn from the professional classes, is torn between its loyalty to the monarchy and the evolution of monarchic politics, working toward the destruction of the parliamentary class; the Jansenist consciousness is therefore a condemnation of a radically bad world, and a world,

183

moreover, that there is no hope of changing. The homology of the two structures is patent. Similarly, the traditional novel tells the story of a "problematical hero," which is to say a character whose values and existence confront him with insoluble problems, which he does not succeed in bringing into full consciousness. This imaginary biography achieves, on the literary level, the transposition of daily life in the individualist society produced by market-controlled production. Parallel to the transformation of economic life and the replacement of a laissez-faire economy (in which the individual can affirm his identity) by an economy of cartels and monopolies (which suppress all the individual's importance), we find the development of modern novelistic forms. The role of the individual character diminishes; antithetical, communalistic, and collective values emerge under the influence of the socialist ideologies. Then, in a second period, all biography vanishes entirely, the individual undergoes a dissolution, giving way to the "novel of the subject's absence." In this way an explanation can be offered of the progression that is found, in Malraux's novels, from *Les Conquérants* to *La Condition humaine*, and from *La Condition humaine* to *L'Espoir*, and which then leads on from the novels of Malraux himself to those of Nathalie Sarraute and Robbe-Grillet. In the case of these latter (and contrary to Roland Barthes, who is aware above all of their pure objectal description and the internal organization of their literary structures), Lucien Goldmann points out that in the fatality of *Les Gommes*, which eliminates all possibility of modification derived from an unpredictable element in the individual temperament, and also in the inertia of *Le Voyeur*, which infects the entire population of the island, we find exact homologues of the self-regulating market mechanisms and growing passivity that are characteristic of the present phase of western industrial societies. But what about the authors, you will ask? What about Pascal? Racine? Malraux? Robbe-Grillet? They constitute a sort of mediation — unavoidable, of course, but nevertheless inessential — between the structures of the work and those of a group or society, which can only be conjoined by means of a single necessary yet simple link. For "the true subjects of cultural creation are social groups and not isolated individuals" (*SR*, p. 11): the strict homology therefore exists between the vision of the world expressed in the work and the vision of the world diffused throughout the group, and not between the structures of the work and those of an individual psyche or life. The psychological relations are infinitely too complex for a study of them ever to succeed in defining this simple and necessary link provided by sociological analysis; and, moreover, for the moment at least, psychology is very far from presenting us with the true unity of a science. "One could therefore, *in theory*, by studying the author's individuality, arrive at a knowledge of the genesis and signification of certain elements contributing to the constitution of his writings. Unfortunately . . . outside the laboratory and clinical analysis, and in the present state of psychology, the individual is in practice hardly accessible to detailed and scientific study" (*DC*, p. 348). It is thus clear why psychoanalysis — whose claims he has examined in a recent study (*SR*, pp. 225, et seq.) — must in Goldmann's eyes be ultimately rejected: the libido remains individual, and has no outlet into history. Although it is useful indirectly, as it were — in that it provides a method of coupling the individual life and the destiny of the group — when psychoanalysis has finished its elucidation of a work's affective and biographical significations, it will still "not have touched or even approached" the literary and philosophical significations of the writings. It would certainly be impossible to deny, then, that Lucien Goldmann is presenting us with a method very carefully worked out to take account of present-day human sciences and the Marxist tradition, and which indeed is intended to provide a synthesis of those two elements.

What are we to think of this method and its contribution to literary criticism? First we should note that in the mind of its creator, sociological explication in no way constitutes the whole of literary criticism. The former, it is claimed, makes possible the "elucidation of the relation between the vision of the world and the universe of beings and things within the work"; the latter, "the elucidation of the relations between that universe on the one hand and on the other the specifically literary means and techniques that the writer selected in order to express it" (*DC*, p. 350). In short, by collating Goldmann and Picard we should

185

arrive at the "total criticism" that our age cries out for. Needless to say, Goldmann has allotted himself the lion's share in the partnership; just as in the Middle Ages philosophy was required to be the handmaid of theology, so literary criticism could never be anything more, from Goldmann's standpoint, than a subsidiary discipline (like psychoanalysis), whose task is the elucidation of details — though admittedly important ones — in accordance with the directives provided by sociological research. It is hard to see how it could be otherwise: since the marshaling and use of the expressive techniques is wholly governed by the vision of the world they are aimed at revealing, literary criticism, as envisaged by Lucien Goldmann, is inevitably secondary, or at least second in line, to sociological investigation, whose reports it must wait to receive before setting to work itself. Very well, the relations of sociology and aesthetics having been thus defined — in accordance with precisely the same schema as in the case of psychocriticism — what are the results, and in what way are they an advance over those of traditional literary research?

Curiously, and for reasons which will gradually become clear, I shall be forced to repeat here, with reference to sociology, what I have already said about psychoanalysis. The *descriptive* stage and the *explicative* stage — as inseparable in Goldmann's mind as they are in Mauron's, since it is the explanation of their genesis that renders full comprehension of the structures possible — are in practice not merely separable but separated and, what is more, of very unequal value. Once again, it is not my intention in this essay to judge the individual talent of any critic, or to provide a general picture of criticism today: I am solely concerned with evaluating the different methods that are presently vying for the researcher's attention, and also with assessing the philosophy of literature that these methods put forward or imply. When I express doubts about a method, I am no more disputing the personal merits of its promoter than I would be endorsing them if the reverse were the case. The contribution made by Lucien Goldmann's work is not in question here; his researches have in very large measure renewed our understanding of Pascal and Jansenism, perfected the invaluable concept of the tragic vision, and thrown a new light on the development of the modern novel.

186

It is to Goldmann that we owe our most penetrating analyses of Malraux and Robbe-Grillet. But to what does he owe that power of penetration? On what level does it operate? For Goldmann, the answer is beyond doubt: like any scholar or scientist he believes that he owes his results to his method, and this structuralist-genetic method, as its name indicates, is valid precisely because it is able both to isolate the essential structures of a literary work and to give an account of their genesis. My answer will be a different one. As was the case with psychocriticism, everything original, forceful, and true in Lucien Goldmann's sociological criticism invariably occurs on the plane of comprehension and phenomenology, in other words, the plane of internal study. His fine chapters on Pascal's tragic vision (God, the world, man); his original and striking association of Jansenist and Marxist dialectics, which holds good even in the very contrasts between them; his remarkable analyses of paradox, the wager, or the conjunction of opposites in the *Pensées*; his treatment of the formation, evolution, and dissolution of the revolutionary ideology in Malraux's works seen as the principle of their fictional development; all this, and many other things beside, fall exclusively into the domain of internal study and structural description. Obviously such study and such description involve the deployment, by a modern critic, of detailed psychoanalytical, sociological, or philosophical concepts and insights either unknown to or spurned by traditional research, and which make it possible to reveal essential significations in the literary work hitherto neglected or omitted. But as soon as it is a matter of making the transition from comprehension to explanation, or of taking the model of intelligibility constructed within one or other of the positive sciences and applying it in its entirety to the decipherment of literature, then things never fail to go wrong. Our observations in the case of linguistics and psychoanalysis will now be verified in the case of sociology.

The central methodological problem facing any criticism that attempts to isolate the unity and coherence specific to works of art, that is, to comprehend them as an organization of concurrent structures, is that of *dissection*. Lucien Goldmann is the first to show awareness of this: "It is clear that if in order to gain knowledge of the real structure of human and historical life it is necessary to dissect it into *significant* structures, the researcher is faced with innumerable possibilities of making erroneous dissections of the body of empirical data presented" (*DC*, p. 106). Once again we come up against the obstacle, already encountered earlier, of skeptical fragmentation, the shattering of truth into a multiplicity of truths that can no longer be fitted together again and leave our global knowledge disarticulated and helpless. But Goldmann turns this difficulty itself into his solution: "Faced with the large number of possible wrong dissections of the object and the small number of valid ones, it is the exclusive quest for *significant* totalities that to my knowledge constitutes the researcher's only valid guide" (ibid.). Put in different terms, the good dissection is that which will lay bare ensembles of a kind that will integrate the maximum possible meaning. This definition coincides exactly with that given by Roland Barthes of the validity of a critical method, and I for my part accede to it gladly. The problem is now therefore this: Does the type of criticism offered by Lucien Goldmann, in the name of a Marxist sociology rejuvenated by his structuralist additions, integrate the greatest quantity of literary meaning, and is his dissection therefore the right one? For me, there can be no doubt that the answer is in the negative.

First it must be observed that this "dissection" claiming to achieve a "significant totality" starts with an arbitrary decree: "A valid positive study of the *Pensées* and of Racine's plays presupposes not only an analysis of their internal structure, but in the first place their insertion into the currents of thought and affectivity that lie closest to them"— in this case, Jansenist thought and spiritual beliefs — which must then, in their turn, be put back into the context of the economic, political, and social situation of the *noblesse de robe* (*DC*, p. 110). Please note the "in the first place" and the order of priority it implies. All research, in practice, must admittedly begin with a vicious circle: it is the question of which came first, the chicken or the egg. Facts must be comprehended by means of a hypothesis, but the hypothesis, in its turn, can be justified solely by the facts. It is no good attempting to deny the existence of this circle; what we must do is attempt to break out of it by employing the dynamic of a concrete procedure that will approach the facts, as the Russian intelligentsia did the people, with the intention of molding itself to them with ever-increasing intimacy and of correcting itself through its contact with them. In this respect it must be accepted that any interpretation is, at the outset, arbitrary, since it is giving signification, in Roland Barthes's phrase, "a stamp on the brake" by making a choice as to which level of signification is to be focused on. But it nevertheless remains inadmissible that there should be a *priority* of hypothesis over facts, for that would mean destroying the very dialectics of knowledge, which is defined by its two-way traffic: the nature of the desired signification having been established, the meaning cannot then be *imposed* on phenomena; the meaning must, on the contrary, and this is phenomenology's very essence, be allowed to emerge — provided, of course, that it is in fact there. It is thus inadmissible to decide *in the first place* to insert Racine's plays into the structures and spiritual beliefs of the Jansenist societies; on the contrary, one must first show, by means of internal analysis, that Racine's plays *do indeed have a Jansenist meaning* (something that a number of critics have denied absolutely), since without this, to insert them into the Jansenist structure, justified solely by the sophism of historical proximity, is nothing more than an arbitrary decision, and the legitimate hypothesis no more than a piece of fallacious question-begging. And this is precisely what happens. For whereas in Pascal's case Goldmann actually *showed* the Jansenist meaning of the texts, in the case of Racine he merely *supposes* it, by contagion as it were. And unfortunately the "setting" of the meaning thus obtained becomes a dubious *dissection*. Having laid bare his meaning, he is then reduced to slicing some of it off; after dissection comes amputation. Having decreed in advance what in a work is or is not essential, in the name of an external criterion — the concept of the "vision of the world" that the sociologist claims as his touchstone for defining that work's "coherence"— Goldmann then decides, without further ado, that we can "leave aside" *Alexandre* or *La Thébaïde* from Racine's work (*DC*, p. 23). Yet Mauron's analyses, among others, have clearly established the thematic affinity and kinship of these early tragedies with those that follow. Apart from the fact that such a sudden hop, skip, and jump over two whole plays is difficult to justify on the purely empirical level, we all know, since Leibniz, that any habit begins with the first performance of the act in question. The first attempts of any writer, though they are often imperfect, are always revealing. I think we should therefore look rather more closely at this curious right the critic has here arrogated to himself of wielding the censor's scissors in order to guarantee the success of his "dissection."

The new criticism is very fond of talking about the unity or coherence of works; but talking about it, or even establishing its existence, is not everything: it still has to be defined, so that we know where to find it. In practice, of course, there are various types of coherence, according to the level of signification upon which one fixes one's attention: the researches of Roland Barthes, for example, accord primacy to a coherence of a formal and lucid type, those of Charles Mauron to a coherence of an unconscious affective type. But though it is certainly a choice made by the critic that decides which among the multiplicity of significations will reveal the essential meaning, this choice, though free, cannot for all that be arbitrary: the basic condition that limits it (a condition that all critics agree in accepting) is that *the meaning thus chosen shall integrate the largest quantity of significations possible, and even, at the limit of possibility, their totality.* Moreover it was on the strength of this very principle that I felt justified in criticizing the formal coherence put forward by Barthes, because it failed to include the transcendent dimension of literary language, which constitutes one of that language's major meanings; and similarly, in the case of Mauron's psychoanalytic coherence, I objected that the rigidity of its conception excluded all possibility of comprehending the variations and development specific to the themes, thus depriving the work of the meaning it acquires through its becoming. In this respect, the definition of coherence put forward by Lucien Goldmann seems to me equally crippling. Because for him, in fact, a work of art is no more than the expression, in a specific language (that of literature, or painting, or sculpture, etc.), of a "vision of the world" that is equally expressed in philosophic and theological works, or in the varied manifestations of everyday life (*DC*, p. 301). The question that then presents itself is: How do we find out in what the specificity of the literary language consists, or, what *differentiates* it from other languages? We have already heard the reply: the literary or philosophic work is defined by "the maximum possible consciousness" that it confers upon a social group's vision of the world, a vision that exists in a confused or diffused state in each one of that group's members. The great creator, in the realm of mind, is the man who succeeds in producing "an imagined universe that is coherent, or almost strictly coherent, and whose structure corresponds to that toward which the group tends as a whole; as for the work, it is, among other things, either poorer or more important insofar as its structure diverges from or comes closer to a strict coherence" (*SR*, p. 219). Given this point of view, historico-sociological analysis, if carried sufficiently far, will also provide the "criterion of the aesthetically valid work" (*DC*, p. 350). But what Goldmann does not seem to have noticed is that in positing this necessary link between sociological analysis and an aesthetic criterion, although he has succeeded in establishing a bridgehead in the realm of aesthetics, it is at the expense of leaving his sociological flank wide open. Because if the aesthetic criterion thus obtained should prove inadmissible, then it is inevitable that the sociological analysis contributing to its definition must likewise be suspect.

In the first place it is necessary to point out, and deplore, the confusion that Marxist thought constantly introduces — in aesthetic as well as ethical matters — between judgments of fact and judgments of value.[9] The dialectic employed here is supposed to consist precisely in the ability to move *objectively* from one domain to the other: "No value must be recognized or admitted except insofar as that recognition is based upon positive and objective knowledge of reality, just as all valid knowledge of reality can only be based on a practice — and that means on the explicit or implicit recognition of a body of values — in conformity with the progress of history" (*DC*, p. 98). The values are based on objective knowledge; the objective knowledge is based on values, which, in their turn, are "in conformity with the progress of history," which is to say provided with an objective foundation. And thus, the imputation is, the circle is closed, the circuit of objectivity completed by a dialectic in which facts and values are all merely moments in one single process. But in fact we are dealing here with a fundamental sophism, one that exists not merely in Goldmann's method of procedure but in Marxist philosophy in general. Marxism is right, needless to say, in attempting to articulate the field of reality intelligibly with that of the possible, for man: value must always presuppose the insertion of a human project into reality. But to say that there are no human possibles other than those founded on reality is in no way equivalent to being able to *extract* the possible from the real by any process you care to name, even a dialectical one: there is no passing here from one state of being to another state of being other than through the mediation of *nonbeing*, by an absolute qualitative leap which refers to something outside the sphere of being, to the upsurge of existence. If, as the analyses of Heidegger and Sartre have shown, consciousness is precisely that nullifying apparition in the heart of being, it is because any human project implies the negation of given reality in the name of a possible reality, a reality, in other words, that is not yet *in being*. And the "not being yet" is not simply a latent kind of "already being." The colors in tubes of paint do not "become" a painting in the way that clouds "become" rain. There is no process that enables the transition from the paints in the tubes to the finished painting to occur by a dialectic of becoming: that "possibility" is something that the paints, in the strictest sense, *do not possess*; it comes to them from beyond the world, bestowed by a free and unpredictable invention, by a human project, which alone can transcend the real toward an *authentic possible* or *value* (that which "is to be," as determination of the being that is not already contained in it). Thus the circuit of objectivity, in which the Marxist was cautiously attempting to enclose himself, is exploded by the upsurge of subjective existence, which by radical negation of fact, and by that negation alone, produces value. Even the conservative ideology of "acceptance of facts" and the *amor fati* are *transcendences*, and thus negations of fact as simple fact, just as much as Marx's desire to "transform the world" or Rimbaud's "to change life." No "objective knowledge," as such, can provide the basis of a value, since value resides wholly in that surplus of meaning that consciousness invents and projects beyond given reality. (Moreover, if values were provided solely by knowledge resulting from scientific investigation, there could never be any value in any immediate and absolute investment, such as love.) Inversely, no aggregations of historical values can ever provide a *valid foundation* for scientific knowledge, whose truth, though it may manifest itself in history, is of a strictly nonhistorical order. The exact truth is that knowledge can aid (but not justify) the choice of "realizable" values, which is one choice among many (the tragic vision, as Goldmann shows, implies choosing the unrealizable). Similarly, the historical adoption of certain values (rigor, detachment, rationalism, etc.) can facilitate, but not provide the foundation for, the progress of scientific knowledge. In short, objective significations and significations that bestow value can never at any point merge into one another, since they belong to radically distinct sectors of being. If there is any intelligible articulation between them, then it is provided not by the mediation of any process, but by an *agent*. Moreover, by claiming to give normative judgments the surety of objective judgments one ends up losing everything just when one thinks one has found the winning system: the two scales cannot be confused with impunity. One may think that one is conferring all the weight of fact upon one's selected values, but the osmosis works in the opposite direction, and what one is offering as a judgment of fact is really *nothing but a disguised value judgment*.

The "strict coherence" that sociological analysis reveals, according to Lucien Goldmann, and which may supposedly be used *at a later stage* as an aesthetic criterion, is in fact, *in the first place*, an aesthetic choice that is guiding, or rather misguiding, the sociological research. Let us look for a moment at the type of coherence implied by the "vision of the world" as Goldmann uses that phrase: it is "the *conceptual extrapolation* to a stage of *extreme coherence* of the real, affective, intellectual, and even motivating tendencies of the members of a group" (*DC*, p. 349). In sum, the sociologist and the artist are seen as traveling, albeit along different paths (abstract language or literary language), toward the same goal: the most rigorous possible expression of a vision of the world; if they meet, that is because their fundamental procedures eventually merge into one. It consists, essentially, of *working from ambiguity toward clarity.* "It is precisely the fact of *not accepting ambiguity*, of maintaining despite and against everything the demands of reason and clarity, . . . that constitutes the essence of tragedy in particular and of the classical mind in general" (*DC*, p. 70). This definition of a "classical" aesthetic gives us the key to the entire undertaking: far from it being the formulation of an essence isolated within the facts by cultural analysis, this "classicism" of the left, just like the classicism of the right proclaimed by Maurras and his followers, is merely a historical fiction concealing a personal choice: "It would not be incorrect to term classical, in a very broad sense, all those literary and philosophic works centered upon rational comprehension, and romantic all those that turn away from reason in order to take refuge in the affective and the imaginary" (*DC*, p. 52). At the heart of this would-be definition there lies a simple postulate: "rational" study is directed toward reality, whereas "affective and imaginary" activity takes us further away from it, because the real, as the Hegelian phrase tells us, is simply the rational. But in fact, nothing could be less correct: rationality is not the entire content of reality; feeling and imagination are *developers* of the world: when steeped in them, reality reveals its being, at another level than that attained by reason, but not an inferior one. Far from the life of the emotions serving as a refuge from the concrete, it is on the contrary a certain form of rationalism that is used as a defense for the mind against reality. The "coherence" we are supposed to find lying at the end of our sociological analysis is nothing more than the initial prejudice of an intellectualist aesthetic working on *the presupposition that art employs the same fundamental procedure as science.* Whereas in fact, their coherences and procedures are diametrically opposed: in the first place, the coherence of art is not of an intellectual but of an existential order (cf. chapter 4 above); second, art does not work from the complex to the simple, from the ambiguous to the clear, but from the simple to the complex and from the clear to the ambiguous. As we saw earlier (in chapters 4 and 7), it is precisely a certain type of ambiguity whose richness justifies and defines literary language. "Classical clarity" is a false clarity invented to suit the needs of a cause, and my arguments used earlier against Picard's "classicism" (cf. chapter 4) hold good against Goldmann's "classicism" too. Moreover it is no coincidence that the revolutionary attitude should have espoused reactionary prejudice in the field of art: in an attempt to bypass the individual in order to reach the universal one inevitably ends up granting preeminence, in the field of literary expression, to the evident (and rationally communicable) significate to the detriment of the latent (and affectively experienced) significate. But the coherence obtained in this way strips the artwork of its flesh, so that we can go into ecstasies over its skeleton. Goldmann's "vision of the world" is no more than an intellectual "schema" arrived at by extreme simplification and extrapolation, the product of a distillation whose recipe consists in boiling off the literary content so that one is left with a residue, at the bottom of the retort, that is the essence of literature. Because even though we may accept as true the notion that the fatality and passivity present in Robbe-Grillet's novels represent analogous structures to those of the self-regulation and reifying mechanisms imposed by the neocapitalist market, all we are really accepting is the isolation of one *possible sociological signification of those works* (there are others: one could demonstrate the affinity between the author's fictional material and the collective myths of the contemporary imagination), and certainly not *their literary meaning*. Because literary meaning, according to my analysis, cannot be obtained by granting arbitrary preeminence to a particular order of significations, but only by achieving the convergence into an intelligible unity of the greatest variety of human significations. To adopt the reverse procedure ineluctably leads to a certain number of errors.

For a start, by cutting the work off from its affective roots in its author, or by dissipating that affectivity in the transparency of an intellectual signification, Goldmann's curious materialism — as the result of an excess precisely the reverse of Mauron's, who saw Racine's plays as one long nightmare — presents us, at the ultimate point of literature, with the clear radiance of an idea. But this idea is nothing more, at best, than a *formula*. Obtained by abstraction of the sensorially perceptible qualities of the work, it fits Racine in his entirety into the Jansenist law of the "world-rejected: world-accepted," or Robbe-Grillet into the economic law of the elimination of the individual. Anything that sticks out beyond this literary bed of Procrustes upon which the author's writings are laid is peremptorily lopped off: Goldmann's vision decides where Racine's vision shall start and finish. *La Thé baïde* and *Alexandre*, onto the scrap heap; the expression of a useless or unimportant life and soul: everything that does not fall within the frame constructed in advance by the critic's "coherence" is decreed insignificant. Yet Freud has taught us that in the human domain just the opposite can be true: what is insignificant on the surface does in fact signify. The detail, the fragment, can indicate and express a man just as well as the perfectly finished chapter, albeit in another way. By thus pruning away all that is concrete in order to achieve an abstract coherence, far from revealing an author's originality, one merely shows up his *banality*. If we are to accept this strange conception — and strange is an understatement — then writings of average or low value would be correspondingly more difficult to analyze than great works, "because they are the expression of particularly complex average individualities, and above all because they are rather untypical and unrepresentative" (*DC*, p. 349). Which makes the writer of genius into a sort of spokesman or standard-bearer, simple and transparent to the piercing eye of the sociologist, whereas the imbecile has all the opacity of the great mysteries. Déroulède, a mediocre poet if ever there was one, with his muddled and inconsistent imagination, would defeat Goldmann's sociological investigations entirely, whereas Rimbaud, the very model of a typical and representative personality, as we all know, would be an only too easily digested prey.

This being the case, why do we have literature anyway? If the entire interest presumed to exist in an imaginary universe derives from the rigorous depiction of a vision of the world, and if criticism's task is to trim and prune away its details until that vision of the world becomes apparent, why go to the trouble of reading dense and difficult works when a history or political economy textbook would suit the same purpose better? Reading Goldmann, one scarcely feels that there is any difference (and he doesn't seem to feel any himself) between a creator of literature and a philosopher, between Racine and Pascal: why should there be one, since every great author is a hawker of ideology? And in consequence the critic has a tendency to mix poets and thinkers together; we find Goldmann citing their names quite indiscriminately in his lists.[10] The analyses of Roland Barthes retain all their force when applied to Goldmann: in literature, what is said forms an indivisible whole with a certain way of saying it, and criticism can never be the abstraction of a quintessence that is common to ten other modes of expression. Nor will it avail at this point, in order to restore the specificity of literature, to appeal to an urgently coopted "aesthetic"; lacking any internal link with the sociological analysis, any such aesthetic is not juxtaposable to it, and "total criticism" is not, after all, just Goldmann plus Picard. The notion that it is possible to isolate a vision of the world, and beside it, quite separately, techniques intended to express it, is a pure fiction. There is at the outset a man, a writer, in whom a certain vision engenders his individual means of expression by means of a specific process creative of the work — and it is that, before all else, that criticism should strive to mold itself to and recapture.

And sociological analysis is totally unable to perform this fundamental task. Having begun by distorting any internal study of the texts by using a criterion of coherence external to the work — and moreover erroneous — it is inevitable that the "dissection" Goldmann proposes should prove, in use, both restrictive and crippling. By borrowing the "tragic vision" schema discovered by a study of Pascal, and by grafting it directly onto Racine on the strength of the postulate that all Jansenist thought always produces the same structures,[11] the resulting analysis of Racine's plays, instead of revealing their concrete structuration, succeeds, in fact, merely in *destructuring them*. For the next stage will be to dissect the plays in accordance with the "primacy of practical reason" characteristic of the tragic vision (simultaneous acceptance and rejection of the world, with the various dramatic combinations obtained by placing the emphasis on one or other of those terms). Here we see the process actually at work. Racine's plays being, by definition, tragic, they will be deciphered by means of an a priori view of them that is not derived from internal analysis but presupposed by a conception of tragedy. Corneille,

197

on the other hand, being "pre-tragic," will be accessible to a "psychological" approach. But in fact, since La Bruyère, we know that exactly the opposite is the case: what his famous phrase means — and in this sense it remains perfectly true today — is that Corneille's drama is totally governed and defined by the primacy of an ethic — what Goldmann would call a "practical reason" ("men as they ought to be"), whereas the Racinian universe, as Mauron pointed out once again quite recently, is situated below the realm of values, at the level where man accepts himself, without self-modification, from the hands of nature ("men as they are"). Restructured by the sociologist's decrees, Racine's drama swiftly ceases to be dramatic. Thus *Andromaque* is no longer a conflict between a set of characters to whom Racine has given a specific being in a particular situation: "There are only two characters present in the play: the *World* and *Andromaque* and a character who is simultaneously present and absent, the *God* with two faces embodied by Hector and Astyanax" (*DC*, p. 354). Oreste, Hermione, Pyrrhus, all nonexistent illusions; Hector and Astyanax, the hidden but true reality (like God). It is a wonderful play, no doubt, and very moving; but unfortunately it is by Goldmann, not Racine. Just as Mauron substituted for the concrete conflict of Racine's characters an argument between psychoanalytic concepts, so Goldmann replaces the complex conflicts between individual existents with the very simple contradictions of his dialectic schema. The *real* characters are no longer those that the eye perceives upon the stage, but those that criticism discerns behind the text. Now finally disencumbered of his theatrical and psychological existence, the new kind of character is one that can be inserted, not into the texture of a play, but into the coherence of a vision of the world. What does it matter that Pyrrhus, as both Mauron and Barthes have shown, is one of the rare *positive* characters in Racine's plays, a man seeking to free himself from fate? Since there can be no question of dilly-dallying over subtleties of psychological analysis, Pyrrhus, Oreste, and Hermione must all be tossed into the same sack, I mean into the same category of "The World," characterized by "passion without consciousness or greatness" (*DC*, p. 355). It is in vain that Racine tells us, in his second preface to *Britannicus*, that his efforts were mainly directed at depicting Agrippine,[12] and, of course, Néron, the "budding moster," in the setting of their Court; it is in vain that he presents Junie as a character external to this central tableau, an almost adventitious addition, as it were, who is not mentioned until the very end and then, as with Aricie, only in order to justify her existence.[13] Racine is mistaken. The last shall be first. "The subject of *Britannicus* is the conflict between Junie and the world, and the play will end only with the resolution of that conflict" (*DC*, p. 367). It is of no concern that this last statement is a flagrant departure from fact, since the Burrhus's cry of "Would to the Gods this prove the last of his crimes!" that ends the play indicates clearly enough that the central character, whose curving descent to perdition is mirrored in the whole movement of the play, is the same one who threw his sinister shadow over the very first line: "What! while Néron lies in easy sleep . . ." It is of no concern that Junie, like Monime or Aricie, belongs structurally (since structure is the order of the day) to that group of pure — and minor — characters in Racine's female world whose contrapuntal role in relation to the great sacred monsters is evident enough. None of that matters: the tragedy must center entirely on Junie, for the simple reason that logic — not the logic of the play but that of the explicative schema — demands it. And similarly, in order to allocate the various characters satisfactorily to the requisite groups he has defined in advance, Goldmann sticks to the old "Aricie-pure-girl-from-convent" and "Hippolyte-a-stranger-to-love" conceptions, whereas in Racine all innocence is always already contaminated, and the pounding of virgin hearts derives from the selfsame poisoned spring as do the most sinful passions. (It is a striking fact that the signs — or rather the symptoms — of love are described in exactly the same kind of terms when they afflict Hippolyte as when they afflict Phèdre.) It would be possible to give any number of similar examples. But there is no point in going on: if the requirements of sound method are to be observed, no dissection of a work can with impunity dispense with a thorough psychological analysis at the dictates of a directing principle specific to the critic, or substitute the intelligibility of a theoretically established dialectic for that spontaneously given in the concrete relations between a work's characters.

All that, however, is not the most serious part. I am less concerned in fact with laying charges of *excess of dialectic* than with complaining of a *lack* of it. After all, much can be forgiven in the way of errors of detail if they are the concomitants of a living understanding of the whole. If the explanatory principle provided by a study of visions of the world were truly *genetic*, if it enabled us to grasp the origin and the variations of the themes, if it provided an account of the development and the becoming of the works, then it would scarcely matter that such and such a piece of interpretation turns out to be, like any interpretation, disputable. What is truly unfortunate is that this dialectic, which the author, good Marxist as he is, perpetually invokes, is in fact nonexistent. Because it fails to situate itself on the level of aesthetic creation, because it fails to comprehend that a vision of the theatrical world, for example, cannot be governed by the same type of coherence as a philosophic or political vision of the world, the dialectic proper to literature vanishes and is resorbed into the general dialectic of history. Although Goldmann's criticism sets itself the task of revealing the unity and totality of a dramaturgy — that is, the evolving process by means of which one play conjures up another, replies to it, and transcends it, in accordance with an internal dynamic that organizes and orients each play around broad axes of signification — in fact at every important juncture of that drama's development, at exactly those points where dialectic comprehension should be brought into play, it breaks down completely. Instead of the tiger in his tank that Lucien Goldmann promised, he is running the motor of his stuttering dialectic on the flattest, stalest dregs of literary history, the leavings already used by Mauron to furnish Racine's unconscious. Just as the evolution of Racine's drama, as seen by psychocriticism, leads us back beyond Freud to dear old Mornet, so the structuralist-genetic method entails a regression, back far beyond Marx, to Taine. Do we want to understand the bond that links *Anromaque, Britannicus,* and *Bérénice*? Well, those three tragedies all simply transpose onto the literary plane "the doctrine and experiences of the recluses as they were at the time of tragic Jansenism before 1669" (*DC*, p. 419). And what is this profound change that occurs, as Mauron also points out, with *Mithridate*?

200

It is due to the "convergence of a certain psychic state in the poet and the political situation at that moment (*Pax ecclesiae* since 1669, national union, war against the Dutch . . .)" (p. 406). Do we want to know what occasioned the transition from *Phèdre* to *Athalie*? "The soundest explanation of this development in Racine's drama seems to me still to be found in the parallel development that Jansenist thought itself was undergoing at the same time" (p. 442). And reference is made to the new Arnoldist pietism. Though in a Marxist as opposed to the previously encountered Freudian form, we are clearly once more confronting the notions of *Racine-the-reflection* and *drama-as-transposed-social-history*. It is elsewhere, in a *parallel* development, that the secret of any development specific to a literary work will be found.[14] But this "parallelism," like the psychophysiological parallelism of old, still remains to be explained. Because it is absolutely not intelligible in itself. In order to render it presentable, the walls of this Lansonian edifice have been given a coat of fresh Marxist paint; it is on the basis of its roots in the "contradictions within the *noblesse de robe*" that we must comprehend the development of Jansenist thought, a development that in its turn governs the plays of Racine. "It would be fruitless to insist at length on the link between the economic and social situation of higher officials in the seventeenth century, simultaneously attached and opposed to a particular form of the state, absolute monarchy . . . and the tragic and Jansenist ideology of the essential vanity of the world and of retreat into solitude providing the best path to salvation" (*DC*, p. 133). It is paradoxical that Lucien Goldmann considers it "fruitless to insist" on the nature of the link that permits him to insert his ideological structures into sociological structures, when we remember that this insertion constitutes for him *the very crux of his explanatory method*. Even supposing that literature simply "transposes" a social reality, it still remains necessary to throw some light on the modalities and the *meaning* of such a complex transposition of the real world into an imaginary one: yet on this all-important point Goldmann's sociology, like Mauron's psychocriticism or Mornet's literary history — as opposed to any true dialectic — has nothing to offer apart from *relations of derivation* based upon a simplistic "postulate of analogy" already so often impeached in the past. It is also curious that the schema of these contradictions within the *noblesse de robe*, used by Lucien Goldmann to explain Racine's drama, is likewise employed by Bernard Dort to explain the drama of Corneille (*Pierre Corneille, dramaturge*, L'Arche, 1957), which is, it must be admitted, somewhat surprising. The very least one can say is that those contradictions besetting the *noblesse de robe* certainly have broad backs, and that "explanations" as convenient and as loose as this, far from being self-evident, cry out to be explained in their turn.

It cannot be denied that class contradictions did in fact exist in the seventeenth century, as in others, and that literature, which is not made in heaven by the angels but on earth by men, must inevitably have lived those contradictions out in its own way. But the important thing is precisely to comprehend that *own way*. Although all human activity is historical, what is essential is that we define the *nature* of its connection with a history of which it is not just a product but also a continuing producer. The "reflecting-reflected" schema that we inevitably encounter sooner or later in Marxist explanations, whatever the mediations introduced between the terms, is the reverse of a truly dialectic comprehension. For what we have to comprehend is how, given a certain social and political situation as a starting point, various human undertakings proceed to construct various meanings (literary, pictorial, scientific, etc.) which, once constituted, *create their own specific and autonomous domain*, inseparable from the historical development within which it occurs yet at the same time irreducible to the general process of that history. It is certain that without the advances made by rationalism, without the rise of the middle classes, and also without certain individual psychic dispositions, Pascal would never have invented the calculus of probability; and to explain that invention from this point of view does mean inserting it into certain precise historical and psychological structures. But its true meaning, which is to say its specific value, can emerge solely on the *scientific* plane, and is arrived at by its insertion into an ensemble of mathematical structures, and not of historical or psychological ones. One wonders why it is constantly necessary to remind the psychoanalyst or the sociologist, where literature is concerned, of truths self-evident to the point of banality in the field of the sciences.[15] If to explain a literary work is, as Lucien Goldmann claims, to comprehend it in terms of its genesis, then the explanation must satisfy two prime conditions: that the genetic process itself shall be fully intelligible, and that it shall preserve, through its genesis, the autonomy of the completed meaning.

And the sociology of literature, as presented by Goldmann, seems to me to fail in this double duty. To begin with, the model of intelligibility it offers us is, in itself, unintelligible. First, because it wavers between two formulas. At one moment we are told that what we must do is establish a "homology" between the structures of the literary work and those of certain social groups. Then later we are told that we must "insert" a signifying structure into a larger structure, and that this insertion will constitute the transition from comprehension to explanation. The author does not seem to notice that these two procedures, though offered as equivalents, and mentioned one after the other without any distinction being drawn (*SR*, p. 223), are in no way identical. In reality, the second represents an attempt to palliate the defects of the first. Let us look at the "homological" relation first: the mechanism of fatality in Robbe-Grillet's *Les Gommes* is the homologue of the self-regulating market mechanisms found in the capitalist system as it is today. We won't worry about whether that is true or not; the important thing here is the type of comprehension implied by this type of relationship. And in fact, homology is plainly a simple semantic variant of the "parallelism" we met earlier in connection with the development of Racine's theater: the structure of the literary work reproduces, which is to say reflects, the structure of the real world, just as, in psychophysiological parallelism, the thought processes correspond to the processes of the brain, each within their respective configurations. In other words, although the series are parallel, they are in no way equal, and one serves as a basis for the other: there is the phenomenon and then the epiphenomenon; the structures of the brain and then those of the thought, the structures of society and then those of literature; the second term always being comprehended in relation to the first. This structural homology thus establishes a simple relation of derivation "work-from-society," "*Les Gommes*-from-

203

neocapitalist-market," without *any intelligible mediation* between the two orders of reality, one of which is a mirror of the other. Without even going back here over the fact that the sociological signification thus revealed in no way exhausts the work's literary meaning, *who* produced *Les Gommes?* Since the true creative subject is not the individual but the group to which he belongs, what group can reflect the *total* signification of the mechanisms of the capitalist market, taken in its totality to the extreme point of abstraction Goldmann reduces it to? The "new novelists" do not constitute a concrete group in the sense that the Jansenists did in the case of Pascal or Racine. If we are to be logical, then it would have to be our entire society that constructed this total vision of the overall dimensions of our society — the fatality of *Les Gommes*, the passivity of *Le Voyeur*. And that would be absurd, since no individual, no group is commensurable with the signifying totality of a society, especially as long as it remains split up into classes. In other words, this structural homology has no meaning, even from the standpoint of structuralist-genetic sociology itself, as long as the concrete problem of its insertion remains unresolved.

Everything, theoretically, would be resolved if we could find some mediation for Robbe-Grillet equivalent to that provided by Jansenism in the case of Pascal or Racine, and we could achieve the transition from an empty homology to a significant insertion. Unhappily however, as we have seen, sociology throws no light whatever upon the nature of this insertion, which is assumed to be self-grounding; it is fruitless, we are told, to insist on the link between the situation of the higher officials in the seventeenth century and Jansenist ideology. All the same, let us insist. The contradictions of a class torn between its attachment and its opposition to the monarchic state provide us with a *political* signification; the Jansenist ideology of the world simultaneously rejected and accepted presents itself as a *religious* meaning given to life. If these significations are in fact linked, then what can the nature of that link be? The homological principle is not going to answer that question. For although it is true that we have two parallel series, we still don't know how to conceive the relation between them. Are we going to use the simplistic methods of

204

traditional Marxism and simply reduce the religious meaning of Jansenism to the political meaning of the class contradictions? All the objections made earlier against psychoanalytic reduction hold good, mutatis mutandis, against the reductions of historicism (cf. section 1 of this chapter). Not only would such a reduction violate the principle of dialectic thought on which it claims to be based, by making the superstructure into no more than a pure and simple reflection of the infrastructure, in accordance with the schema of common or garden materialsim; but it would also destroy the specificity and autonomy of the significations, an autonomy and specificity that are granted in the case of science, and which we must therefore also confer on other activities. Man dreams, acts, or writes: that in no way refutes the specific reality (and in consequence the individual interpretation) of the dream, the action, or the writing. But, when all is said and done, the agent is the same. Psychology, politics, and aesthetics are all founded upon the same subject. If these various activities intersect, if there does exist an intelligible relation of analogy or homology between them, then it is because they are consolidated and connected *at the outset*, at their very bases, *by the human existence from which they spring*. Without this concrete and preliminary convergence, the subsequent diversifications of the praxis will give rise to nothing more than parallel significations, incapable of ever being connected, so that the "contradictions of the noblesse de robe" and "the ideology of Jansenism" are doomed to sit staring at one another to all eternity like two china dogs on a mantelshelf. The only reality is men, individuals, Pascal, Racine, or others, who have each of them experienced, similarly and differently at the same time, a certain historical situation, projecting their possibles from this common historical ground and creating, this one the calculus of probability, that one tragedies, this one a theology, on the basis of their singular existences. The only comprehensible coordination of the various signifying structures is therefore *exactly the opposite of* Goldmann's contention that: "every valid object in the human sciences, and that means every relative signifying totality, is comprehended in its signification and is explained in its genesis by its insertion into the spatio-temporal totality of which it is a part" (*DC*, p. 105). What is in fact required

205

is not to insert the individual existence into an external framework, in which it will receive clarification by a process of dissolution; on the contrary, what we must do is to insert that external framework into an individual existence, in other words, to see *how the infinite multiplicity of the significations offered by an objective situation receives its meaning from the human project that assumes it*. Needless to say, this human project in its turn is not a mysterious entity but a way of assuming a situation; one can no more explain the project by the situation than comprehend it entirely divorced from it; the two terms are both implicated the one in the other, and the true dialectic must be that which will link them together in a process of perpetual transcendence, not that which spirits away the term that irks it in favor of the other. The real trouble is, in fact, that if the true motive force of historical dialectic is not, as Goldmann would have it, the exteriorization of interiority, but the interiorization of an exteriority, then the model of intelligibility provided by the human sciences, and sociology in particular, forfeits all its efficacity and ceases, to use the terminology now in vogue, to be "operative."

It is no coincidence that Lucien Goldmann's undertaking should run straight into the same difficulty as Charles Mauron's: the impossibility, for scientific thought, of comprehending the singularity of subjective existence. Just as Racine's personality was subjected to such rapid dissolution in the impersonal laws of unconscious psychic mechanisms, so the author's individuality is here a mere catalyst, enabling the objective structures of the group to become visible behind the works. In both cases, consciousness as an individual mode of existence possesses no intelligible ontological status. In the first place, there is no science that is not general, and the human sciences cannot, in the creation of their models, evade that rule; second, there is no science that is not objective, and to a scientific approach man must necessarily appear as an object. Whether it is a question of studying man's body, psyche, or social behavior, science cannot constitute itself other than by giving the dimension of the *for-other* preeminence over the *for-itself*. No science is possible unless the knowing consciousness of the scientist annihilates itself in order to constitute the object known, and this hiatus necessarily subsists, even when that object known is man.[16] What all scientific thought (unlike the relations that link literary activity with its creations) is doomed never to be able to encompass within the science it constitutes, is precisely itself in the process of constituting that science. This being so, the scientist, *as an individual,* is always unwanted and left out by his own research: he exists outside it, an encumbrance to himself. Hence, confronted with his personal existence, that "escape complex" that I condemned in the theoretical determinism of Freudian psychoanalysis. And we meet that same complex again here, magnified out of all proportion by the vast methodological and philosophic apparatus of Marxist dialectics; merely latent in Mauron, with Goldmann it becomes aggressive and bellicose. And since it is situated at the very heart of the vast ensemble of present-day researches aimed at transforming literary criticism into a science of literature, it is appropriate here to flush out and, if I may so express it, corner this "scientific" pretension in the area most essential to literature and most foreign to science, in order to scotch it once and for all.

Just as there is no science that is not general, so there is no literary expression except by the individual. Books do not write themselves; *someone* writes them. It is no good trying to explain this "someone" away as an impersonal "One," as the "Id" of the unconscious or the "We" of the collective unconscious; it is no good struggling, however hard, to rid ourselves of that irksome individual, the author. The prime and disconcerting truth remains intact: without an author, no works. And so, given this intrusion of a singular destiny into the pure and harmonious interplay of their laws, critics are obliged to make the best of it — albeit not without considerable intellectual contortions. The psychoanalyst will manufacture a distinct personality for the writer by importing a few well-chosen details from the cupboard of literary history into his unconscious. But how is the sociologist to solve the same problem? In his happiest moments he will establish direct homological relations between the literary works and social groups, thereby doing without the author altogether. But this optimum result, as we have seen, induces a merely transitory euphoria: he still has to insert the work *into* the group, because

207

he can't just leave them standing there face to face, like an object and its reflection in a mirror. And it is at this point that he inserts the tragic structure of Racinian drama into the extremist current of Jansenism, the extremist current of Jansenism into the overall history of Jansenism, the overall history of Jansenism into the history of the *noblesse de robe* in the seventeenth century, the history of the *noblesse de robe* into French social history in general, "and so on" (*SR*, pp. 223–34). So that logically, in order to comprehend Racine's plays even better, we must then insert French social history into that of Europe, that of Europe into seventeenth-century world history, seventeenth-century world history into the history of civilization, the history of civilization into the history of the Earth, the history of the Earth into that of the Cosmos, and, if possible, the history of the Cosmos into that of the divine Spirit, or failing that, into the great adventure of Matter: it is all very well going on like this from insertion to insertion, but as Aristotle once said, "one has to stop."[17] And another thing: if we want to understand Racine's plays, why not start with Racine? What seems perfectly obvious to the simpleminded reader is just what the critic with his full panoply of sociological weapons finds difficult: have we forgotten that the author doesn't exist, and that "the real subjects of cultural creation are social groups and not isolated individuals"?[18] The only trouble is that having failed to base the works themselves in the solid foundation of an individual existence, the explanation, drawn irresistibly upward, is finally lost among the galaxies. So the sociologist is forced to return to earth and modify his first formulation with a second: it is "the social group — through the creator as intermediary — that proves in the final instance to be the true subject of creation" (*SR*, p. 217).

So now we have the writer resuscitated in the role of "intermediary" and slipped in, to facilitate matters, between the works and his group. But unfortunately this role of intermediary still requires explanation, and there no help is forthcoming. Goldmann's thought begins to waver at this point. There is of course the solution — always tempting — of treating it as a miracle, and that is the one opted for first of all: the writer gives maximum consciousness to the tendencies diffused within his group because

208

he is "an exceptional individual." This formula obviously has considerable attraction for its author, since he repeats it as much as three times (*DC*, p. 27). But too much is no better than too little: just now the individual did not exist; now he is a superman, and the intermediary has become a medium. All we asked for was an explanation and we are offered a supernatural phenomenon. As Barthes prettily puts it, these days almost no one but positivists believe in the Muse. But that explanation won't do, as it turns out; so the sociologist looks around for another. And it is at this point that the second miracle occurs, contradicting, as it were, the first. This exceptional individual must be made to step back into line, because scientific thought does not recognize exceptions, only rules; and the science upon which the sociologist finds himself forced to fall back is none other than that very discipline he previously rejected because of the distortions it imposed on cultural facts: psychoanalysis. *Mithridate*, you will remember, was the fruit of "the encounter between a certain psychical state in the poet and the political situation at that moment": just as it takes two to make love, so to make literature it takes an "encounter" between a political situation and a psychic state, and this it turns out, on reflection, is where the sociologist can make use of the psychoanalysis he had prematurely scorned: "The only usefulness of psychological and psychoanalytical analyses in literary criticism — and a rather circumscribed one, what is more — seems to me in their ability to explain why in a given concrete situation, in which a certain social group has evolved a particular vision of the world, a particular individual has proved particularly fitted, thanks to his individual biography, to create a conceptual or imaginary universe" (*SR*, p. 227). This is very ungrateful of Goldmann, and the usefulness of psychoanalysis isn't as circumscribed as all that, since it removes a very nasty thorn indeed from his foot by providing him with *the only concrete mode* of inserting sociological structures into a literary work, through the at last intelligible mediation of the author. Rival siblings transformed by force of circumstance into Siamese twins, Freudian psychoanalysis and Marxist sociology are from now on to form a united front: you scratch my back and I'll scratch yours; you give me the individual and I'll give you society. But alas,

209

like even the most beautiful girl in the world, psychoanalysis can only give what it's got; and, even more inevitably, it's not going to be able to give the very thing it most notably lacks: a method of comprehending the unique and the basis of individuality (cf. section 1 of this chapter). Besides, I'm not at all sure that this sudden association is going to prove such a good thing for the sociologist: he is going to find that the psychoanalyst will seize on that vision of the world of his, defined as a "maximum of consciousness" in the artist, and push it straight down into the unconscious. For instance, Robbe-Grillet never for a moment suspected while writing *Les Gommes* that the fatality in his book was an acting-out of capitalist self-regulating market mechanisms: in this respect his novel presents itself as the *disguising*, by means of successive images, of a truth that he himself has not grasped; the meaning of *Les Gommes* is to be deciphered in the same way as that of a dream. But in that case, how does one think a *maximum of unconscious consciousness*? Psychocriticism, more modest in its demands, contented itself with a *minimum* of consciousness within the unconscious (cf. note 2 of this chapter). And the question arises whether the definition of the "vision of the world" ought not be modified. Is it perhaps arrived at, not by an extreme conceptual extrapolation on the part of the writer, but on the contrary by an obscuration of the concept with all the density of the writer's imaginative life? But that would mean reversing engines and starting to work from the clear toward the ambiguous in literature, instead of from the complex toward the simple. So that ultimately Goldmann's hesitation at taking psychoanalysis to sociology's bosom was well-founded: the cavalry galloping up to save him turns out to be a Trojan horse. So is all hope gone? Must he definitively renounce all attempt to provide an intelligible conception of the author's role as "intermediary," of the individual's mediation in creations whose essence is collective? No. Because here the third miracle occurs. What could not without shame be asked for from the Muse, or without peril from the Unconscious, must ultimately be provided, the sociologist decides, by Structure. Structuralism is about to save Marxism at the eleventh hour. The individual, impossible to pass over in silence, however much one may wish to, and too costly to acquire from psychoanalysis, is going to have to be quite simply (and economically) manufactured by the sociologist himself from sociological structures — transmitted directly from producer to consumer: "Each of these groups acts on its consciousness, thus contributing to the engendering of a unique, complex, and relatively incoherent structure" (*SR*, p. 216). So there we have it: the groups "act" on consciousness and "engender" its structure. At last the model of intelligibility sought with such perseverance is in our grasp: "The relation between the creating groups and the work usually presents itself in accordance with the following model: the group constitutes a process of structuration that builds up in the consciousness of its members a complex of affective, intellectual, and practical tendencies directed at achieving a coherent answer to the problems posed by their relations with nature and their interhuman relations" (p. 219). Instead of a brain that secretes thought, as in old-fashioned materialism, we have a "process of structuration" that "builds up tendencies" within a consciousness. A rose by any other name . . . Very simple isn't it? Once you've thought of it.

Simple yes, but in practice too simple. The procedure works beautifully, and the gap is neatly closed: that irksome Individual, having been omitted at the outset, is now liquidated upon arrival. Moreover this "process of structuration" has classical guarantors, and today's structuralist Marxism is simply a translation of Engels's old-fashioned Dialectic of Nature into more fashionable terms. By a process or by a dialectic, *thought* is "engendered." But we still need to know *who thinks* the thought. The problem is not a new one for Marxism: in the great debates of the late forties, Sartre and Merleau-Ponty persistently and urgently pressed Naville or Lukács for a *Cogito* which was stubbornly refused them — as a woman, despite the tenderest of sieges, may refuse her final favors. By a strange paralogism, which consists in illegitimately transposing into the ontological domain an attitude that is perfectly legitimate in the ethical domain, the rejection of individualism leads to the negation of the individual, and the condemnation of egoism to an inability to comprehend the Ego. Goldmann's genetic-structuralism does not evade this confusion either. When he is asked "who thinks?" he replies "one thinks."

"The great defect of most psychological research has been to treat the individual too often as an absolute subject" (*DC*, p. 25). So no Cartesian Ego, or Kantian, or Fichtean, or any other kind of ego. "The subject of action is a *group*, a 'We' . . ." (ibid.). Very well, but what is this "We"? Is it perhaps a collective consciousness? No, that too is a myth. A collectivity is "nothing but a complex network of 'interindividual' relations" (*SR*, p. 214). But then what are "interindividual" relations between individuals who literally do not exist as such? How is it possible for a reality to emerge from the relating of terms that are themselves unreal? We are told: ah, but that's precisely what dialectic is. To which the only answer is: no it's not. Dialectics is not a form of conjuring, it cannot make fullness from the void, it does not consist in pulling the rabbit individuality out of the hat of collectivity with a murmured "abracadabra."[19] If the I as Cartesian substance is a myth, the We as real subject is a deception: there is no We other than the plurality of I's.[20] Of course, this plurality is not a pure summation of independent units; the fact of existing in the plural is a fundamental dimension of each I. That coexistence contributes to the fashioning and structure of human existence no one will deny; but conversely, one cannot think coexistence other than upon the foundation of individual existence — anything else is just fantasmagoria. Although they are empirically contemporary and simultaneous, ontologically the I is anterior to the We. Marxism here confuses, to the detriment of any intelligibility, what in Heidegger's terminology we should call the ontic and ontological spheres. If there is indeed a *Mit-sein* or "being-with" that is the foundation of human community, then it is as a structure of a *Da-sein* or man's being there in the world. Or, to use Sartre's terminology, the "for-the-other" appears on the ground of the "for-itself." Put more simply, the only *concrete insertion* of man into the world is that achieved through consciousness of self: that consciousness is the absolute beginning, on the basis of which man emerges into being in the world, among other men, and by means of which the outline of a subsequent dialectic of man's relations with nature and history becomes possible. "When Marx's prime maxim and golden rule postulates: 'It is not men's consciousness that determines their being but, on the contrary, their social being that determines their consciousness' (Preface to the *Critique of Political Economy*), one can only reverse his proposition entirely: if history comes into being on the ground of existence and existence on the basis of consciousness's structures of being, then it is inevitable, ultimately, that it should be men's consciousness that defines their being, including their social being. A result that in no way implies a return to an idealist philosophy of the Cogito, or in any way diminishes the primary importance of economic relations, but does make them into human relations." What I wrote earlier in reply to the Sartre of *La Raison dialectique* ("J.-P. Sartre et le mythe de la Raison dialectique," *Nouvelle Revue Française*, November 1961, p. 880), I repeat now in answer to Goldmann. Only what we are bound to call a *radical perversion of the meaning of the concrete* (which, moreover, unlocks the secret of that strange intellectualist "reduction" to which Goldmann subjects literary expression) makes it possible to perceive the *abstract* in the immediate[21] and the *concrete* in the result of a "process of dialectical conceptualization.[22] As materialism goes, isn't that a really fine example of idealism? And doesn't it look as though someone is taking a mischievous delight in combining the difficulties of both systems? Just as the concrete is the immediate and total presence of self to self, mediating all other possible relations, so the concrete in literature is the abounding and inexhaustible richness of the work, its dense, opaque *Da-sein*, and not some formula that one arrives at by "conceptual extrapolation." And that being so, one must make a choice, not necessarily for or against Marxism, but certainly within Marxism: *one must choose one's Marx.* There is the Marx of the *Holy Family* who wrote: "History does nothing, possesses no great wealth, fights no battles. It is rather man, real and living man, who does everything, who possesses, and who fights. . . . History itself is nothing but the activity of men pursuing their goals." And there is the Marx who wrote in the preface to the first edition of *Das Kapital*: "My viewpoint, according to which the economic development and formation of a society appears as a process of natural history, is less able than any other to render the individual responsible for the relations of which he remains socially the creation." Marx rightly points out, with exemplary clarity, the ineluctable philosophical — and methodological — choice to be made: between an activity pursuing its aims and a process of natural or social history, between men who make history and a History that makes men. We must choose one or the other. A dialectics that moves from the objective to the objective, turning the subjective into a passing and inessential moment, is a pseudodialectics whose phraseology is merely failing to conceal what is in reality a return to a naturalistic causality. Goldmann's sociology does not escape this dilemma: his choice is betrayed by his constant — even obsessive — desire to engender the literary work from social relations alone, just as a certain kind of psychoanalysis claims to derive it solely from a psychological nature, *thereby doing without an author*, or in other words an individual, free, meaning-creating consciousness. And this is not just a theoretical problem that is of no interest outside purely philosophical discussion: this decision to comprehend human facts in the third and not the first person is, as Barthes would put it, a "fatal wager," one that engages every step — or false step — that is taken in literary analysis. It also has an important bearing — though this falls outside our province here — upon the practical comprehension of man that certain human sciences in their present state of development are attempting to achieve. What may be legitimate for scientific thought, which apprehends man as object, cannot be so for literary criticism, which apprehends man as existence.

The necessity, not of refusing to attempt a genetic comprehension of cultural facts, but of conceiving such a comprehension in terms of projects rather than of a process, imposes itself for a twofold reason. For a genetic explanation to be satisfactory it must, as I have said, fulfill two conditions: first, that the genetic process shall itself be fully intelligible; second, that it shall preserve the autonomy of the completed meaning. In fact, explanatory schemas of the scientific or objectivist kind, since they render the concrete genesis incomprehensible by the elimination of a free subjectivity, inevitably end up by destroying the specific value of the cultural creations they are applied to. We have already seen how psychocriticism, by reducing the religious meaning of Jansenist thought to its supposed psychological meaning, was in fact destroying all possibility of any authentic theological speculation: from the moment you posit the products of the human mind as the end product of a single process, their surface diversity becomes a mere disguise, and interpretation will consist in reducing the multiple to the common denominator that engendered it. The sociology of visions of the world, having replaced the Unconscious with History, runs into exactly the same difficulty as psychocriticism. Since its explanation is obtained by inserting signifying totalities into external spatiotemporal frames, *all intrinsic signification is dissipated*, so that the explanation consists in annihilating all that the comprehension had revealed. So we find Goldmann writing that there is "ultimately no valid history 'of philosophy' or 'of philosophies,' but only study of philosophic thoughts as the expression of an individual life and consciousness plus a history of society in which philosophic thoughts appear both as expressions of individual consciousnesses and of class consciousnesses" (*DC*, p. 107). It would be difficult to express with greater ingenuity the fact that, once the psychological genesis (expression of an individual consciousness) and the social genesis (expression of a class consciousness) have been established, there is really nothing left of philosophy at all, unless it be simple as an *index* revealing the presence of a psyche or a society. The very notion of philosophic *truth* no longer has any meaning, and the history of philosophy can no longer be the study of the emergence and disputation, in and through history, of philosophic significations *valid as such*. Except for one miraculous exception: the philosophy of Lucien Goldmann, which can no longer be simply regarded as the "expression" of an individual consciousness and a class consciousness, like all the others, but is suddenly *true*, since it is in the light of its truth that all previous philosophic attempts can be deciphered as illusions. Just as the psychoanalytic system was the only form of thought possessing a valid and true meaning, independently of its genesis within the psychoanalyst's unconscious, so the Marxist system constitutes, in history, the emergence of an absolute truth, one that makes it possible to relativize all the others: this unjustified and absurd privilege that "scientific" thought insists it possesses — namely, the privilege of constituting an *advent* that is not reducible to an *event* — must either be denied to scientific thought or extended to other activities of thought and, in particular, to literary creation. It is impossible to remain content with the "historical admiration" that Goldmann, in the wake of Renan, offers us all over again, his socialist historicism looking oddly like bourgeois historicism's twin: "It is on the basis of a historico-sociological analysis that the philosophic signification of the *Pensées*, the literary and aesthetic signification of Kleist's plays, and the genesis of both become susceptible of comprehension as cultural facts" (*SR*, p. 228).[23] Although Pascal's *Pensées* or Kleist's plays may appear as mere dated "cultural facts" to the sociologist (that is one of their possible significations, or let us say one of their dead significations), those works only achieve integration into true, in other words living, culture insofar as the human appeal with which they are charged is still as urgent as ever, and the view of the world they offer still as pregnant. The drawback with all such "historical admiration" is that the very changes of history itself make the permanence of the admiration incomprehensible. Whereas psychocriticism at least has at its disposal the recurrence of unconscious patterns through the ages to provide an account of this permanence, historicism has no fixed point at all to clutch at in the flux of history. In order for a philosophy or a work of art to retain their value beyond the particular circumstances surrounding their birth, or, to use Goldmann's phraseology, beyond the spatiotemporal frame in which they are contained, there must be, in the heart of history, *a transhistoric dimension of being and comprehending*. In one curious passage, which to my mind is sufficient to weaken and perhaps jeopardize his entire undertaking, Lucien Goldmann himself puts his finger on the heart of the problem: this possibility of survival on the part of a philosophy or work of art "rests" he says, "on the fact that they always express the historic situation *transposed* onto the plane of the great *fundamental* problems that are posed by man's relations with other men and with the universe. And, since the number of humanly *coherent* answers to this ensemble of problems is limited by the structure of the human individual himself, each such answer corresponds to different and often contrary historical situations" (*DC*, p. 30). The analysis is admirable and I would not wish to change a word of it: but where in heaven's name is Lucien Goldmann going to find in his philosophy the means to base a trans-historicity of historical situations on the structure of the human individual himself? Since the avowed purpose of a "materialist and dialectical" method (p. 14) is to show subjectivity to be the infinitely complex and distant outcome of objective relations, the *necessary structure*, which is to say the ontological foundation suddenly required for the human individual, transcending his conditions as an historical manifestation and himself providing the justification for them, is *strictly unthinkable*. Indeed, Goldmann does hurriedly exorcize this specter, so frankly but imprudently summoned, by deferring the solution of the fundamental problem of "the typology of visions of the world" until the necessary long historical and empirical study has been made — in other words until the second coming. The very lacunae of the objectivist approaches provide an "impression," as it were, of the comprehension that is required to fill the hollows of inadequacy they leave. And since, where human behavior is concerned, the type of intelligibility that we are persistently forced toward is one that entails the laying bare, as a foundation for other structures, of the structures of existence itself, it is now time, after tarrying so long in the company of formal logic, linguistics, psychoanalysis, and sociology, to direct our gaze at last in the direction of Jaspers, Marcel, Heidegger, Sartre, and Merleau-Ponty — in other words, toward the existential philosophies.

Part Four
CRITICISM AND PHILOSOPHY

BEYOND THE
HUMAN SCIENCES

SINCE polemic too often consists in distorting an opponent's thought the better to defeat it, and since this is a work of contestation and will certainly be contested in its turn, this is a good moment to pause for a moment and sum up our findings so far. There will be no lack of opponents, of this we may be sure, who will jump in to condemn my position as "anti-scientific" and "irrationalist." In themselves, such accusations would leave me indifferent, but they are in fact false. So I had better spell it out: a refusal to construct the model of intelligibility for literary criticism in accordance with those found in the human sciences is no more to be "against science" than the rejection of a traditional and outdated type of comprehension entails being "against literary history." To be against science or against literary history would scarcely make any more sense than to be against the air we breathe or the food that provides our energy. Two observations are therefore necessary here. First, far from minimizing the contribution of the various scientific disciplines to the knowledge of literature, I am on the contrary convinced of their necessity. As with man, the products of his culture have their objective aspect *as well*, and must be included, as such, within the province of positive researches, guided by the modern disciplines, Whether we are concerned to refine and increase the precision of our historical tools still further; whether we are concerned, at one extreme, with articulating our comprehension of a literary text with the structures of the society within which it came into being, or, at the other, with the linguistic structures of which that text makes use, nothing can replace the indispensable factual accuracy and detail that can be provided solely by literary history, sociology, or linguistics. And if it is true that every work is in its way a spiritualized biography, then how can we reject the invaluable insights provided by psychoanalysis? Or equally, if we wish to study a tragedy or a sonnet, how can we dispense with a detailed knowledge of the laws that governed those genres, and the reasons for their formation, from their first appearance to their decline? If we wish to probe the question of a poem's power to cast a certain spell over us, how can we ignore all the research done on the analysis of sounds and rhythms, the critical attempts made to chart the point at which poetic language comes into being within our ordinary language? There is therefore a vast domain open to rigorous aesthetic research, from the study of the genres right through to modern stylistics and phonetics. Far from contesting the utility of these various disciplines, I have used them as the basis of my attempted analysis of "literary meaning." If literary expression is indeed the fusion of a multiplicity of different meanings into a single body of writing; if its aim is to provide for itself, in the form of language, the equivalent in richness and depth of total human existence, then it is evident that every signification of any particular order (historical, sociological, stylistic, psychological, etc.) requires its elucidation by the particular science into whose field it falls.

In this respect — and this is the second observation — the examples I have chosen to discuss (Roland Barthes's metacriticism, Charles Mauron's psychocriticism, Lucien Goldmann's sociology of visions of the world) in no way exhaust the possibilities, with respect to literary criticism, of the different disciplines from which these authors have taken their inspiration. In the work of Leo Spitzer, for example, we find an approach to the facts of linguistics very different from that of Roland Barthes; Jungian psychoanalysis, in the work of, say, Maud Bodkin, produces quite different results from Freudian work; the conception of sociology and anthropology found in the work of Gilbert Durand, oriented toward the study of the great imaginative and mythic archetypes, is antipodal to Goldmann's Marxist researches. And the experimental work carried out by such people as Paul

Delbouille, investigating the powers of suggestion possessed by sounds in poetry, has nothing in common with work in the field of historical aesthetics as conceived in the manner of René Bray or Jacques Schére.[1] I have not attempted in this essay to provide a complete account of all the various scientific methods, any more than I have been trying to paint a systematic picture of the present tendencies in literary criticism. In three selected areas that seemed to me particularly representative of the main ideological currents of the day (structuralism, Freudian psychoanalysis, Marxism), I have attempted to isolate certain *types of comprehension* of human facts, and therefore of literary creations, that radically engage the destiny of criticism. Whatever the variations in the scientific methods and theories used, and in their point of application, the problem that concerns me here — one that is of an epistemological order — remains unchanged.

On this primary question my position is clear: I reject none of the aid, none of the insights that the various human sciences can and must contribute to clarification of the various significations of literary expression; on the contrary, I welcome them with open arms. But on the other hand, what I do absolutely deny is *the competence of any particular human science to discern and define the unity and totality of the significations that form the meaning of a work.* In other words, the coherence specific to works of literature does not, as a matter of principle, lie within the grasp of the types of coherence available to scientific knowledge. Some would say: "in the present state of scientific knowledge." But I disagree. I say: in no matter what circumstance and by definition. The various scientific disciplines can establish no relations among themselves other than those of *exclusion* or *juxtaposition*. By dissecting its object in accordance with its particular viewpoint, by throwing light on the aspect it has chosen, each science reveals a series of significations and laws incapable of being integrated into the other significations and other laws revealed by other sciences. Structuralist linguistics excludes, as does formal logic, any transitivity or any precise link with the real. Psychoanalysis, on the other hand, begins by reestablishing that link and anchors it in the immutability of an archaic psyche, whereas Marxist anthropology, granting preeminence to the processes of history,

223

locates the comprehension of the human in the ever-changing heart of social contradictions. Moreover, the significations isolated by linguistic, psychological, or historical analysis all have one particular thing in common: *they are all true, and all true at the same time; yet they are powerless to articulate themselves intelligibly one with another or to intersect within their object.* In order to achieve a global comprehension of that object, the very most they can do is to add their various viewpoints together and juxtapose the disciplines. Thus, as we saw, Lucien Goldmann believes he can arrive at a total criticism by collating sociology and aesthetics here, sociology and psychoanalysis there. But a collage is not a marriage in any sphere: significations that are foreign to one another and never intersect have nothing to link them *from within.* It is no more possible to create "total" criticism by mixing together a pinch of psychoanalysis, a dash of aesthetics, and a good dose of history than it is to create "total" theater just by enlivening a script with music, ballet, and even the odd fragment of cinematic projection. Since the form of criticism toward which contemporary scholarship is moving is, by common consent, *that which will integrate the greatest possible quantity of meaning*, it follows from this that no model of intelligibility being employed in the human sciences can be applied to literary criticism as a whole; because those models are arrived at either by the exclusion of other and equally legitimate significations, so that one is *losing* the greatest possible quantity of meaning, or by the simple addition of various possible meanings but without integrating them.

It now remains to be explained why this inevitable and irremediable obstacle should not be immediately detectable, and why so many critics continue, and will continue in the future, to base their hopes of instituting a total analysis of literature on one particular science — history or sociology, linguistics or stylistics, characterology or psychoanalysis — which they then constitute in practice as so many rival interpretative imperialisms: there is a war of the sciences going on as well as a battle of the critics. To the general reason provided by the universal prestige of scientific thought in the mid-twentieth century — though this is something that dates back to the mid-nineteenth century — there must be added, in my opinion, another and more specific reason, which has to do with the very nature of the new sciences that have recently been evolved under the name of "the human sciences." These sciences are in fact distinguished by the particularity, clearly perceived by Lucien Goldmann, that unlike the physical sciences they entail a partial identity of the subject and the object of their research. And it takes only the slightest of shifts — under the influence of a very understandable temptation — for this *partial* identity to become in its own eyes the *total* identity that is required, as I have shown, by a true epistemology of the subject-object relations in literary creation (cf. chapter 8, section 2). From the moment that the *comprehension* of a certain sector of human activity claims to have become empowered to offer an *explanation* of man, the scientific method involved suddenly begins to claim that it has achieved the status of a philosophic system. We have observed this process in action both in the case of psychoanalysis (chapter 8, section 1) and of Marxism (section 2).[2] By some abrupt metamorphosis, one that Ovid omitted to describe, the scientist suddenly finds that he has sprouted a philosopher's wings:

> I am a bird; look at my wings . . .
> I am a mouse; long live rats!

That quotation from La Fontaine, much loved by Barthes, sums up the situation nicely. I am a bird: I can offer you a bird's-eye view of the human condition in all its unity. I am a mouse: I can give you the bone of science to nibble. Freudianism and above all Marxism, now followed by structuralism, are all vying with one another at having one's cake and eating it too. To no avail however. Though perfectly justified as means of practical and theoretical investigation in certain areas (affective relations or social relations), which are amenable to positive and empirical enquiry, they can elevate themselves to the status of philosophy only by hardening the objectivity necessary to a scientific method into a *philosophy of objectivity*. What they are doing is to use this "partial identity" of the subject and object of knowledge upon which the human sciences are based — but which they can never transcend toward a total identity — and use it in one direction only, finally resorbing subjectivity into an objective system and thereby ridding themselves once and for all of the encumbrance of consciousness. This methodology, hypostasized under the name of philosophy, is therefore always in fact a materialsim, the orientation of which varies according to the originating science but whose metaphysical postulate always remains the same. And this postulate is not merely false (something that remains open to discussion), but it is a self-delusion (something that is incontestable). The philosophy we are being offered, so the theory goes, is based upon a science, and therefore has the advantage of being "scientific"; and at the same time, freed from earthbound origins, can blossom into a metaphysical synthesis. This operation is in fact doubly fraudulent. Although claiming to provide us with a "scientific philosophy," it consists, to begin with, in giving us, instead of science, merely *a* science, as though the fundamental problem of contemporary epistemology were not the very fragmentation of the sciences, the plurality and conflict of methods and approaches that no conceivable synthesis can overcome. With imperfect sleight of hand we are offered as the principle of synthetic comprehension a "philosophy" incapable of achieving its own synthesis. (Hence the often aggressive rivalries between the various sciences, with each one claiming for itself the right to transmute its status of concubine to philosophy into that of legitimate spouse; though what results, at best, is squawking polygamy.) Meanwhile, at the behest of a contradictory and perverse humor, at the very instant when one scientific method is being granted unearned preeminence over all the others, by being endowed with the prestige of primary philosophy, the very possibility of any philosophy at all is being definitively destroyed by the proclamation that the only valid form of knowledge is science. Half-lion and half-goat, half-science and half-philosophy (each half destroying the other), this fabled monster "scientific philosophy" supposedly extracted from — or imposed upon — the human sciences is in fact nothing more than just that — a chimera.

10

THE LINKED DESTINIES
OF CRITICISM AND
PHILOSOPHY

WHAT we must do then is look for philosophy where it is, at its simple starting point in the very foundations of being, not at its destination in the elaborate structures of knowledge. Though there does remain one preliminary question that some will not fail to ask: why on earth should we look for philosophy at all? And why do we need it to guide the reflections of literary criticism anyway? Philosophy in the culture of today has a status that can at best be called ambiguous: a deposed queen, beside the sciences she tends to cut the figure of a poor relation, invited out of charity, and seated at the very bottom of the table. And yet some aura of royalty must still float about her, since any conception of the world, even if it be a product of the positive sciences, cannot wait to proclaim itself philosophical. From Sextus Empiricus to Jean-François Revel, people have inquired with skeptical smiles: Who needs philosophers? And especially since there have been scientists. In every century, with La Mothe Le Vayer and Bayle in the seventeenth, Voltaire and Diderot in the eighteenth, Comte and Marx in the nineteenth, all the Viennese, Anglo-American, and other varieties of scientism and positivism in the twentieth, philosophy has been constantly interred anew, only to rise from its own ashes every time like a true phoenix. For some, the word "metaphysics," like the word "mystic," if not laughable is obscene: if you happen to utter it you are surrounded by shocked indignation. The same enlightened minds will then go on to offer us thought secreted by brain cells, by the coupling of two acids, or reflexes that combine mechanically to produce human behavior. All that, of course, is not metaphysics. What is it then? Oh well, we'll say it's philosophy if you insist, but serious, scientific philosophy, mark you! But enough of such silliness. Any overall and articulated vision of the relations of man with the universe, any formal system of the relations of existence and being, is a metaphysics, whether we like it or not. As in everything else, there are simply good metaphysics and bad. The bad are invariably those that dare not speak their name.

Can we, ought we to pursue the tasks of literary criticism in total isolation from any metaphysical preoccupation? Baudelaire did not think so, and rightly said that "criticism borders at every instant on metaphysics" (cf. section 1 of chapter 11 below). Yet it is a view held by many thinking minds, some of them impervious to argument, others open. The rejection of all "ideology," the fear of all "engagement," do not surprise me in certain academic minds: they are part of such men's intellectual comfort and also, it must be admitted, of their professional training. But I am, on the other hand, pained to encounter this same stubborn prejudice in a man as enlightened as Robert Kanters, in the article full of both lucidity and good will that he recently devoted to the "battle of the critics" (*La Revue de Paris*, January 1966). I hope therefore that he will permit me to try to change his view. "Literature," he writes, "is perhaps the longest and densest discourse that the human mind has ever addressed to itself; the art of criticism is the art of making that discourse speak." One could not hope for a more exact or a more concise definition. But the author quickly adds: "This presupposes a total absence of theoretical prejudices. . . . Whenever criticism bases itself upon a predetermined philosophy, say that of Aristotle or that of Taine, or upon a general more or less scientific theory, such as that of Marx, or Freud, and tomorrow perhaps that of M. Lévi-Strauss, it dooms itself to the impossibility of attaining a value as criticism greater than that of the philosophy or theory in question; and indeed it is likely to have a slightly lesser value, since the transposition and the application are always approximate." At the same time, however, unlike the academics mentioned earlier, Robert Kanters has a mind wide open to his age; he wants a criticism that will keep open house, one that "must

228

be able to profit to the full from the contributions of all the disciplines, old or new." I must therefore ask him how, in the total absence of theoretical presuppositions, which is to say in that state of total and willed ideological nonpreparation he recommends, it is in any way possible to derive any genuine profit from the disciplines that urge themselves upon contemporary critical attention. Because clearly one cannot profit from the human sciences, or from a philosophy, simply by the accumulation of intuitions gleaned at random under the influence of what Spitzer so accurately terms the critic's "eudaemonist sensibility." It is certainly not necessary, I agree, to belong to the Communist party or to have been psychoanalyzed in order to make use of Marx or Freud, but it is essential to have given some thought to the problems that Marxism and Freudian psychoanalysis involve; such philosophic reflection, which M. Kanters presents as not merely cumbersome but actually fatal, is something that we must have, quite literally, at our command. The existence of any more or less coherent body of thought implies a theoretical framework, and criticism is not, any more than literary creation, an intuitive thunderbolt: it presupposes a work process; it must be constructed. Thibaudet rightly drew distinctions between spoken criticism, artistic criticism, and academic criticism. These different criticisms have different laws. And a criticism dealing with totalities, as modern criticism aims to be, has its particular requirements: specifically, it requires that everything it contains in the form of implicit postulates shall be made explicit; that those "theoretical prejudices"— lurking in all thought willy-nilly — shall be dragged out of the darkness in which we were keeping them safely hidden in order to become clear and fully formulated theories.

But every time a theory is used as the foundation of a particular criticism it leads to catastrophe, because that criticism dooms itself in advance to the impossibility of attaining a greater value than that of the philosophy, and will probably have even less value. So wouldn't it be better just to let our theories remain lurking there undisturbed, like the complexes that lie beneath an incurable neurosis? I think not. For one thing, whatever the circumstances, is criticism ever historically less relative than all these theories that supposedly threaten it with destruction if it places its reliance on them? *Either way*, there is nothing more easily dated, nothing quicker to become stale and obsolete, nothing more fragile than critical commentaries; they all end up on the same great garbage tip, and what Voltaire said about Corneille, La Harpe about Racine, Sainte-Beuve, Lemaître, Faguet, or Lanson about the various classics, has scarcely any interest today except for thesis writers avidly picking through the jumble to find scraps for their card-index boxes. One needs to be an optimist indeed to believe that criticism could attain greater value or longevity without philosophy than with it. But in any case, whatever we may say or do, literary criticism and philosophy are both constituents, implicit or explicit, of the ideology secreted by every age. And not to have an ideology is simply a particular form of ideology: positivism. Their destinies are therefore linked: inseparable in principle, they are never separate in practice. Criticism has nothing to lose by openly acknowledging its solidarity, its alliance with philosophy. Indeed it has everything to gain. Ah, but theories pass, you may say. True, and criticism too. But the fact that a vision of man has been transcended does not therefore mean that it was never anything but a distorting prism. We are back to Sartre's passage about Blanchot (quoted in chapter 6). His own emotions, his own cast of mind, his own philosophy incline the critic toward such and such an interpretation rather than some other, but they also serve him as instruments of elucidation. And I would claim that, of all those instruments, a conscious and organized philosophy is likely to be the most accurate: thanks to the influence of Bergson, Thibaudet achieved a better understanding of the profound unity of Flaubert's personality, which had previously been seen as split into a "realist" half and a "romantic" half; thanks to his reflection on Heidegger, Blanchot was better able to apprehend the meaning of Mallarmé's Nothingness. And to go back to the examples put forward by Robert Kanters, criticism has not really done so badly out of its association with Aristotle, whose philosophy has provided us with the only conception of tragic action and its catharsis that still stands up today. (Moreover, Aristotelian philosophy is still far from having exhausted its virtues, and is at this moment, as we know, particularly in the United States, providing the inspiration for a whole school of literary criticism.) Similarly, Taine succeeded, not despite his philosophy but because of it, in making a far greater contribution to the advance of modern criticism, through his search for an articulated and total explanation, than men like Lemaître or Faguet with their verbose impressionism. Is a close relationship between criticism and *a* philosophy therefore without danger, and are the fears Kanters expresses without foundation? By no means. With theories, as with everything else, there are good and bad applications. We have already observed, in previous parts of this book, what havoc the *strict application* of a doctrinal position can wreak in the criticism of particular works, and Robert Kanters would not find it difficult to turn my own analyses around and use them against me. Is the situation hopeless then? I do not believe so, and we shall see later on that, in the inevitable and desirable relationship between theoretical thought and literary practice, the fact, so clearly perceived by Kanters, that "the transposition and the application are always approximate," is not what dooms but what *saves* criticism (cf. section 3 of chapter 11 below).

Far from a philosophic method of procedure being harmful to critical research, the conclusion, or if you prefer, the central principle of this essay of mine affirms precisely the converse: *that a thorough intellectual investigation of literature is either of a philosophic order or it is nothing.* This is not an axiom that I have summoned down from the empyrean of Ideas as a starting point; it is a hypothesis that has been evolved, like any hypothesis, within the matrix of a personal experience and that I believe has been gradually confirmed and verified by the facts. Present-day criticism, I said earlier, is characterized, empirically and theoretically, by a striving toward a unitary and totalitarian comprehension; it postulates, as the focus of various significations, as their locus of intersection, a certain fundamental meaning, immanent in each work taken as a whole but to be found in complete form solely in the works as a totality. This quest for coherence defines what I have termed a "literary phenomenology," which sets itself the task of describing structures inherent in the object under investigation. But we soon run into a double contradiction. On the one hand the structures isolated in this way are neither convergent nor susceptible of juxtaposition; there is no "structure of structures" within which they merge and harmonize. The quest for coherence explodes into incoherence, the search for unity into disjunction. And on the other hand, the objectivity of the structures refers back to the subjectivity of the critic, in other words to his way of comprehending man, which is in practice a personal choice, a metaphysical option, even — indeed above all — in the case of those who believe they have eliminated Self in the cause of their System.[1] Moreover, there is no choice that can comprehend all the others, there is no "comprehension of comprehensions." After the notions of unity and objectivity, must we now see the notion of truth exploded? Earlier, against the successive solutions of relativism, then against Roland Barthes's formalism, I believed myself correct in maintaining the notion of a truth lying at the heart of literature and, a fortiori, at the heart of criticism. But what kind of truth exactly is involved here? Since we have rejected one by one the models of interpretation provided by the evidence of personal taste and by formal aesthetics, and since we have dismissed the models of intelligibility offered by the historical as well as by the human sciences, all we are left with as a foundation for critical truth, by elimination as it were, is the reflection that also provides the foundation for philosophic truth.

First, their epistemological status is the same. Whereas literature is defined precisely in the multiplicity of its signification within its expressive unity, criticism cannot attain this unity *already given* in its object by any objective method: similarly, no diversification of explicative schemas of the world will succeed in providing an account, in any way, of the unity concretely given in the totality of the real. In this postulated yet always undiscoverable "truth"; in this will to systematic comprehension that never succeeds in closing itself into a system; in this passionate quest for a Unity that has been irremediably shattered into plurality; in this discipline that is, by definition, the "science of resolved problems" and that never succeeds in resolving them; in all this, who does not recognize not merely philosophy but also criticism? This status as radical and untranscendable *ambiguity*, assigned by Merleau-Ponty to the perception of reality and serving as constant horizon for the philosophic quest, is something we have already encountered in our analyses of literary expression, and it also circumscribes the field of critical inquiry. But I must make one thing clear at this point: when I speak of philosophy I mean the *existential philosophies*, to which I have frequently alluded in preceding pages without ever confronting this particular problem squarely. For me, the very progress made by modern philosophy, since Jaspers, Heidegger, and Marcel, not to mention their common ancestor Kierkegaard, or Kierkegaard's ancestor Pascal, begins with the awareness of its inevitable failure. The world in which we live is that of single reality and fragmented truth: no knowledge is commensurable with being; the rational apprehends no more than fragments or facets of the real — discontinuous profiles that no ultimate conceptualization can integrate. In consequence, and not without regret, we must regard all the great rationalist structures of the nineteenth century, from Hegelian idealism to dialectical materialsim, as so much bankrupt stock. Unlike scientific theories, which constitute knowledge in a predetermined area of the universe, philosophy, human reflection on our total being-in-the-world, must henceforth always begin with the comtemplation of its not-knowing.

To invoke its kinship with philosophy understood in this way is no soft option on literary criticism's part. It is in fact the reverse of the intellectual complacency that can, and often does, characterize the application to literature of various instruments of knowledge evolved within the scientific disciplines. As J. Starobinski so acutely remarks, "philosophy has the superiority over the human sciences of possessing a great cognizance of the risk and the lack of foundations of its enterprise" ("Les directions nouvelles de la recherche critique"). None of its inquiries, it is true, can lay claim to the certainty possessed by objective truths; but what it can do is to fill in precisely that lacuna which any objective research must leave forever gaping: the locus of its apparition or coming into being, which is to say its ontological link with the subjectivity of the inquirer. Though there are human sciences, there does not exist, even in our dreams, a Science of Man, an absolute body of knowledge that could resorb into itself the contingent subject producing that knowledge. There is an existence of the scientist, but not a science of existence. So that we are left with nothing but this fundamental and uncomfortable situation of ours — "this shattered world," in Marcel's words — which we must strive to comprehend. To reflect on our condition means in the first place to *reflect it*, by repossessing it at its maximum of virginity and totality, at its source, in its primal upsurge. This reflexive description (in which you will have recognized phenomenology) is a return to the absolute point of emergence of all reality, where being unveils itself for a consciousness, but where consciousness apprehends itself as suspended in being. The return to this focal point, which is the procedure specifically characteristic of philosophic thought, I shall term, in opposition to the objectivist theories, the return to the Cogito. No longer the lovely and pellucid Cartesian Cogito, that serene and sovereign possession of self in a thought-substance, but an obscure clarity that gives the world back without constituting it, condemned to construct the diversity of its meanings upon the foundation of a primal nonmeaning; the rational activity that then follows does not dissipate this primordial and ambiguous level of the concrete, but on the contrary posits it as necessary: the sole locus, if not of constructing at least of testing truth, remains the perceived world or, if you like, the natural world. The real does not lie at the far end of a dialectical conceptualization, as Goldmann's Marxist rationalism would have us believe; the real is the irrecoverable and immediate origin of that conceptualization. We therefore need to apply the same treatment to Marxist dialectic as Marxism did to Hegelian dialectic and "get it back onto its feet": the immediate is not the end result but the foundation of mediations. For this prereflexive Cogito, revealed by reflection, is not a motionless contemplation of self by self within a consciousness: it hurls consciousness in its entirety out of itself, into the world; it defines man by the concrete projects — preception and praxis — that his awareness of a future imposes on him; it constantly transcends the real that invests it by the invention of possibles; in short, it is movement and the principle of movement. The Cogito does not therefore lead to the apparition of a disembodied thought, but to that of a practical intention situated within being and history. (It was with good reason that Freud defined man in terms of "desire," and Heidegger in terms of "care": the Cogito calls the world into being not by a knowing intention but, fundamentally, by an affective tension.) It does not provide us in any way with a human essence, but with an existence in the process of forming itself, by each one of its acts, even though it can never be summed up and seen as complete in any one of them. So this Cogito, as gradually isolated and defined in the course of our analyses, does not provide the philosopher with a panacea, an Open Seasame, a magic recipe that will serve to *explain* anything. All it provides is a means of *comprehending* how the various significations brought into play by the various human activities can be articulated one with another, not as the totality of an objective Knowledge that will form that unattainable "structure of structures," but as projects that are so many partial expressions of the fundamental situation of one and the same thinking and acting subject.

However, nor does there exist any "comprehension of comprehension," any standpoint this subject can take up in order to apprehend himself as a signifying totality: as Sartre puts it, consciousness is a "detotalizing totality," and it would be futile for a philosophy of existence to attempt to encompass the total of human significations, in other words to constitute itself as a universal system. The fact that Sartre, as a philosopher, has striven, not only in *Being and Nothingness* but also in his *Raison dialectique*, to recapture in consciousness that totality which can never be anything for him, as a man, but "detotalized" is at once his greatness and his failure. It is indeed, we may say, the greatness and the failure of all philosophy. This is why I have referred throughout this book to existential philosophies in the plural: no reflexive Cogito is capable of dissipating the ambiguity at the very source of the unreflected Cogito in any ultimate illumination. Every approach throws light on one facet; each philosophy apprehends one meaning. No philosophy can grasp all the meanings and all the facets. But this fundamental failure on philosophy's part is also the source of its progress: it is because philosophic research can never reveal any but partial truths that it is able to continue its advance; it is because it can never isolate any but ambiguous significations that it is bound to contradict itself. As Georges Gurvitch clearly perceived in his *Dialectique et sociologie*, true dialectic, at the level of human existence, is never a coupling of clear and clearcut antinomies, of distinct concepts, elegantly overcome by their synthesis after the fashion of Hegelian or Marxist rationalism: it is infinitely more fluid; it "implies reciprocities, ambiguities, and contraries in equal measure, not to mention complementarities and mutual implications." So there is in fact a history of philosophy, the meaning of which depends not upon the individual philosopher's psychology or upon class conflicts, but upon the nature of philosophy itself. Philosophy cannot be anything but a succession of contrary yet complementary efforts in which what is denied is (in contradistinction to what happens in science) in a certain way preserved, in which the distinct or adverse truths, including those of science, must learn to coexist, though without ever uniting or merging. Philosophy in this sense is therefore the history of philosophy, on condition that it be understood once and for all that this historicity is not an exteriority but the fulfilment, in history, of an autonomous human activity; and on condition also that this historical relativism can only by error become a pure skepticism: "There is no *one* philosophy that contains all philosophies; philosophy in its entirety is there, at certain moments, in each philosophy. . . . Thus the truth, and the whole, are there from the beginning — but as a task to be accomplished, so that they are also not yet there" (*Signes*, p. 161). Such is the narrow but firm status that Merleau-Ponty, reflecting upon the history of philosophy, assigns to philosophic truth: starting from the immediate, it is enriched, but also made complicated and contradictory, by an infinity of mediations; a phenomenology of the real transcends itself, but also destroys itself, in the open dialectic of a history that has no term. Partial and biassed truth of a totalizing process constantly continuing and never finished, progressive apprehension of consciousness of self through all the density of the world and history, yet never achieving coincidence with it: such is the mode of comprehension offered to us by philosophic reflection. For minds that thirst after the absolute, it's not much. Philosophic meaning, like literary meaning, is an ambiguous meaning; what the philosopher means always goes beyond the confines of what he says. And it is thanks to this fact, no doubt, that Aristotle and Hegel still survive in Heidegger and Marx. But this ambiguous meaning is also, in the last resort, a "frustrated" and, one must confess, a frustrating meaning. Not science, yet striving to be knowledge; lying outside all methods, yet of its own decision methodical; seeker after a concrete absolute, yet doomed to the relative abstract; systematic cogitation on the impossibility of systems — philosophic reflection, though not conducive to comfort, is nevertheless imperative. Probably the highest point at which the human need for clarity and wisdom is given affirmation, this moment of man's greatness is also that at which, in all its nakedness, his weakness is most fully revealed. Philosophy — an activity far more noble and absurd than those of the Don Juan or the actor, as Camus once put it — always still to be done, ceaselessly undone and again attempted, stands eternally in the presence of its task like Sisyphus in the presence of his rock.

Connoisseurs of "objective" and "strict" truths will hardly find it to their taste, any more than adherents of ineffable certitudes. One must make one's choice: "A concrete philosophy is not a happy philosophy" (*Signes*, p. 198). Neither objective nor subjective, philosophic truth is to be found, like the existence it reflects, at that simultaneously distinct and obscure meeting place where consciousness and the world emerge and define one another, the one for the other and the one through the other, in the Look and in Desire. And it is this type of truth, so limited and so demanding, this global and open model of understanding, that I believe is precisely what can and ought to be offered for use in literary criticism, *as soon as it ceases to be merely a series of questions about literature in order to become a radical questioning of literature.* It may be said that this shift in interest and orientation is precisely what constitutes the transition from the old to the new criticism, as well as the best definition of the distinction between them. As long as one continues to ask oneself questions *about* the work, which is to say, as long as one continues to constitute it as an object, then one will continue to receive, according to one's particular bias, a certain quantity of objective replies. And insofar as every work presents itself as an object, the significations thus arrived at are perfectly legitimate. Man too, from one whole aspect, is an object. But — and this we have been able to verify experimentally as it were — no objective signification can achieve the synthesis of the others and provide an intelligible articulation of them. This is because man and his cultural creations are those specific types of existents, at once radically objective and radically subjective, that I have referred to in previous chapters as "false objects" or "object-subjects." Although wholly *there*, in bodily behavior, the pages of a book, the paint on a canvas, their *meaning* is always *beyond* these external foundations for the consciousness perceiving them. These different meanings are nevertheless not merely scattered at random: they group themselves together and combine to form the meaning of a human action, of a play, of a painting. This meaning has by gradations, albeit continuously, been indicated in the course of the preceding fragmentary analyses, which it is now time to collate into a whole.

11
CRITICISM AS EXISTENTIAL PSYCHOANALYSIS

1. THE WRITER'S COGITO

When the critic ceases to ask himself questions about the work and instead *questions the work*, or in other words replaces the question "What are the significations of this work?" by the question "What does this work signify?" the work, as object, melts away. For the aesthetic object is not a thing but "a special mode of confrontation with the Other" (Doubrovsky, *Corneille*, p. 20; cf. chapter 4 above), and its structures do not form a whole except insofar as they are the expression of a "structuring consciousness." Nor can this consciousness be simple intellectual consciousness: true coherence is to be found at the affective level, and aesthetic communication at the level of experienced reality. Merleau-Ponty, referring to those intellectual constructions the great philosophies, could say with justice that "system, explanation, deduction, none of these have ever been the essential. These arrangements expressed — and concealed — a relation with being, with others, with the world" (*Signes*, p. 199); and this is even more true of literary creations. If there is indeed a "vision" that supports the work of art from start to finish (cf. the discussion near the end of chapter 4 above), that vision is not an intellectual view, one that could be contained in a formula; it is, for the writer, "the total convergence of his being in his work" (cf. the end of chapter 6) — the totality of the endeavor in which a man strives to *say* what his condition as a man signifies for him (cf. the end of chapter 7). But to say, here, is not the same as to state; it does not mean simply putting ideas into circulation so that a commentator will later be able to condense and catalogue them. The ideological content itself is always carried by those deeper relations "with being, with others, with the world," and if language always means more than it says, if what the writer says attains its full sense through what he does not say (chapter 4), this is because every signifying arrangement, as Merleau-Ponty wrote in an earlier quotation, both "expresses" and "conceals" those fundamental relations it aims at making manifest.

Given that this analysis is correct, it furnishes criticism at one blow with both its end and its means, its justification and its criteria. And also its limits. If, in Robert Kanters's phrase, criticism consists in "making that discourse [literature] speak," then it can only be with the result of *repeating* what that discourse has said already and said better. If we dismiss criticism-paraphrase and criticism-chat, in short the nonexistent form of criticism that traditional criticism all too often is, true criticism is that which *adds* to the work, and which *adds itself* to the work as opposed to being resorbed into it; it is neither a stand-in nor a reflection. Not that it constitutes itself as a screen between text and reader: that is the forte of personality criticism, in which the critic is expressing himself with reference to other writers. Though meaningless in the hands of mediocre writers, this secondary kind of literature is certainly not without interest when produced by interesting minds; but Barbey d'Aurevilly the critic is still Barbey d'Aurevilly the novelist. If criticism wants to be an illuminating comprehension of literature, justified in itself, though not for itself, its role is made clear by the very nature of literary creation: since any expression is at the same time manifestation and dissimulation, *criticism will consist in revealing what is hidden and in linking what is given to what is concealed, in an effort to isolate the totality of the expression.* And in order to avoid all misunderstanding, let me emphasize that although this totality remains to be isolated, and the critical process to be undertaken, this is not as a result of some kind of failure on the part of the author; it does not imply that he has somehow or other been unsuccessful in achieving his ends and therefore needs outside help. The justification of criticism is not dependent upon an imperfection in literature itself, which would mean that a supposed perfect work could, in an ideal world, dispense with all supplementary elucidation for the reason that it would contain its whole meaning in

240

itself. But the totality of the meaning is always, and in principle, *in suspense*, both as a result of the nature of language and as a result of the work's ontological and historical situation (cf. chapter 4). At no point, even supposing him to be the author of the most lucid work ever produced on this earth, could a writer possible succeed in formulating its integral meaning.[1] In this respect, and at each moment of history, the critic — and every reader, in general — is the writer's midwife. And instead of the ad hoc parturition offered by banal chat in some booklined and dusty back room, new criticism — unlike the old — intends to "deliver" meaning by the use of adequate and precise instruments. And at this point I must state that critical analysis appears to me, in the exact sense of the expression invented by Sartre, as an *existential psychoanalysis*. Psychoanalysis — the knowledge of what in another is hidden from that other, or of what that other is hiding from himself — places the critic in the same situation vis-à-vis his text as the psychoanalyst vis-à-vis his patient. In both cases, what is involved is rendering the totality of a human behavior pattern intelligible, by achieving a perception of the link between obvious significations and latent significations, and by replacing the global organization of real or imaginary activities, themselves imperfectly coherent or manifestly contradictory, within the context of the fundamental project that underlies and supports them. Existential psychoanalysis: this fundamental project cannot be seem as stopping short at the level of the libido; even sexual relations themselves are a repetition and integration — on the psychosomatic plane specific to them — of deeper relations, with being, with others, with the world. In order to decipher these relations, an existential psychoanalysis will naturally turn to the philosophies of existence, and it is in this sense that present-day criticism seems to me so notably involved with and dependent upon the researches of contemporary philosophy. The latter is in fact striving to *elucidate*, on the theoretical level, the same primary relations of man to reality, the same total meaning of a human condition, that literature *projects* in an integral and therefore an ambiguous form on the imaginary plane. Within the field of their common exploration, philosophy and literature have a relation of *greater consciousness of* and *greater fidelity to* existence respectively.

241

The specific and irreplaceable work of literary criticism therefore consists in endowing the authentic and transhistoric truths of literature, at a given moment of history, with the maximum of consciousness.

A certain number of consequences result from this, as well as a number of difficulties, which I have no intention of passing over in silence, since criticism understood in this way consists much less in providing new solutions to old problems than in posing new problems — which it is not always able to resolve. Let us begin, all the same, with the advantages that can be chalked up to its credit. If we consider the type of comprehension established by philosophic reflection, it is evident that though it does not for a moment neglect the contribution of the various sciences, the task of science is not that of serving as a clearing house for scientific information. Just as it was never the handmaid of theology, as the old saying went, so philosophy is not now the handmaid of science; it is striving, on the contrary, to do something that science could never do: integrate the contradictory multiplicity of the procedural forms of knowledge by grasping that knowledge at its point of origin, as a relation of being, in such a way that its various degrees (affectivity, perception, science) can be articulated one with another in accordance with the ontological structures they reveal. Similarly, criticism cannot afford to ignore the significations revealed by the various positive studies of the literary texts. Its task, nevertheless, does not consist in attempting the impossible summation of those significations, but in placing them, establishing their hierarchy, articulating them in the only intelligible way possible: by relating the multiple aspects of the literary work to the *signifying intention* that animates it, supports it, but also passes through it and transcends it (see below). For the comprehension of a work cannot simply *bring itself to a halt* at the work taken in isolation, as it were, and explore it as though it were a wholly self-enclosed reality, as Picard expresses his wish to do when he naïvely criticizes the new criticism because it searches for its significations "elsewhere" than "in" the work: the work does not exist *in itself* (and this is why no objective approach could ever provide the key to its unity); it has not been given, once and for all, like an ensemble of *spatially coherent struc-*

tures that are simply *there* and present themselves to us all of a piece, in a book and on a stage. It is no coincidence that the objectivist approaches rely upon the exploitation of a certain number of *spatial* metaphors: Picard and his "literary structures"; Barthes and the "organization of forms"; Mauron and the "networks" of images; Goldmann and his "structural homology." If a true thematic analysis, as I said earlier, implies the dynamic comprehension of the unfolding and becoming specific to the themes (cf. chapter 8, section 1), this is because the existence of the literary work is itself constituted by the convergence of a twofold duration: that of the creative consciousness and that of the observing consciousness. *Andromaque* is not a spatial but a *temporal* existent: the play, strictly speaking, only exists insofar as Racine, in writing it, and at every moment of its duration, carries over, synthesizes the meaning included in the previous moment and transcends it toward the moment that follows, without the total meaning at any moment condensing itself and becoming wholly available at one single point. At the same time, *Andromaque* also exists only insofar as I read or see the play — in other words insofar as I constitute it, line by line, scene by scene, as the horizon of my successive apprehendings, receding and disappearing even as I advance toward it; at no moment can I lay my hand on an object whose synthesis exists somewhere *already*. So the meaning of *Andromaque* is, as it were, the vanishing-point of my experience of it. Thus both from the point of view of the creative and that of the observing consciousness, from that of the writer as well as that of the critic, we may say both that the meaning *lives in the work* (it is nothing outside that assemblage of words, as the picture cannot be outside the aggregation of its paints), and that it is always *beyond its immediate materiality* (it exists only in the synthetic unity of an apperception). Let us now try to unravel as quickly as possible the methodological consequences of this fundamental situation for literary criticism.

The domain of the work's "materiality" is, by right, the province of the objective disciplines. Fom the establishing of the text to the examination of its stylistic coherence, from the study of aesthetic canons to that of the history of genres, Racine belongs at a primary level to the scholar, to the linguist, to the lexicographer, to the literary historian, to the aesthetician. It is absolutely impossible to dispense with their services. At a second level, Racine's work appears no longer in its *objectal* but in its *documentary* reality: here we are already dealing with a meaning that constitutes a synthesis, since it groups the diverse material aspects together by subsuming them in general signification: Racine as witness of an age and a civilization (Taine wrote: in these plays in which he speaks of neither his times nor his life we find the history of both his life and his times); Racine as individual manifestation of a certain current of Jansenism and a certain aspect of the class struggle; in short, Racine as a moment of History, in which literary history, religious history, and general history all intersect. But this historical or sociological meaning synthesises Racine's theater as a document, not as a literary work, since it is defining that theater's interest within a significating framework *external to its inner intention*, which is not historic at all but transhistoric. Through his history and my history, as through his life and my life, Racine is speaking to me of man's fate; Racine is questioning his human condition and my human condition. Without in any way denying the other meanings, but by arranging them in a hierarchy, placing them and also "putting them in their place" as secondary in relation to a primary intentionality which must now be isolated and brought out, literary criticism proper truly begins at the moment when we cease to take literature as an object that is there simply for our delight or our study, and discover in it the richest and most complete expression of a *metaphysical experience* — of the total meaning that human experience takes on for one man.

I can hear the outcry from here: what did he say? Metaphysical! We cannot shrink from words because there are fools in the world. Let me quote you this passage from Baudelaire, writing about the arts: "Since they are always the beautiful expressed by each person's feeling, passion, and fantasy, which is to say variety in unity, or the various faces of the absolute, criticism verges at every instant on metaphysics." If it is accepted that we are using this term in its most precise acceptation, in the context of the modern philosophies of existence, and that we strip it of any medieval aura of omniscience, then the ultimate meaning that we were seeking as a foundation for literature's subsidiary and multiple significations, the unifying principle of comprehension that has been the object of our quest, is nothing other than *the metaphysical intention that is at the living heart of literary expression*. Do I hear more cachinnations from our intellectual village-idiots? So what about *The Italian Straw Hat*? What about *La Dame de chez Maxim*? they cry through their mirth. Are we to look for a "metaphysical meaning" in those delightful comedies, and must we imagine Labiche and Feydeau writing metaphysics as M. Jourdain did his prose, without knowing it? Once more, let us set the record quite straight. In order to give an expression a "metaphysical" meaning there is absolutely no need whatever to assume the inspired pose of the Musset statue that once stood outside the Comédie-Française; nor is there the slightest need to make sententious use of a philosophic jargon uttered in solemn and scholarly tones. Laughter contains an awareness of the human condition in its generality just as much as does anguish or tears, as Rabelais knew full well when he said that "laughter is what makes man man." It is this same awareness of generality that defines, by its presence or its absence, the *quality* of humorous expression, that in fact distinguishes Labiche, the skillful craftsman, from Feydeau, the true artist. Feydeau's disarticulated puppets present us, in their hypnotically choreographed frenzies, with an articulated vision of human absurdity — a vision already foreshadowing those of Ionesco or Beckett — whereas the sedate intrigues of Labiche's sedate burghers never take us beyond the level of pure entertainment. Whatever the aesthetic means employed, varying as they must do with genres and times, tastes and temperaments, whether it is a question of comedy or tragedy, poetry or novel, of seventeenth century or twentieth century, the only authentic criterion of literary value — because the only immutable one — is *the unity and depth of the vision of the world that a work or a body of works presents us with*. But this "unity" is not that of an abstract principle, of a theoretical theme that a writer's work must eternally reiterate in marginal variations; the "depth" is not some ineffable and mystic virtue; nor is the "vision of the world" a conceptual schema achieved by the reduction of the work to its essence. Although the new criticism often seems to be speaking one identical language, or employing identical formulas, those formulas in reality change their sign according to the meaning one gives the individual words. From the viewpoint I have taken, to resume the analyses scattered through the earlier part of this book, if every human existence calls into play, and into question, its fundamental relations with being, with others, with the world and God, then its *unity* can only be an affective and concrete thematization, accompanied by a greater or lesser degree of theoretical consciousness; the *depth* of the literary work is simply the richness, the convergence through their teeming abundance, of the various levels of symbolic expressivity; and lastly, the *vision of the world* is the ultimate meaning, the final taste that his being has for a man ("nuptials" for Camus, "nausea" for Sartre), on the basis of which literature is evolved and philosophies constructed — those with "scientific" pretentions as well as the others. Camus expressed it admirably in his preface to *L'Envers et l'endroit*: "A man's work is nothing other than the long journey he makes back via the detours of art in order to rediscover the two or three simple and great images upon which, that one first time, his heart once opened." Criticism too is a long journey made to rediscover those images, but made via another route. In the literary domain, which is what concerns us here, a great work is one that by the texture of its language, the concatenation of its themes, the deployment of its images, the subtle interplay of statement and subtext, in short, by using all the apparatus of a complex rhetoric, evokes for us, and through us, the total meaning that can be achieved, at any moment of history, by the absolute mystery that his own existence always remains for man.

Far from neglecting historical and aesthetic considerations (two criticisms often directed at the new critics), the approach I am proposing, under the name of "existential psychoanalysis," provides an intelligible foundation for aesthetic and historical significations by making possible the living experience of communication between reader and writer, despite the variations in expressive techniques and the changes in historical situations. The type of comprehension that literature requires is thus of a quite different order from that of the great explicative systems, which the works must always be "fitted into"; the only valid meaning, on the contrary, is that which we "draw out" of them. "When you have explained Racine in terms of his age, of his environment, of his childhood, there will then remain *Phèdre*, the inexplicable" (*Saint Genet*, p. 222). *The inexplicable*: the word Sartre uses must be taken in its strict sense. *Phèdre* is literally inexplicable, because it is the starting point, not the destination, of any possible explanation, and because, contrary to the old rationalist myth, there is no explanation that could finally explain itself, no method that could ever close the circle of its own knowledge upon itself, like a snake swallowing its own tail. As I have said elsewhere, "just as there is no scientific explanation of perception, because all science and all explanation are constituted upon a primary foundation of the already-perceived, so artistic reality is wholly given and defined by the primary contact with the art object" (*Corneille*, p. 16). There can therefore no more be a *standing back from the work* in criticism than there can be a *standing back from the thing* in perception; for natural as for aesthetic perception, the meeting with the object is an absolute beginning. "The subsequent classifications, comparison, relations, and constructions of purposeful thought are possible only on the basis of this primary, untranscendable, and irreducible presence" (ibid.). *Critical comprehension can therefore only make the work explicit and never explain it.* We cannot, as Goldmann believes, begin with a "phenomenology" of the products of literature that will isolate their internal meaning and then, with the aid of a "genetic explanation" salvage the meaning of those products and as it were re-manufacture" them as the result of this process: this notion is merely a philosophic chimera, a mirage that Bergson analyzed to perfection under the name of "retrospective illusion." Explanation of the scientific kind posits the world *before* consciousness and the world *without* consciousness: it conjures up the earth, then man upon the earth, then consciousness in man. Similarly, one can posit France in the seventeenth century, the contradictions in its history, Jansenism, the life of Racine, and at the end of it all, *Phèdre*. But the whole point is that scientific procedure is abstract, whereas philsophic thought is concrete: there is in fact no "earth," no "man" other than for a consciousness thinking their apparition retrospectively. Concrete reality, the absolute starting point — on the basis of which one can then evolve all the atoms with little hooked arms or all the neutrons and positrons one likes in order to provide an account of reality — the concrete reality, I repeat, is the *act of consciousness* for which and by which, even in the case of the scientist, the world is constituted. Similarly, the primordial focus of all meaning, the untranscendable *terminus a quo* is *Phèdre*, and it is only on the foundation of this contingent existent that we can go on to establish all the necessary links required by theoretical elucidation.

Although *Phèdre* is not a thing that has fallen from the sky, a fragment of matter arrived here from some interstellar region and whose origin, once its chemical composition is known, we must proceed to deduce; although, as I have said, its coherence is not that of a spatial object but that of a temporal synthesis, a synthesis by means of which the consciousness of both writer and reader are perpetually transcending the immediately created or perceived meaning of each moment toward a total meaning, it is still essential to realize that this meaning is never at any moment *given*: it is at every moment, and for always, in abeyance. The signifying totality we know as *Phèdre* is forever open. Just as an act, taken in itself, is incomprehensible unless it is linked to a man's other acts, and those other acts in their turn have no meaning except insofar as they express the direction of a life, concretized by each one of the acts it is true but revealing itself in them without exhausting itself, in the same way, each fragment, each part of a work (and all apprehension of a work is fragmentary and compartmentalized) does not become truly comprehensible until replaced in *the overall movement that sustains and articulates each of its discontinuous moments*. Which is why the critic confronts an author's works in the same way as the psychoanalyst confronts the acts of a life: work and act are temporary syntheses, symbolic expressions of the overall impulse of an existence. *To comprehend* a work is to make oneself one with that impulse; to explicate the meaning of a work is to show how it manifests itself; to *analyze* a work is to connect the various significations it possesses (stylistic, aesthetic, historic, etc.) to the fundamental project that alone pro-

248

vides it with its intelligible unity. To define that project or that impulse means very strictly, for the critic, to *rediscover in the writer the prereflexive Cogito* that the philosopher has revealed to us, which is to say the primal apprehension of the world and other by the consciousness, and the affective relations it enters into with them. But this Cogito (and here there is an all-important difference between classical psychoanalysis and existential psychoanalysis) is not an immutable Cogito, and the time it experiences is not a reiterative but an inventive time: as Sartre said, referring to Genet's choice of being a saint and a criminal, "this double decision does not remain inert; it lives, it changes, it enriches itself over the years, it is transformed by its contact with experience and by the dialectic of each one of its components: it will be our task to follow it in its development" (*Saint Genet*, p. 67). In this respect, Raymond Picard is right to decry a form of decipherment that would transform the variousness of literary creations into a continual reworking of a single theme: this type of interpretation, of which Jean-Paul Weber's "instant-psychoanalyses" present the ultimate caricature, can indeed be dangerous, as we have seen in our analysis of the more serious researches of psychocriticism. "You should have changed if you wanted to remain yourself": that magnificent, albeit unjust, remark made by Sartre to Camus expresses perfectly the fact that if man is free, then to live is also to change in order to remain faithful to oneself. Although one part of existential psychoanalysis is *retrogressive*, in that it works back toward a fundamental complex, part of it is also necessarily *progressive* and is directed at apprehending the act or the work as *a transcendence and not a reflection* of that "complex." Far from reducing thematic variations to an eternal common denominator (which is what the explanatory and objectivist approaches do), we have to understand that change is not the surface appearance but the very being of existence. However, if change is not just random scattering of incoherent significations, if it has a meaning, a direction, if it follows a certain line, that is because it conceals within it a unifying principle of its own variations, not in the form of a cause producing effects but as a project that has perpetually still to be, which is to say to choose itself and to invent itself among its possibles, if needs be in opposition to itself, in an endless continuity of new situations. Rather than the unity and the totality of the meaning of a life or a work, we should therefore talk of a *unification* and a *totalization*, since it must be clearly understood that we are not dealing with a static entity, an essence. but with a dynamic and a becoming.

This theoretical aim once posited, what are the practical means that present themselves for its realization? We are already in firm possession of the general aim of our research: having started from the work as a body of literary structures, as the organization of a certain language, or, we may say, of a certain very precise style of utterance, we are referred on from *what the work says* to *what is said by the work*, to all that it expresses beyond all that it states, to all that it does not utter and that nevertheless lies at the heart of what it is saying: this work of linking the explicit and the implicit, which is specific to criticism, delivers the work of its total meaning and gives to the language its dimension of being-as-bearer-of-significations. If writing is a way of being, then it refers us on in its turn to the presence, in it and through it, of the writer. The style of the work therefore indicates an author's choice of being; it tells us the way in which one human existence has integrated and expressed the totality of its concrete relations with the world.[2] The work mediatizes a whole series of biographical, psychological, historical, and sociological relations that the various positivist studies have revealed and apprehended at the level of *analytic* thought; it is now a matter, not of rejecting or ignoring those findings, but of thinking them *synthetically*, of grouping them and linking them together dialectically, of integrating them into the project of an existence, since after all, conscious existence is nothing other than the unifying tendency gathering scattered significations together into a global meaning of life, or "vision" of the world. It is quite obvious that this vision of the world is not a closed system and that it communicates — even if only by the use of a common language, albeit the kind of language without literary content that Barthes would term an *écriture* — with the social and historical universe. In this sense all literature, as Goldmann claims, is indeed the expression by an individual of the structures of a group. But this same literature, looked at from another point of view, by its use of certain images or myths, is expressing the great mental archetypes studied by psychoanalysis and anthropology. Existential criticism does not reject any of these data, any more than it rejects the biographical and historical elements provided by traditional research: it is simply another way of comprehending and organizing them. Instead of working from the inside outward, from the isolation of autonomous significations to their insertion within objective frameworks, in which they are negated, it works in precisely the reverse direction: first it shows that literature, like the existence it is manifesting, absorbs and resorbs into itself the events of the individual and collective life (and not the reverse), and then it shows how they are symbolically digested and assimilated, as it were, in order to constitute the flesh and texture of the work. In a word, instead of being the exteriorization of an interiority, *critical comprehension is the interiorization of an exteriority*: the very act of the Cogito is nothing else but that, yet it is everything; or, more exactly, it is the condition and the foundation of everything.

2. THE WRITER'S LIFE AND HIS WORK

The question that immediately poses itself here, however, is the very same one we were forced to put to Lucien Goldmann earlier, when his philosophy said, "There is thought," and we asked, "Who thinks?" Given my standpoint, who cogitates? Is this "Racinian Cogito," which I see as the central focus of all the subsequent significations of a body of tragedies, really that of Jean Racine? If so, then in order to apprehend his work we should need to work our way back through his biography in all its density, albeit a piecemeal density as history presents it to us, and the meaning of the work would be the meaning we would have reconstructed by reconstructing the man. And this, as we shall see, is as much one of the temptations of existential criticism as of academic criticism. But it must be resisted: the Cogito, if reconstructed in that way, from scratch and from the outside, would be no more — like the psychoanalyst's hypothetical Racinian Unconscious — than pure conjecture. And in any case, the decipherment involved would be less literary than historical in

251

nature; in literature, although the work does refer us on to the author, it is not as a man in general but as the author of the work under scrutiny. You may say that the same existence is involved in either case, and that a man is not a cat with a multiplicity of lives. True. What J. Starobinski has written of Rousseau applies to all other writers: "Rightly or wrongly, Rousseau did not consent to separate his thought from his individuality, his theories from his personal destiny. We have to take him as he offers himself, in that fusion and confusion of existence and idea" (*Jean-Jacques Rousseau*, preface). Since, as our previous analyses show, the expressive coherence of a work is always, through the cohesion of its language, of an existential order, it goes without saying that the literary and biographical meanings coincide — that they are, at a certain level, fused and confused. But unless it is to founder in a total syncretism, literary criticism must know exactly what it is looking for, and be certain, in this confusion, not to lose sight of its proper object. The elements of interpretation, if one may so put it, are always the same, and everything lies in the way we arrange and order them. When Flaubert exclaims: "*Madame Bovary*, c'est moi!", what we must establish is whether the important thing is to study *Madame Bovary* in order to understand the man Flaubert, or whether it is to use our knowledge of the man Flaubert to achieve an acuter understanding of *Madame Bovary*. In practice, needless to say, there is a two-way traffic of thought from one of these poles to the other, but we still need to know which fundamental direction we ought to impose on our research. And for the literary critic, it seems to me, there can be no doubt what the answer should be: *the circuit of comprehension works from work to author, then back to the work, and not from author to work then finally back to author.* Let me repeat: without a known author there can be works; without known works there is no author. On this point, critical comprehension is epistemologically the converse of historical comprehension: *first* the tragedies; *then* Racine. In this sphere the primacy of the work is absolute. Not that the work does not refer us on, if it is to be understood, to a multitude of significations (including biographical ones) that it mediatizes: but those significations are of interest to criticism solely insofar as they are

252

integrated into the work, and they must not be allowed to disintegrate the work. In short, if a total criticism is to achieve an intelligible relation of the meaning in a literary creation with the fundamental project of a life, then its role is to make a comprehension of the life serve the comprehension of the work, and not the converse, since the only Racine we can meet on the plane we are occupying is the Racine that exists in and through his tragedies. The tragedies are, for us, the first and last point of contact that we have with him as a writer. One can also of course be interested in Racine as a courtier, as a man of letters, as a secular witness to a certain Jansenist spirituality, etc. If that is the position we take up, then immediately the "essential-non-essential" relation is inverted: the works are nothing more than an index — one of many — that refers to a man whose real activities in an objective world one wishes to recapture. That is a perfectly legitimate attitude: it is the attitude of the historian or sociologist. It has nothing to do with that of the literary critic. Criticism cannot therefore be a biography, now narrated by the philosopher instead of the psychoanalyst, onto which the writings will have to be attached somehow, here and there. Because the writings are *the only signifying totality*, to use the structuralists' language, that it is the task of criticism to know.

On this all-important point, Lanson is right — as opposed to Sainte-Beuve and also, in some measure, to Sartre — when he says of Sainte-Beuve: "For instead of employing the biographies to explain the works, he employed the works to constitute biographies. He treated the masterpieces of literary art no differently from the hurriedly penned memoirs of a general or some woman's epistolary effusions; all this writing is pressed into the same service: he uses it as a stepping-stone toward the soul or the mind, which is precisely to eliminate the literary quality" (*Hommes et Livres*, preface). Not that Sainte-Beuve, in his turn, is quite in the wrong: we must also comprehend the "soul" or the "mind," and there can be no question of reverting to some quasi fetishism of the "literary thing," that object-worship of which Raymond Picard has set himself up as high priest. It is simply that this "soul" or this "mind" cannot be fully grasped other than in that special form of communication, through that irreplaceable and privileged mode of

253

expression constituted by the successful work of art. Inevitably lying in ambush for all "biographical" criticism, therefore, whether traditional, Freudian, or Sartrean, there is the danger of putting a masterpiece, a rough draft, or a paragraph from a letter all on the same plane on the pretext that they are all contributing equally to a complete picture of the author. Rough drafts, letters, and biographical details are interesting solely insofar as they permit us to understand the masterpieces better. And if I am asked why we should attribute a particular value to the "masterpiece," which affects the whole direction of criticism, why we should decide to treat *Athalie* and a general's memoirs or a woman's epistolary effusions differently, this choice that constitutes texts as unconditional ends and some texts as simply means of access to other texts, then this is my reply: because the means-of-access texts are merely speaking to us of *a* man, whereas the end texts are speaking to us, through a man, of *man*. The mere omission of an indefinite article is a slight thing, it might be said; but in the absence of that "a" all literature resides.

Because either literature confers on the singular, and without leaving the singular (which is what distinguishes it from philosophy) a universal value — or it is not literature at all. I will take what seems to me a significant example. In a penetrating article devoted to an attack on "the thematic illusion" in J.-P. Richard (*Temps Modernes*, May 1963), Otto Hahn poses the problem extremely well: "The image divides and reforms, ramifies and takes on new qualities. . . . In his work on Mallarmé, Richard has set himself to unraveling their proliferation. . . . At the same time, he has described the qualitative structuration of the real: is that not the essence of the work of art? There we see the illusion rearing its head." Hahn's objection, as a good Sartrean, is as follows: "One of the particularities of the *For-itself*, taken in itself, is that of being incomprehensible. In order to discover its signification it must be confronted with an objective reality. . . . There are indeed themes in Mallarmé's work, there is indeed an organization of the images, but neither the themes nor the organization of the images are describable in isolation from the real impulse that has produced them." So far no comment. But Hahn adds: "The theme has no interest other than through the way in which it is connected to the real world on the one hand, and through the way in which it is oriented by the project on the other." But the whole problem (which involves the very essence of literature and, in consequence, of criticism) is precisely that of knowing whether the way in which a theme is connected to the real world is indivisibly one with the way in which it is inserted into the life and the project *of the author*. Otto Hahn, less a follower of Sartre in this than of a long critical French tradition, seems to think it is. Thus, he tells us, "this well-concealed faun gazing out at the lovely naiads" is only comprehensible as a poetic theme when replaced within the life of Mallarmé, whose sexuality was of a timid and voyeuristic kind, and whose erotic life, strongly feminine in character, led him to dream of peacock-women, Lesbians caressing one another, etc. I believe that there is a confusion here between two planes that criticism must keep distinct, on pain of seeing its object disintegrate before its eyes: that of anchoring art in reality and that of art's own reality. It is quite evident that Mallarmé's images are not absolutes, entities emerging mysteriously from some unknown region, like the sensations of empiricist philosophy. The image, in its *genesis*, can be comprehended solely in terms of its relation to the real, a relation not of the "reflecting-reflected" but of the dialectic type, as a symbolic projection overcoming personal contradictions. But can we conclude from this that the image's *interest* — which is to say, ultimately, its *value* — resides in the way in which it is inserted into the author's project? To do so is to ignore the fact that the human world extends far beyond that individual project in every direction, and that the excess of the former over the latter is precisely what constitutes the *imaginative meaning* capable of extension and repossession by others. For the *meaning* of the image of the Faun in fact lies wholly in the symbolic surplus it presents over and above its *signification* for Mallarmé; it lies in its "oversignification." While the Faun may embody for its author the erotic reaction of a hypnotized yet timid sexuality, in a reader accustomed to welcoming laps and easy conquests that same Faun will produce the quite different experience of an *impassable gulf*: for example that which in Don Juan's case separates all the women he has so easily conquered from the eternally elusive Woman perpetually sought-for in them and yet for ever unattainable. The beauty of Mallarmé's theme, its value (irreducible I repeat, to its genesis), lies in its having transcended its occasional cause in órder to present to any man *a signifying image of his own condition*. And this is why the mark, the only mark of a great work, is that it offers a form of experience susceptible of universalization. There is a specifically *Mallarmean* meaning of the image, it is true, and criticism must explicate and define it, but on condition that it is directing its attention through and beyond that limited meaning to *all the human meanings* it draws to itself, rather as a fire, once started, draws the surrounding air into itself. Moreover, Otto Hahn, even at the risk of contradicting what he has said before, goes on to express this admirably: "The reader pours his own experience into the formal construct of the work of art. . . . And one has understood just as much when one has fueled that formal construct with one's own experience as when one has fueled it with the real experiences of the author."

But in that case, J.-P. Richard has suddenly been proved in the right by his own critic, since the aim of his research is to describe the internal organicity of a network of symbolic qualities. We must therefore correct Hahn's formula — "neither the themes nor the organization of the images are describable in isolation from the real impulse that produced them"— and say that they are not describable in isolation from the *imaginative impulse* that animates them. Needless to say, an imaginative impulse is also a real impulse, but the reality that transmits it is above all, for each individual reader, *his or her own existence*. It is also true that in molding itself to the imaginative impulse of the work the reader's consciousness is coinciding *partially* with the existence of the being who engendered it. This is why comprehension of the theme includes explication of its meaning for its author, or, if you prefer, establishes its genesis. But no theme has value except insofar as comprehension is here exceeded by a resonance that induces a second zone of comprehension, *the only essential one*, in which the reader's own experience goes from self back to self, passing through the author's experience on the way. When as is often the case, the relation between the work's imaginative universe and the author's real project cannot be made explicit, this zone of essential comprehension is not destroyed or harmed; which provides us with a reductio ad absurdum test of the argument: when we *know* nothing or almost nothing about the author, as with Shakespeare or Corneille, their writings *speak* to us no less for that, and it is for that *voice in the work* that criticism is listening. In such cases, the totalization of meaning that criticism aims at is, quite simply, less complex and less complete to the degree in which a whole order of significations has evaded it. In the terminology I have been using I would express this by saying that referral to a biography as an ensemble of personal events is *one of the significations* of the work, and a necessary one (without an author, no work), but inadequate nevertheless as a foundation on which to constitute the *global meaning* for which we are searching, since that global meaning absolutely requires the active presence and participation of an Other.

This does not mean that whenever possible we should avoid any attempt to establish intelligible relations between writings and writer — a process for which I personally have always stressed the need. Since this book rests entirely upon the conviction that the internal cohesion of literary works is sustained by the coherence within the individual and concrete existence (there is no other kind) that is searching for itself through them, it goes without saying that the literary meaning and the biographical meaning must, as I have said, coincide at a certain level. But the question is: at what level? This is not merely a theoretical problem but a practical one, since it involves the technique of our literary analysis itself; so we must examine it more closely. "Employing the biographies to explain the works," in Lanson's words, is easily said, but *how*? Here we would do well to listen to Proust's still valuable warning against Sainte-Beuve and, indeed, against the major temptation of a whole long tradition in French criticism: "A book is the product of another self than the one we reveal in our habitual life, in society, in our vices" (*Contre Sainte-Beuve*, "Idées," p. 157). Only the adherents of a certain kind of literary history believe they can resolve the problem, at minimum expense, by thinking they will find the meaning of a book in a grand total of all the external details, biographical ones in particular, that may be concealed within it: such a use of "biography" is, as has been clearly seen, the surest way not of explaining but of murdering literature (cf. chapter 4 above), because it ignores a primary fact: that in the transition from the plane of reality to that of imagination a radical transformation and restructuration of the meaning occurs (cf. chapter 4, note 4). Now, if the coincidence between biographical meaning and literary meaning is never given by a relation of exteriority, if a book is not translatable word for word into an objective language, is not commensurable with the real actions and gestures of its author (and that is what Proust means when he speaks of "another self"), there is a very good reason for it, and one that Roland Barthes has perfectly summed up: it is that what we have here is "a relation between *all* the author and *all* his work, *a relation of relations*, a homologic and not an analogic correspondence" (*Essais*, p. 250). In a word, if literary and biographic meanings do ultimately coincide, they can only do so on condition that the nature of biographical meaning is totally changed.

Traditional criticism's error here is its belief — parallel to its belief that it can arrive at a comprehension of the work by laying enough notes and footnotes end to end — that it can interpret a life simply by aggregating episodes and anecdotes. Or rather, it imagines that it is respecting the truth of a life by refusing to interpret it. It was in this spirit that Raymond Picard attempted "not to judge," "not to draw conclusions," "not to reduce to a unity" — a unity that would be "factitious"— the accumulated facts of Racine's life, on the pretext that Racine himself "can scarcely be said to have introduced into his life the logic and the lucidity that we believe to be evident in his aesthetic creation" (cf. the beginning of chapter 5 above). Naturally enough, between a "biography" conceived as a mere succession of disjunct or superficially linked empirical facts, and a "logical" and "lucid" body of works, one cannot expect there to be any common scale of measurement or even any thinkable communication, unless it be a tiny detail in the life timidly pointing a hesitant finger once in a while at some detail in the works. It is thus basically upon the very same principle that traditional criticism will sometimes pay exclusive attention to the work because it cannot find sufficient meaning in the life, and at other times pay exclusive attention to the life because it cannot find enough meaning in the work. In both cases the principle is absurd and, as far as comprehension is concerned, crippling: it consists in imagining that one can interpret either a life or a work by limiting oneself exclusively to *the facts*. (Hence the mythology of "prudence" and "objectivity" that we have already encountered more than once). But in fact, since Freud, we know — though that does not seem to include Picard and many of his colleagues — that in every life, even in the most apparently disordered, there is an internal logic, even when the individual concerned has not "willed" it to be there (again that myth of "willed meaning" in the life as well as in the work). Not that the willed meaning, in both cases, does not exist; but is is partial and superficial, it neither grounds nor covers the signifying totality of a life or a work, and no life or work has a meaning other than as a signifying totality. It is completely futile to refuse, as the positivists of the "detail" school do, to *totalize* the meaning of a life on the grounds that it would be impossible to reach a *correct total*. It is the very conception of man itself that must be changed here; if, as Sartre has shown to be the case, human reality is a "detotalized totality," this means both that our existence is a permanent impulse toward totalization and that, despite this, the attempted totalization never achieves a total. Every moment of my life projects both before and behind it a certain meaning which is its moving horizon, and on the basis of which my past or my future can be constituted. But, this meaning, which makes it possible to identify and unify this life as *mine*, beneath its surface dispersion, at any moment, is nevertheless neither apprehendable nor formulable in its integrality; it is *present*, but without being *there*. None of my actions is comprehensible in isolation from this meaning, though the meaning is never wholly given in any one of my actions (cf. section 1 of this chapter). We cannot renounce the attempt to apprehend it without also renouncing the attempt to comprehend a man and rendering his activities as a whole nonsignificant; nor can we grasp it as we grasp a *reality*. The reality of a life is a sequence of actions and gestures both discontinuous and partly obscure to the very person who performs them, in short, a series of open and ambiguous significations that do not make up a total meaning except when halted by death — whether the momentary death of the retrospective survey in which one draws up the balance sheet of one's existence by halting it arbitrarily at some temporary horizon, or else the veritable death that hands us over without appeal to others, in which case the halt is final and the horizon definitive. In any case, the "meaning" of a life, which I live concretely as the implicit unification of my acts, is from the point of view of theoretical knowledge a possible that is projected, by me or by another, *onto* my life, whose events then play the role of an analogue. The meaning of any human life therefore exists, very precisely, as an *imaginary quantity*. It is on this level alone that an intelligent — or merely intelligible — biography can reveal it, and never on that of objective reality.

We must be very careful indeed here to avoid the gross error of confusing the imaginary with the fictive or the illusory. The illusion, on this point, must be laid at the door of a certain rationalism: just like emotion (cf. the discussion of ambiguity and clarity in section 2 of chapter 8), imagination is a way, not of *veiling*, but of *unveiling* the real. For the imaginary does not stand in opposition to the real as false does to true but as the virtual to the actual. And for man, existence is at no level actuality: it is not a concatenation of full and separate instants, causally linked after the model of phenomena, and belonging in consequence to an order of reality susceptible of a scientific explanation. To the degree in which concrete existence is always open, is always "still to be," remains perpetually to be fulfilled, it projects itself into an imagined existence in which *it gives itself symbolically that which it lacks, as the implicit thematization of the meaning of that existence* (cf. the beginning of chapter 8). The imaginary being nothing other than the means by which consciousness presentifies, either in anticipation or memory, the objects it lacks to fulfill its desire, so the meaning of a life is nothing other than the signification of that plenitude of being of which existence is perpetually the lack. What we must understand, however, is that this plenitude can never be denoted otherwise than by means of a symbolic language. For far from being error or occultation, the symbol is the *truth* of my concrete life. This is what Freudian psychoanalysis has so clearly understood when it employs the imaginary life as the *cipher* of the everyday existence: such and such a dream is the cipher in which such and such a secret desire — orienting my entire behavior — is being given to me; so that by "deciphering" the dream the "reality" of that desire is revealed and also, in consequence, the "true" meaning of my behavior. Though psychoanalysis must take care here not to fall dupe to its own language and underlying rationalism: it can and it must speak *as though* the psychoanalyst's activity consisted in going beyond symbolic meaning, in showing what is *underneath it*; but that is simply a requirement of a purely practical and therapeutic order, in that it enables the patient to become aware of the real meaning of his own behavior, which he has been concealing from himself. But we must nevertheless understand quite clearly that *this real meaning is in its turn a symbolic meaning*, that what lies "beneath" a symbol is another symbol. To pass from a state of mental sickness to a state of mental health does not mean suddenly ceasing to maintain symbolic relations with the world, so that nothing is then left but rational relations with it: it only means changing an affective structuration that leaves the individual isolated — incapable of connecting with himself, with others, and with the world — into an emotional investment that conforms with the values of personal survival and collective life. But existential psychoanalysis, unlike the clinical variety, is not attempting to "decipher" such or such an ensemble of practical behavior (sexual or other), in order to substitute a "good" symbolism for a "bad" one. It is attempting to elucidate the signifying totality of a life, which is to say, as we have seen, to articulate that life in all its multiple manifestations as the dynamic realization of a certain imaginary scheme, and in consequence there is no language of "reality" that could ultimately replace the symbolic cipher; there is no objective truth that could dissipate the subjective apprehension of the real. The "desire to be God," which Sartre names as every man's ultimate project, is itself no more than a symbol of symbols; it leaves no "remainder" after the symbolic constitution of all experiential relations. When existential psychoanalysis attempts to "decipher" the meaning of a life, there can be no question of its translating symbolic significations into a nonsymbolic or rational language, which seems to be the ambition of Freudian psychoanalysis. (Needless to say, scientific language too, like all language, is symbolic. But the symbol of logic is a univocal sign, subject to set, precise, and objective transformations. The two types of symbolism are radically different.) The notions employed by the philosophies of existence, "being," "having," "doing," are absolutely not univocal concepts after the model of scientific concepts; but the language of philosophy makes a more acute comprehension of the concrete possible here precisely because its concepts retain sufficient ambiguity to give an account of human reality, while nevertheless possessing sufficient clarity to permit an articulated and intelligible description of it. To analyze an existence, therefore, is always to transcribe one order of symbolic significations into another, without ever going beyond the boundary of symbolic expression itself. If such analysis is not futile, and if the process of comprehension is possible, that is because *certain languages* permit a more thorough and systematic integration of human meanings than simple everyday language.

Dreams and desires are not literature. Whereas a childhood incident, a traumatic accident, revealed by such and such a biographical detail, may provide the "key" to my behavior, it is completely useless, not to say absurd, to seek such "keys" to literary creation. (And this is why the application of classical psychoanalysis to the comprehension of works is, ipso facto, limited.) Insofar as literature is *total* language, which is to say a language aiming at expressing the totality of human relations to being, to things, and to men, it cannot be explicated by *partial* languages, which is what the various clinical forms of psychoanalysis must always remain. No biographical detail, no "character trait," none of those "facts" of which scholarly research is so fond, can ever, as such, reveal the meaning of a work: only the whole of a life, as signifying behavior, can be brought into intelligible relation with the whole of a work as an expression of that behavior. From this point of view the meaning of his work, for a writer, is nothing other than the meaning of his life, *as he presents it to himself synthetically in the act of writing.* The writer is the man who, by "bringing his existence to the imaginary" (as we say that metal is brought to white heat), by transferring it into the matrix of language, calls his own particular language into being, against the background of a common tongue, as a siglum of his total Self. It is Proust once again who has grasped better than anyone the essential procedure of writing: whereas the bad writer "does not see his own thought, which is still invisible to him, but contents himself with the crude surface that masks it from each one of us at every moment of our lives," the true writer is he who rejects "the ready-made expressions that are always put into our minds by what comes to us from others — and from the least good among them — when we wish to speak of something, unless we go down into that deep calm where thought *selects the words in which it will be reflected entire*" (*Contre Sainte-Beuve*, p. 365). Far from being the creator of mirages and illusions, authentic writing begins by rejecting the banality that obscures man's true condition from him (an occultation that is the very purpose of that "everday chatter" denounced by Heidegger), and constitutes itself as *total reflection* of the meaning of being; it brings up to the surface, in the texture of its discourse, the symbolic meaning that perpetually haunts the writer's existence. By bringing existence and language into the most intimate communication possible, literature becomes that which gives, in its words, precisely what the writer's life is the lack of: it is the *cipher of the truth* about a man and about the world, as it appears to that man. But this cipher is never, strictly speaking, "decipherable," in other words, translatable into the "right" language. If that is criticism's secret goal, then it may as well abandon it here and now. In its relation to literature, criticism can never aim at a higher degree of *truth*, but only of *consciousness* and *explicitness*, since after all, any language, including that of criticism, is ultimately not resolving the mystery of being but, as Proust quite rightly says, reflecting it.

In practice then, a writer's life and work appear to the critic as homologous systems of symbolic relations, both constituted by one and the same existential dialectic working across a link between the imaginary and the real that I have been trying to define. It is now easier to understand that ambivalence noted by Lanson, that Janus-like possibility — whose two aspects tempt

263

literary criticism turn and turn about — of using biographies to throw light on works, and works to throw light on lives: in fact, the amounts of meaning radiating from work toward life and from life toward work are equal, and a truly synthetic criticism will be able to pass intelligibly from one order of significations to the other. In theory, it is permissible for the critical procedure to operate in both directions, to pass back and forth from one symbolic system to the other, since they are linked by a relation of significating reciprocity. (Sartre did this in his admirable *Saint Genet*, which will be examined in a later volume.) If, in practice, the present work grants an absolute preeminence to the symbolic network formed by the work, that is for two reasons, neither of which has any connection with the sort of "aesthetic" fetishism found in the sacred cult of Literature presided over by our middle-class vestals: literature is the most complete revelation of existence, nothing more, nothing less. And that is why there is always priority of work over author. For a technical reason in the first place: a valid work (that is its definition) always forms and includes a signifying whole, whereas our knowledge of lives, even when it is not frankly nonexistent, is too fragmentary to make a strict synthetic apprehension possible. But above all, although the comprehension of a life and that of a work are homologous, they are in no way analogous; the first has a fundamentally historical dimension of being, the second a transhistorical one. And this is the appropriate place to clarify a distinction that has guided my inquiry throughout. It is a distinction that has probably found its clearest expression at the end of *La Nausée*, when Sartre's Roquentin decides to give a meaning to his life by writing: "It would have to be a book: I don't know how to do anything else. But not a history book: history talks about something that has existed — no existent can ever justify the existence of another existent. My mistake was in trying to bring M. de Rollebon back to life. Some other kind of book. I'm not sure what kind — but you would have to be able to sense, behind the printed words, behind the pages, something that doesn't exist, something above existence." It is odd to find Sartrean existentialism converging on this point with Proustian essentialism: "The matter of our books, the substance of our sentences should be immaterial, not taken just as it is from reality, and our very sentences themselves, and the incidents too, should be made of the transparent substance of our best moments, when we are outside reality and outside the present" (*Contre Sainte-Beuve*, p. 368).

What exactly is meant here? That historical communication with Others is always halved in value, in comparison with literary communication, simply because it is deprived of all reciprocity. Critic and historian are both faced with texts, with signs, of which they then attempt to establish the meaning. But historical comprehension in no way implicates the historian in the object of his study, unless it be by virtue of that partial coincidence of subject and object that is the characteristic of any human science. Historical meaning lies at the far end of the historian's researches, aloof from him, lost for ever in the radical contingency of that which "will never be seen twice." The communication is one way: it goes from the historian to the signs, which receive their meaning from him without ever denoting him in return. I can elucidate the life of Caesar, or the age of Charlemagne, without that elucidation throwing light upon my life or upon my time, unless it be very vaguely, either as a "moral lesson" based on the "nothing human is foreign to me" premise, or else as a simple relay of cause and effect leading indirectly from the past to contemporary history through the thick filter of intervening ages. In other words, in historical comprehension our contact with others, instituted in a cognitive form, remains a hypothesis in which the system of signs remains eternally open; the contact is inevitably a fragmentary contact, even though it may consist in giving an overall meaning to separate parcels of meaning. Even if I attempt to unify Racine's life and work in their process of symbolic totalization, even if I succeed in bringing these two systems into communication in a satisfactory way, it nevertheless remains true that I shall identify myself *much more immediately and fully* with Hermione or Pyrrhus, and *never in the same way* as with Racine. This is because the meaning of a life is always irreducibly singular and contingent, a prisoner of historical separation, whereas the meaning of a work, even though it is situated within the narrowest cultural, geographical, and linguistic limits, is in theory as in fact fundamentally susceptible of universalization. Hugo gave the best explanation of this power of universalization in his famous cry: "Ah! mad reader, you who believe I am not you!" Taken to the biographical letter, that is absurd: Hugo is not me. Nothing, or almost nothing, of what concerns the individual Hugo concerns me. And yet, in his work, Hugo is indeed an alter ego. The writer, as I said before, is a man who finds *himself* by finding his language; but, in that selfsame process, he finds *us*. And that is why literary communication, unlike historical communication, is two way.

Why and how, in literary communication, though never in historical communication (and all biography is a form of history), does the *self* of the writer become the *you* of the reader? Camus observed in *L'Homme révolté* that, "except for the thunderbolt moments of plenitude" (and that such moments exist may be doubted), "all reality is unfinished for them [men]. Their acts escape from them into other acts." Conversely, "the striving of great literature seems to be to create closed universes or finished types." One could indeed say of all authentic literary creation what Camus said of the novel: "What is the novel, if not that universe in which action finds its form, in which final words are spoken, beings bestowed on beings, in which all life takes on the aspect of destiny." This closing of the work does not contradict its openness — a quality which, with Roland Barthes, I have always accounted a prime necessity. On the contrary, in my opinion the former provides the latter's foundation. For in this case the openness, or, if you prefer, the ambiguity, is of a quite different order from historical openness and ambiguity. For history, openness is a lack, ambiguity a privation of meaning: the "data" of an individual or collective history will never "speak" sufficiently for the imaginary meaning by means of which the historian unifies them to become a necessary meaning. In the case of art, on the contrary, the openness and the ambiguity bear witness to an excess of meaning: there is too much meaning in the work for any focused attention to grasp it whole. Barthes put this very well in his recent critical survey: "A work is 'eternal' not because it imposes a single meaning on different men but because it suggests different meanings for a single man, who always speaks the same symbolic language through multiple ages: the work proposes, man disposes" (*Critique et vérité*, pp. 51–52). And for the work to propose, or even for there simply to be a work, it is necessary, as Proust and Mallarmé before him rightly said, that there shall have been a *metamorphosis of language*, a transition from the "poor" language of everday banality to the "rich" language of literature. This transition, as Camus sensed, is that from a *contingency to a necessity*. The openness of the work coincides exactly with the closedness of its language, that is to say with its totalization. Sartre's Roquentin dreams of an enterprise "beautiful and hard as steel"; Proust speaks of "drops of light cemented together": both metaphors express the same literary essence. If I identify myself with Hermoine and Pyrrhus, not with Racine, that is because by means of his imaginary creation the author has transcended what was necessarily unfinished in his own existence: he has constituted his work as the completed meaning lacking in his own life; his work is his contingency transcended into a necessity; his life plus what it lacks; or, in Camus's words, his life "taking on the aspect of destiny," though I would myself prefer: *taking on the aspect of the symbol*. Because the necessity here is not that of the concept; "the last word" is not a univocal and clear reply: and that is what I meant when I wrote (in the last part of chapter 7) that in literature every answer becomes a question, every question an answer. The necessity is totally of an *expressive order;* it lies solely in the depth of the experience induced by the organization of the signifying forms: every *strict* symbolic language, which is to say a language closed in on its own signifying network and presenting itself as an imaginary *universe*, joins and rejoins within itself both personal myths and collective archetypes; it speaks at the same time of the whole of one man and the whole of man. The cipher invented by a writer in order to express his existence *in its totality* must of necessity involve my existence too; it is the cipher of my existence also. The imaginary thus becomes the vehicle of a transhistory, in which the real self of the reader finds itself in the process of rediscovering, through the language of the work, the author's symbolic self. "If we wish to attempt to understand it, that other self, then it is in the very depth of ourselves, by trying to recreate it within us, that we can succeed in reaching it" (*Contre Sainte-Beuve*, p. 157). This being so, there can be no other path for criticism than the one Proust signposted. Because of literary communication's very nature, critical analysis is an *analysis immanent in the work*, as long as we are quite clear that this immanence, indissolubly closedness openness at the same time, is the dialectization of a multiplicity of transcendent relations, totalized in the unity of a symbolic utterance, at once fixed for all time and eternally responsive. There are those who will find this analysis "complicated." It is certainly not complicated enough. It takes certain professors of literature to believe that the problems of literature are simple. When Raymond Picard lavishes his would-be irony on the errors of the new critics who regard the literary work as "a collection of signs whose signification is elsewhere," it does not seem to have even occurred to him that the signification is always "elsewhere" than in the sign, since it is relation to an object indicated through that sign; and when he continues, still in his ironical tone: "and, of course, this *elsewhere* lies at the very center of the work, since it is the work's raison d'être" (*Nouvelle critique*, pp. 113–14), he is giving a precise definition, in his very ignorance, of the process of interiorization of exteriority that constitutes the essence of any subjective apprehension of the real. The *here* of the work, as a specific type of "interiority," is no more than a certain imaginary mode of denoting and organizing *elsewheres*.

3. THE COGITO OF THE CRITIC

If the unity of Racine's drama refers us on to that of a Racinian Cogito, and if, as indicated by our analyses in the previous section, this Racinian Cogito cannot be reached other than in and by means of Racine's plays, we are now led back to our first question: is this Racinian Cogito, which is not the Cogito of Jean Racine, that of his characters? That would be to forget that Hermione, Orestes, and Pyrrhus are not real existents: the only Cogito that can be apprehended in them is that of Racine as he writes, the actor as he or she plays, or the reader as he reads *Andromaque*. "Existential psychoanalysis" is easily said; but psychoanalysis *of whom, by whom, why*, and *how*? Here are the elements of my own answer to these questions on the theoretical plane. In the first place, the only Cogito that criticism can know is *that of the critic in the process of reflecting on Racine's plays*, in other words, the Cogito of *reflection*. If, as shown by our previous analyses (section 1 above), the work acquires consistence by a synthetic unification — in the heart of my own temporality — of the discontinuous experiences by means of which it gives itself to me in a succession of profiles, then it is indeed true, as Raymond Picard bitterly laments, that "the work is no longer in the work" (*Nouvelle critique*, p. 114); as Corneille's Sertorius said of Rome: "it is wholly where I am." Which does not mean, of course, that I in any way at all "invent" the work, but that it *constitutes itself*, literally, *through me*. For the work has never been "in" the work except in the wholly illusory sense cherished by a simpleminded realism. In the first place, on the level of perception, although the work taken as an aesthetic object does indeed exist outside the consciousness, as book or canvas, that object has no meaning, any more than any thing, other than through and for a consciousness: it is the critic's consciousness that in this respect, like any perceiving consciousness, constitutes the meaning as it uncovers it. It is through my looking that this blue, this green, this red form a colored structure, by my reading that the dried ink on the pages becomes Racine's lines. But that is not all: the work of art is imaginary, its materiality is nothing more than the analogon of a meaning that goes beyond it. This colored structure does not become an annunciation or a crucifixion; this dried sediment does not speak of hope or grief except insofar as a human look projects its own possibles into them and transcends their crude materiality. The meaning of the painting is always in suspense on the painting, or rather beyond the painting, never "in" the painting. The meaning of Racine's text is not "in" Racine's text: it is no more than the infinite reverberation, prologation, echo, on every level from the most immediate to the most subtle and most distant, of the human experience that is radiating toward us through a specific language. Whatever he does then, the critic is in the full sense of the word the *developer* of the work: there is no work other than through him (which is, moreover, why modern writers, having grasped this fact, are now attempting to assign to the reader in an explicit way the creative role that he has in any case always and inevitably played.) Nothing could be more futile than the fantasy nursed by those critics who are so terrified of their own shadows that they dream of "effacing themselves in the presence of a text that did not wait for them in order to exist" (letter to *Le Monde*, 13 November 1965).[3] Epistemologically this self-effacement is a piece of silliness, morally it is cowardice. It is impossible to posit Racine and his works for oneself as entities existing in themselves, so that all you have to do is stick them all together again, using some method that will ultimately vanish of its own accord — a self-liquidating summum that will leave nothing behind but a number of objective significations glittering in all their purity. The only reality is the consciousness of the critic (or else of the historian) focusing, through the totalization of his own experience of the texts or stage representations, on a signifying totality that he apprehends only in fragments and at variable levels of comprehension and perception.[4] In other terms, articulating the various meanings of Racine's drama in order to reconstitute its inner process cannot be anything, for the critic, but the unveiling, by means of a reflexive examination of himself, all that he discovers, all that seeks to escape him, in the course of his patient and passionate quest. Put very precisely, the Racinian Cogito, which must be laid bare if we are to grasp the profound coherence of Racine's plays, is the critic's Cogito molding itself to the type of existence that manifests itself and communicates itself through the relations that are lived out by Racine's characters and reexperienced, reworked, *reflected on* by the critic's consciousness.

We must therefore not be afraid to go on and say that psychoanalysis of Racinian drama is *psychoanalysis of the psychoanalyst*. (This is also true to a certain degree of Freudian practice, since any decipherment of man, however objective it tries to be, inevitably has its reference point in the subjectivity of whoever undertakes it, and is thus what Barthes, borrowing from psychology, calls "a projection test.") This untranscendable situation of fact explains why no criticism, as I posited earlier, can lay claim to an objective type of truth. Nor, however, is there any question of returning to some sort of ineffable "subjective" truth. Criticism is not a whirling dervish dance. If, in accordance with our postulate, a work of art is nothing but a particular mode

270

CRITICISM AS EXISTENTIAL PSYCHOANALYSIS

of the apparition of the other, then our analyses so far mean simply this: the "meaning" of a work, like the "meaning" of behavior, is nothing but the synthetic unification by my own consciousness of the manifestations of the Other, against the background of a common intersubjectivity. The consciousness of the Other is never given to me as such, and yet "there is" knowledge of others: literary communication is neither inferior nor superior to this general communication, of which it constitutes a particular case. Although it is never complete (there is neither fusion nor identification with the Other), it does admit *degrees* of penetration and truth, according to the quality of my adhesion, of my responsiveness, of my openness. The relations of the Racinian universe are *reflected* by the consciousness of the critic, we said. Let us add: by his attentive and *equipped* consciousness. Inso far as the critic's Cogito possesses a possibility of self-elucidation more complete at one moment than another, insofar as there is a history, and in particular a history of thought, there is progress in the awareness that can be achieved of the self and of others, or a progressive clarification of the fundamental relations of existence by a philosophic reflection that has achieved a higher degree of maturity and precision.

The synthetic unification of Racine's drama by the critic's consciousness is thus in no sense gratuitous: it does not produce an objective type of truth (no one, unless it be God, "sees into the hearts and souls of men"; no one can claim to know the truth of the Other in the sense that the physicist knows the truths of his molecules and atoms); but it does offer what Merleau-Ponty cogently termed a *concrete grasp*, a possibility of limited and pragmatic verification by ceaselessly renewed contact with its object. So it is indeed a projection test, in the sense that it makes possible the exact and detailed projection of a signifying network that does not just integrate the greatest "quantity" of meaning but also *integrates it qualitatively in an intelligible manner* (1), thereby enabling me to test the concrete validity of the Racinian dialectic that I constitute against the ensemble of different and divergent significations isolated by positive researches. (On this point I therefore take a position opposed to that of Barthes, when he speaks of "integrating — in the mathematical sense of the term-

— the greatest possible quantity of Proustian language" [*Essais*, p. 255]. The "integration" of literary meaning can never be of that type.) It is impossible, nevertheless, to accept the Cartesian optimism of Sartre, who makes this "test" into a sort of scientific proof. You will remember the passage quoted earlier (from *Sainte Genet*, p. 517; cf. chapter 6 above). The critic's subjectivity, in this view, can be used as a "developer" that will make visible the objectivity of the work. "Conjecture, whether true or false, is a deciphering tool. If true, it is filled out by the evidence; if false, it is erased in favor of the fresh paths to which it points." But in criticism, unlike mathematics, there is no object that can come to "fill out" the evidence, no object that will at any point yield up to our consciousness a translucid essence in which the "thing in itself" is given to us in its integrality. In criticism, "evidence" must always remain the evidence *of someone* (whereas 2 + 2 = 4 is the evidence given by everyone, that is, by no one), and what is evident for Sartre absolutely does not have to be so for another.[5] At no moment does a happy conjunction of good subjective "developer" with the being of his object produce an immutable truth that is the "definitive" Racine or Mallarmé. Halfway between the evident and the aribirary, criticism's truth, just like philosophy's, *has never finished its search for itself.* Though partial (always adhering to a subjectivity it therefore remains a particular viewpoint), it nevertheless leads out into reality, which it attains, though without ever being able to spread it out, as though on a table, for observation; it offers a more or less precise, more or less correct grasp on the world of significations at which it aims, without ever attaining a total annexation. This apprehension of a relative-absolute is precisely what characterizes perceptive truth, and criticism does in fact present itself, epistemologically, as a particular form of the perception of the Other. This perception, which I have termed "existential psychoanalysis" (section 1 of this chapter), must be more closely examined, so that I can give more precise answers to the questions posed at the beginning of this section.

1. Psychoanalysis *of whom?* Psychoanalysis of *the work*, and not the *man*; of an imaginary *existence*, not of a real *life*. For the reasons

examined near the beginning of section 2 of this chapter, there is an ontological primacy of work over author, even though, whenever possible, comprehension of the work should progress by way of the nature of its relation to its author and, in a sense, integrate that relation into the totality of its meaning. This dispenses with the double objection that Raymond Picard rightly put forward against the psychoanalytic approach: that it sacrifices the specificity of the literary structures, and that it does so in favor of the dubious reconstruction of a psychic entity that ceased to exist centuries ago, and about which we are apt to know almost nothing. Far from sacrificing the literary structures, it is precisely upon those structures that our analysis will be brought to bear, to the degree in which their coherence expresses a certain vision of the world, which is to say a certain type of relations of existence.

2. Psychoanalysis *by whom*? By a critic, himself situated affectively and historically in existence, a fact that both makes possible and limits the communication between reader and work. The only possible foundation of the permanence of art is the transhistoricity of existential structures (see the end of chapter 8 above). To the degree in which "I" is also the Other, the man of today can still apprehend the human meaning of the Lascaux cave paintings or rediscover the Racinian Cogito. But if the law of perception which states that all disclosure of reality is at the same time concealment of reality is also applicable to the writer, and is the justification of criticism as an acitvity directed at making the writer's work explicit, then that law must also of course apply to the critic himself: his look is not an absolute bird's-eye view, nor is his analysis atemporal. He approaches the work from his own point of view, situated in space and time, rooted in a personal engagement. Everyday language describes a spectator very accurately as being in a "good position" or a "bad position" for knowing something. Similarly, one can be in a good or bad position historically when it comes to evaluating a work. The moments of history are no more equal in value than are positions in space. It is therefore no coincidence that an intelligence as acute as Voltaire's should have been closed to the plays of Corneille; nor is it purely by chance that the Pléiade poets, forgotten for two centuries, should

273

have emerged from obscurity with the romantic movement. There are historical sympathies just as there are individual affinities. Certain periods communicate with one another spontaneously; others lose all contact and remain oblivious of one another. The historicity of criticism is such that at the very moment when it unveils one horizon, it obscures another. It confers vision and blindness in equal measure. It would be wholly futile to look for a single epoch commensurable with all other epochs. No psychoanalysis is innocent; no psychoanalysis is complete. All psychoanalysis offers promise and compromise in exactly balanced proportions.

3. Psychoanalysis *why*? We have already observed that the critic confronts his object in much the same situation as the psychoanalyst does his subject. We must draw the radical conclusions inherent in this fact. Since the critic is concerned with elucidating — to the degree made possible by his new means — a meaning that was not, on principle, *capable of elucidation* to the same degree by the writer (cf. the discussions of lucidity and ambiguity in chapters 4 and 7 above) or by writers of another age, and since the critic's task is to make the discourse we call literature "speak," the critic, far from limiting himself to summing up the conscious intentions and processes of the writer, will often be led to *make the work say the contrary of what its author is saying to us*. In his *Qu'est-ce que la littérature*? Sartre showed quite rightly that, "though it is true that the essence of the literary work is liberty revealing itself, and willing itself to be totally itself, as a summons to the liberty of all other men, it is also true that differing forms of oppression, by hiding from men that they were free, have concealed from authors all or part of this essence" (p. 189). If the liberty of the writer, like that of every man, is a liberty in a particular situation and alienated by that very situation, then literature is *alienated* "when it has not achieved explicit consciousness of its autonomy and submits to temporal powers or to an ideology," and *abstract* "when it has not yet acquired the plenary view of its essence" (p. 190). In other words, if literature creates for itself, in each age and with each writer, its own myth, then criticism's task will be in part one of *demystification*. This in no

274

way entails a diminution in the value of literature: by disclosing the writer's alienation, criticism always shows also *how his work transcends it* (this transcendence is in fact the first mark of great creations); by making the "abstract" view that a literature has of itself "concrete," one is not diminishing but adding to the fullness of its meaning. In this respect I am even prepared to say that the aim of literary psychoanalysis is a *certain cure of literature*, insofar as any psychoanalytic cure, by liberating man from the personal myths in which he has imprisoned himself, restores the man to himself. This notion will provoke a great deal of teeth gnashing among lovers of that eternally pure and immutable form of disembodied Literature that lies embalmed in our textbooks; their kind of love is simply an idealist perversion, a curious necrophilia whose passion is spent on mummies.

Just as the overall meaning of a life, as it appears to another, may be exactly the opposite of the signification consciously willed in each action of it, so the meaning of a literary work is often the contrary of its author's express intention. We know that the politically moderate works of Rousseau, or the determinedly conservative works of Balzac, have a revolutionary meaning when replaced in their historical context. As I myself have tried to show, Corneille's plays, which *intend* to proclaim the triumph of a heroic liberty, are *in fact* the long story of its failure. And if this example of mine is accused of heresy, then I shall be in the company of a most unexpected companion at the stake in the person of Raymond Picard, who is not normally associated with such sacrilegious activities; for he has shown precisely the same thing, as it happens, in the case of Racine. When he tells us that it is "wrongly that Phèdre's consciousness of her responsibility has been opposed to her powerlessness. Phèdre is not truly powerless. She believes herself to be the victim of celestial vengeance; but the gods are nothing other than the personification of our own limits; and Phèdre knows that the demand for liberty is infinite. . . .Phèdre is a witness (Racine, *Oeuvres complètes*, Pléiade ed., vol. 1, pp. 742–43), Picard is offering us a very model of existential psychoanalysis: although Phèdre "believes herself" to be the victim of celestial vengeance, the critic-psychoanalyst demystifies this *false consciousness*; the gods are nothing other than the personification of our own limits (and notice the "nothing other than," so dear to the psychoanalyst, his trademark even.) But this false consciousness is nothing other than a form of bad conscience, or of bad faith. Phèdre *knows* that the demand for liberty is infinite; her celebrated "powerlessness" is nothing but the form her abdication takes. This so-called tragedy of fatality, in which some have tried to find an expression of Jansenism, is in fact a statement on liberty, and "there is much more human-ism in this play than there is Christianity" (p. 743). This very Sartrean analysis seems to me a convincing one, and Picard is quite right about Racine, even though he is *contradicting Racine*. For there can be no doubt that the author, on this point, thinks just as his character does. In his preface, Racine expressly pre-sents Phèdre as being ensnared in her fatal passion "by her destiny and by the anger of the Gods," and, he tells us "her crime is rather a punishment from the Gods than an impulse of her will." It is hardly possibly to be more explicit than that. Racine, like Phèdre, believes in the gods and fate; from *La Thébaïde* to *Athalie*, his entire work exists in order to depict man crushed by his race, by his heredity, by history — in a word, by those gods who in the last plays are finally called God, and beneath whose power human liberty wavers like a taper flame in a hur-ricane. But Racine is deceiving himself and trying to deceive us: "Phèdre is not truly powerless." Racine, like Phèdre herself, and despite himself, is bearing witness on behalf of liberty. So Picard comes along and demystifies him: he restores to Racine Racine's own *truth*, obscured by his own historical alienation and three centuries of stultifying commentaries. In short, Picard fully assumes his responsibility as a critic: engaged, himself committed to the hilt by the meaning he reveals in it, he shows us, to their greater glory, that Racine's plays *mean* the opposite of what they *say*. In doing so he is contradicting himself; but he is psychoanalyzing and curing Racine.[6]

4. Psychoanalysis *how*? Needless to say, when I speak here of "psychoanalysis" and "cure," they are metaphorical expressions, intended to suggest the parallelism of certain procedures and not an identity of means and ends. Parallelism of procedures there

276

certainly is in fact, insofar as criticism, like psychoanalysis, sets itself the aim of acquiring a certain type of knowledge about Another (through the profound unity of intention that draws together multiple and divergent manifestations); insofar too as both presuppose toward their objects an attitude not of detachment, like that of the physicist or chemist, but of controlled sympathy (the psychoanalyst is radically involved in the analysis he performs, as is the critic in his interpretation). But the ends could never be identical; first, because writers are not sick — or if they are then it is a sickness of being, inseparable from our condition and incurable; second, because the critic is dealing with works not with men, or, more exactly, if he is directing his attention at a man, it is the man as he gives himself in his works and not in his gestures or actions. The result is a complete variance in means; whereas the psychoanalyst can encourage his patients to talk away on his couch for months or years, the critic, more often than not, has to understand the "inflections of loved voices long since silenced." Even were he investigating living authors, and even supposing an optimum case in which he is on intimate terms with them, as Sartre was with Genet, that may strengthen but can in no way change the critic's position. The literary meaning of which he is in search still yields itself up to him solely through the written signs; it does not properly exist other than at the level of the writing, or rather, insofar as it is brought back to life by a reading of those signs. Which means that the "meaning" a critic educes can never be as verifiable, in its results, as a psychoanalyst's "meaning". It also means that the critic can never be as complete, since he is working on limited expressive systems which have been given once and for all, invariables constructed in isolation from any suggestion on the part of the investigator. Whereas the physician collaborates with his patient, that is, with a living freedom which is modified thanks to this living contact it experiences, the critic communicates through the written signs with an immutable or at least an imprisoned freedom, with which and over which he has no influence. In consequence, although the critic can assert a *conviction*, he can never legitimately claim a *certitude*. The physician, by using a process of elucidation in which he has the patient's cooperation, can overcome resistances

277

in the other in order to bring him toward a full consciousness of himself; what remains forever *resistant* in what I have termed the unsurmountable ambiguity of the literary work is, precisely, a freedom eternally off limits and out of reach. Artistic creation therefore has a way of evading us that makes any decipherment of it forever conjectural. In this respect, Roland Barthes is right in emphasizing what he terms the *moiré* or "frustrated" nature of literary meaning, even when it seems most evident.

At the same time, the critic does have one enormous advantage over the psychoanalyst: he is dealing with "patients" who present him in their works, *already given* in a latent state, with the very analysis that he is attempting to perform. Whereas the expression of the sick or everyday consciousness is obscured by fantasies or fragmented in unmeaning talk, on which the interpreter must confer from outside the signifying unity they reject, literary expression, on the other hand, represents the deepest degree of consciousness that man can achieve of his own condition: even if that consciousness is partially alienated, the great work always transcends the alienation toward a radical unveiling of human reality. Banality or sickness is the tragedy of meaning in flight from itself; literature is the Advent of meaning finding itself. The critic's task is thereby both complicated and simplified. Complicated, because the fullness of the meaning he is attempting to liberate is always in excess of his attempts. Simplified, because the synthesis of the meaning has already been accomplished for him. And this methodological aspect of "existential psychoanalysis" should be emphasized. It is in no way a question of employing *modern* categories to comprehend *old* works, which would constitute an anachronism and, if carried far enough, an abuse. It was on these grounds that I myself have been criticized for employing a dialectic of Sartrean freedom to decipher Corneille's plays when in fact, I was told, the schema upon which Corneille's attitudes to freedom are framed was a Molinist one. Application of contemporary intellectual instruments in this way to works of the past is, it was added, an arbitrary and antihistoric procedure. So a critic who confined himself to a recent psychological or ontological theory in order to "comprehend" the past would be as ridiculous as those men of science who believe that

278

"good" science, the only science that counts, is always the very latest. This objection would be valid if the instruments of philosophic comprehension were of the same type as those of scientific knowledge, which is to say *external to their object*. But that is in fact not the case, and the best reply to this objection, which Georges Poulet was kind enough to suggest for my consideration in an exchange of letters, is to be found, I think, in a very fine passage from one of his own letters that I hope he will allow me to quote here: "Nothing is easier than to reveal in every age, without forcing, without 'cheating,' a psychoanalysis, a phenomenology, an existentialism that were the creations sui generis of that age. One might even say that the essential function of literature in every age is precisely to constitute itself within the philosophy that is always more fundamental, more inward, more closely linked to human experience than the "official" metaphysic of that same age. This means that there can be no question of injecting the existentialism of Kierkegaard, of Nietzsche, or of Heidegger into Pascal; what we must do is to make visible the authentically existentialist ground that is Pascal's characteristic feature (and which always has been — even for Pascal). "This extremely important passage seems to me to define very precisely the nature of the literary and philosophic communication that is criticism's foundation. It does, however, forget one thing: although the literature of every age may constitute itself within this "more fundamental" and "more inward" philosophy, thus defining that zone of transhistoric comprehension whose existence I for my part have never ceased to argue, it does not follow that the different moments of history are equivalent. To say that history *progresses* from the seventeenth to the twentieth century is to say, as Sartre did of the writer, that man cannot achieve the same consciousness of his own existence in every age, that certain fundamental aspects of his condition are obscured from him by the variable nature of his alienations; the progress of thought, which is inseparable from the movement of history, therefore consists in a process of making the totality of existential structures *increasingly explicit*. Although this does not mean that we ought to transfer Kierkegaard's or Nietzsche's conclusions to Pascal, nevertheless the "authentically existentialist

279

ground" we find in Pascal is not fully apprehensible except in the light of Kierkegaard and Nietzsche, just as we can "recognize" the Cogito in Saint Anselm only because it was later clearly isolated and revealed in Descartes. Since the critic is himself rooted in his own history, his comprehension of the past must inevitably be reached through his comprehension of the present; it is only retrospectively, thanks to the psychoanalysis or the existentialism evolved *since*, that he is better able to grasp the meaning of Racinian analysis or Pascal's existentialism. It is the Sartrean schema of freedom that makes it possible to comprehend what was valid in the Molinist schema, and insofar as literature, in Poulet's own words, constitutes a philosophy that is "more closely linked to human experience that the 'official' metaphysics of that same age," it is precisely the greatness of Corneille's plays that they embody, in an implicit state, a dialectic of liberty that was not to be made theoretically explicit until three centuries later.

To psychoanalyze Racine, to existentialize Pascal, is therefore in no way to commit an anachronism or violate those authors' works. As Georges Poulet rightly observes, a veritable "augustinian psychoanalysis" already exists in Racine and the Jansenists—"a conception of the human being as being composed of a surface and an underneath, the underneath being in itself obscure, impenetrable, and yet the center and determining principle of all our actions and all our thoughts." True, but to understand Racine in the twentieth century does not mean understanding him in terms of *his* psychoanalysis; it means understanding him in terms of *ours*, insofar as ours is a dialectically transcended version of his, which is to say its conservation and also its negation. Our psychoanalysis does not approach Racine's plays from the outside; we do not impose it on them by force: it is simply a reworking *at a historically more advanced stage of elucidation* of the thematization already constituted in Racine's own work. Moreover, this is precisely the same relation as that between Freudian theory and Greek mythology: the former was evolved — on the basis of a new historical situation of knowledge — by a process of reflection on themes in the latter hitherto not repossessed by reflexive consciousness. The same goes for philosophy: as Merleau-Ponty observed, if Descartes, Spinoza, or Leibniz still retain their truth today, it is insofar as our own research coincides with theirs while transcending it. "Despite appearances, the system has never been anything but a language (and invaluable as such) for translating a Cartesian, Spinozian, or Leibnizian mode of self-situation in relation to being, and for the philosophy to endure, it is sufficient that the particular relation should remain problematical, that it should not be taken as going without saying . . . It is this same relation that we are today attempting to formulate directly, and it is for this reason that philosophy feels itself at home wherever it occurs" (*Signes*, p. 199). The various comprehensions of man that constitute this *philosophia perennis* are thus not discontinuous casts of the lead made separately by each age to sound the deeps of our condition. Pascal's truth is not, as Poulet seems to say, given once and for all in Pascal (which would lead us back, in another form, to that over publicized "historical admiration"); history is not immutable, and Pascal's truth, for us, is *truth that has become*: it is that Pascalian relation to being that subsists beyond the explosion and disappearance of the system, and that we, from our point of view, in our situation, can assume afresh. Which leads me to fill in briefly here the outline of the relations between criticism and philosophy given earlier. Although I have claimed that the destiny of the two procedures is linked, that is not to say that they are identical; although it is the task of criticism to search for a type of intelligibility evolved in close proximity to philosophy, criticism and philosophy are nevertheless different. They differ first in their objects: that of philosophy is more general, since it is attempting to repossess the structures of existence in all its manifestations, while that of criticism is directed solely at the expression of human reality in one particular area — art. But neither is literary criticism a philosophy of art, even though it always ultimately implies one: philosophic comprehension, even though it may be concrete, works from the individual to the unversal; critical comprehension, following in this the movement of the literary expression upon which it bears, works from the universal to the individual. What it has to grasp is not the nature of tragedy *in general* but *this particular* tragedy by Racine. Philosophy *abstracts* the human meaning that literature *embodies*. Corresponding to this difference in direction there is necessarily a difference in method and a difference in spirit.

Despite the knowledge that "the System" is impossible and forever in abeyance within history, philosophical inquiry — and this is its characteristic paradox — must nevertheless constitute itself as systematic. Philosophy proper exists only at this price (which is what distinguishes the philosopher from the thinker or the essayist), and from this point of view the reflection of men like Heidegger or Sartre is no less "systematic" than that of their predecessors. This paradox, or contradiction, is the very motive force of an apprehension of the structures of being that must, on principle, strive to be total. Whether phenomenological, rationalist, or Marxist, the "system" — to use Merleau-Ponty's terms again — is the unavoidable *language* of philosophy, even though philosophy is never perdurable other than above or below the level of its system. Can and should literary criticism be systematic in this sense? Such is the opinion of those criticisms which take their inspiration from the human sciences, and which aim at the institution of a language sufficiently rigorous to become a closed and self-sufficient comprehension that will grasp and hold the essential of the work of art within it. Personally, however, I do not believe that the language of criticism can ever become the perfectly articulated logos that the human sciences and philosophy, each in its own way, are striving to be. I have several times been reproached for my *eclecticism*. It is implied that by referring to the "existential philosophies" in the plural, without ever making it clear which one in particular I mean, by making use of categories taken at random, sometimes from Heidegger, sometimes from Sartre, sometimes from Merleau-Ponty, not to mention convenient foraging expeditions back into Hegel or Marx or even Descartes, I am just using anything that happens to suit my ends, to the detriment of all intellectual consistency. "What exactly is your system then?" I was asked one day, exactly as one might ask a card player to make a frank show of his hand. I have no hesitation in confessing that I have no "system" whatever, and that the existential analysis I am championing here neither proposes nor presupposes one. But this fact, which in the philosopher would constitute an essential flaw, seems to me in the case of the critic to be a necessary virtue, and I shall explain why. Criticism can never be the *application* to literature of a method of decipherment evolved *in isolation from it*, in the sense that we speak of the practical "application" of the various sciences. Criticism is nothing but a certain *experimentation on literature* capable of being conducted at various levels. The immediate signification of a theatrical performance is extracted and expressed by the newspaper review; the ultimate signification of a play, or rather its significating horizon, cannot be grasped in the same way. Far from the various significations experienced during the various modes of contact automatically converging to form a happy unity, they are more often than not contradictory, and the search for a global meaning is nothing other than an effort to think and link those contradictions, to situate oneself at a point where one can attempt to *comprehend* them in the very strictest sense, and to *resolve* them. That point, however, is a *virtual* point, not a real one. It is a signpost for our research, not its finishing post. It is, as I said earlier, not a certitude but a conviction; to be even more precise, I would say that it is a *manner of proceeding*. To attempt actually to locate the point where the contradictions are resolved, where the totality of meaning becomes actual, where man becomes diaphanous for man, where the Other is repossessed as Self, and the Self coincides perfectly with itself — even to postulate such a possibility, merely as a principle and an ultimate and under the disguise of historical materialsim or Sartrean existentialism — means a return to the irrational hubris of Hegelian rationalism, the enthroning of absoulute idealism under a cloak of science. We approach the center of a work or life asymptotically, coming ever closer yet never reaching it, for the very good reason that this "center" never at any moment exists: it is always *still to be*. That is the meaning of Merleau-Ponty's objection to existential analysis as conceived by Sartre: "If I have difficulty in recognizing the 'fundamental choice' made by the absolute Descartes that Sartre speaks of — the Descartes who lived and wrote once and for all three centuries ago — it is perhaps because at no moment did that Descartes himself coincide with Descartes: what he is now to our eyes in his writings he became only gradually, by a process of reaction of himself on himself, and the notion of grasping him totally, at source, is perhaps illusory if Descartes is not some 'central intuition,' an absolute character, but an originally hesitant discourse that affirms itself by experience and exercise, that learns itself little by little, and never altogether ceases to aim at that very thing which it has resolutely excluded" (*Signes*, p. 165). This center, the fundamental meaning of Cartesianism, reveals its presence perpetually to the critic, as indeed it did to Descartes himself, as a *horizon* toward which the divergent lines of Cartesianism seem to converge; but the specific characteristic of a horizon is that it recedes when we think we are drawing close to it: one can direct one's path toward it but can never pitch camp on it. To the degree in which the ambiguity of human existence is insurmountable the ambiguity of its concrete expression in literature is unresolvable. We must just make up our mind to that; as Du Bos aptly put it, criticism remains forever an *approximation*.

I would simply add (and it makes all the difference in the world): a *methodical* approximation. I have never believed that literary communication is an ineffable communion, and this book asserts the contrary. Criticism certainly requires sympathy, but a *well-equipped* sympathy, as I said earlier, a sympathy backed up by all the pertinent forms of knowledge its age has to offer. The problem lies in the correct use of that knowledge; because if knowledge without conscience ruins the soul, as Rabelais said, it also ruins art. If it is true that criticism is not the explanation but the making explicit of literary works, then it is the work itself that must indicate the nature of the tools appropriate to its investigation.[7] Roland Barthes saw this very clearly when he wrote that "there are no prohibitions in criticism, only requirements, and also, in consequence, resistances" and that criticism must seek for its own "pertinence" in its object. But if that is so, then it is impossible, as Barthes would like, to be given a clear indication *once and for all*, at the outset, of the particular kind of process needed to make a particular work explicit, so that one can then go on to constitute one's criticism in the form of a circular language endowed with perfect internal coherence. I believe that criticism should renounce this desire for purity and admit to itself what it really is: *a bastard language*. For it is not just generally but at every bend in the road, as it were, that our comprehension

284

must be modeled on its object. Otherwise it will eventually lose sight of that object, and of itself, through its absorption in its own system. It is not such and such a work that requires a psychological elucidation while another demands an ideological approach; it is such and such an aspect, such and such a moment within the work that requires to be understood on the psychological plane, another aspect on the ideological plane, and some on both planes (and many others) simultaneously. The critical gaze is not the eye of a motionless camera, stationed at the correct spot, arranged at the correct angle; it is, in J. Starobinski's apt phrase, a "living eye", which molds its gaze to its object by means of a succession of tentative observations. Criticism is *the continuity of an end sought by a discontinuity of means.* To say that it is "unifying" and "totalitarian" is to say that it remains forever this side of both unity and totality; to say that it is open is to say that it is imperfect. It never isolates an ideal essence; it rediscovers, with more or less success, the movement of an existence. As the philosophic Cogito never repossesses its prereflexivity, so what I have termed the critical Cogito never acquires translucidity. And the best proof is a reductio ad absurdum: whenever criticism attempts to become the rigid application of any kind of system of decipherment (psychological, sociological, aesthetic, philosophic, etc.), it invariably ends up by eliminating whatever in its object resists such application, instead of incorporating that resistance into its account and adapting its own reference grid accordingly. In this respect, however hastily penned, Raymond Picard's objections to "reductive" criticisms are justified, whatever the mode of reduction involved. Their dissection ends up by dismembering the work, their restructuration by destructuring it, their explanation by conjuring it out of existence.

Does this mean, then, that this "methodical approximation" — in total contrast to Descartes's Doubt, which brought the dazzling certainty of his Method into such abrupt and definitive existence — is also to be a *methodological* approximation? I shall be frank and honest with you — yes. To the question at the head of this section — psychoanalysis how? — there is no answer capable of encapsulation in a formula. But what sort of analysis is it that has no method, it may be objected? The analysis

that I am proposing is less a matter of method than of a fundamental orientation of critical research; it defines not so much
a certain sphere of knowledge as a certain climate of comprehension. There is no royal road to the inmost heart of literary works;
no "method" that constitutes a total cover policy; no knowledge,
but a know-how. Since literature is the expression of a concrete
vision of our destiny, and since the various philosophies of existence have set themselves precisely the task of elucidating the
concrete, it seems to me only natural that criticism should make
use of their contribution, which is to say the conceptual tools that
they have forged for themselves and the always limited and partial
answers that they offer. What I am putting forward is therefore
less a *method* than a *frame* for research, inside which the analysis
must maneuver with responsiveness and flexibility. Thus it is clear
that a study of the look in Racine will spontaneously allow itself
to be guided by the study of the look in Sartre, especially since
the relations of aggressivity and sadomasochistic fixation that Sartrean phenomenology reveals are extremely apposite to the world
of Racine's plays. It is this schema that J. Starobinski made use
of in his "Racine et la poétique du regard" (*L'Oeil vivant*). But
Emmanuel Mounier, in his *Introduction aux existentialismes*, has
clearly shown the degree to which Sartre's analysis is both schema-
tic and inadequate: the loving and amplifying look that the poet
directs at being, the look of a Blake, a Hugo, a Claudel, is not
reducible to the outline provided in *Being and Nothingness*; the
critic will thus be forced to turn to other, different philosophies,
personalist or otherwise, if he wishes to remain faithful on this
point to his object. Since no philosophy is commensurable with
the totality of human experience, we shall therefore be led to
look to them all in turn, seeking illumination on that aspect of
human existence which each has elucidated best; we shall be led
to correct Heidegger with Sartre, and Sartre with Merleau-Ponty,
perhaps to return in the end — for works such as those of Corneille which rest entirely upon the human relations of master
to slave — to the schemas so admirably evolved by Hegel. Is the
critic then a sort of invertebrate philosophic animal, a lamia coi-
ling itself around its texts as chance or opportunism dictates?
And how exactly is it going to accomplish this much vaunted

"integration" of significations that neither the human sciences nor history are capable of achieving? How can an ideological position that is not itself integrated ever provide us with the principle of an integration?

My answer is to repeat of criticism what I have already said apropos of psychoanalysis: like the most beautiful girl in the world, it can only give what it has to give. What it doesn't have, and what it can never have, is a theoretical system capable of providing an *actual* totalization of the meanings of a work. It is enough, for its task to be a useful and fruitful one, that it shall possess the principle of a *possible* totalization, which is to say a certain fundamental comprehension of human reality and of the way in which that reality engenders meanings. This, then, is my theoretical reply to the charge of eclecticism. Whatever their differences or divergences, the existential philosophies offer a perfectly defined type of comprehension, within which it is permissible to move to and fro, even in contradictory directions. The real ideological eclecticism in this context would consist in taking a pinch of Platonism here, a dash of Kant there, shaking on a little instant Hegel, and then stirring the whole lot up into a sort of vast and vague Russian salad. (One must distinguish, of course, between such an ideological eclecticism and the procedure that consists, for all modern thought, in the combination and integration of diverse aspects of psychoanalysis, sociology, etc., into the practical and necessary synthesis of a unified comprehension.) On the model of that valid definition of a life as perpetual change within a permanence, the philosophies of existence constitute successive and even contrary illuminations of our fundamental relations all within the frame of a single procedural approach. Their categories, various though they may be, all gravitate around a common center; their contradictions are articulated around the same problems and pass through the same points of comprehension, to the clarification of which they all contribute. Thus, to return to the example already used, an analysis of the look in literature can and should, as the necessity arises, make use of the interpretations of Sartre, of Merleau-Ponty, of Mounier, or of Marcel, according to their pertinence to the work under scrutiny, without this involving the slightest infidelity or the slightest incoherence: the contradictions here are not sterile antinomies of petrified terms (of the spiritualism-materialism, realism-idealism kind), but mobile relations of dialectical complementarity.[8] In short, all that can and ought to be required of true criticism is that it should be a *philosophic semantics*, that it should possess an intelligible theory of meaning, and should be conscious — as far as it historically can be, at the moment in time when it evolves — of the essential relations to self, to others, and to the world on the basis of which all human significations are constituted.

4. WHAT IS CRITICISM?

Rejecting that "criticism of verisimilitude" so justly attacked by Roland Barthes (*Critique et vérité*, pp. 14 et seq.) — a conglomeration of all the platitudes, contradictions, and clichés that go to make up the "good taste" and "good style" of the traditional commentaries — a criticism worthy of the name will thus begin by being an autocriticism. It must have a conscious knowledge of its own postulates in order to lay firm claim to its own certainties. In that lies its rigor, which is in no way a rigidity: it knows where it is going, it knows what it is seeking, or rather the direction in which it must seek. It knows what does and what does not lie within its capacity to find. It knows its limits. It knows that its illuminations will never amount to total elucidation. It knows that it is always concealing to exactly the degree in which it reveals, and that its process of totalization can never, for that reason, achieve a totality of knowledge, or its striving toward unification a unity of meanings. It knows that it is a living and therefore still uncompleted dialectic. True, it knows it has the tools to circumscribe with ever increasing precision the radiant focus at the work's heart (and that is why it implies a *frame* of thought); but it also knows that it can never establish the exact equation of that profound intentionality with all the significations it presents (and that is why it can never be a *system*). Merleau-Ponty said that a concrete philosophy is never a happy philosophy: in this regard, the same is true of a concrete criticism. Both are aware that contrary to the skeptic's belief, there is indeed a truth of the relations of man to the world; but they also know that all

288

expression of that truth is partial and "profiled," and that no summation of all those profiles is possible. We must accept that, as theoretical enterprises go, criticism, like philosophy, is a torture of Tantalus: they both strive every time, with all their might, to make a book "definitive" that never can be so.

To the question asked at the end of chapter 6, "Is criticism's misfortune a tragedy?" we must therefore answer, it might seem, with a frank yes. But to situate the problem, as we have done up till now, entirely *on the level of knowledge*, is to pose it incorrectly. The new criticism is deluding itself no less than the old when it believes itself to stand *in a pure relation of objectivity* to the work, when it sees itself as the basis upon which it is constituting a cumulative and impersonal body of knowledge. The "critic's Cogito," analyzed earlier in outline, would be radically falsified if we saw it as a mere process of theoretical construction: it is first and foremost *a practical undertaking*; it is not a particular type of knowledge, it is praxis. I said earlier (section 3 of this chapter) that an existential criticism cannot be grounded on anything other than the existence of the critic. And we must now follow that statement through to its conclusions. The error shared by many adherents of new and traditional schools alike is to believe that their activity is limited in fact to providing an account of *that which is*: it is implied that once the meaning and genesis of the works have been established — whether with the help of history and psychology or, more recently, of psychoanalysis and sociology, phenomenology and dialectics — there is nothing left for the critic to do, his work now being finished, but to tiptoe discreetly away. That which has been or that which is, it is assumed, is also, by definition, that which ought to be.[9] Racine or Campistron, Molière or Poisson, all are equally products of a universal determinism; each in his place and all together they are contributing to the expression of a culture, of which they appear to us as signs — albeit varying in importance and completeness — that we must then decipher. To believe that is to be totally and utterly mistaken about the very meaning of criticism. Because the critic is neither a lackey nor a spectator; neither "the public's secretary" that Sarcey claimed to be, nor a wan shadow anxiously trying to "efface himself" in the presence of the texts, like all those academic mice scuttling back to their holes at the first chance they get. Nor is the critic a scientist bent over the retorts and alembics in which literature is supposedly manufactured, or a hospital consultant preparing to utter an infallible diagnosis. Old or new, traditional or modernized, "modest" or aggressive, "prudent" or systematic, the critics of objectivity all have one thing in common (and that is why I grouped them together in this volume): they ignore, they wish or pretend to ignore, *the existence of the critic himself*, that irksome individual whom it is their dream to rid themselves of entirely, as science, once constituted, dispenses with the scientist.

This dream is an absurd dream; and this neurotic attitude of flight, already uncovered and deplored in its many different forms in previous chapters, is no more than the slenderest of excuses for evading a primary responsibility. Because as we have observed on numerous occasions during the course of this book, I do not confront a literary work as though confronting the plenitude of an object that is or that has been: the work is *still to be*, and *I make it be*. (The actor, less simpleminded than many critics, knows that any text is always *still to be interpreted*.) And further, we should be misleading ourselves if we were to draw the conclusions of this solely on an *epistemological* plane, as we have done up till now. The meaning that the literary work bears within it is not a dead possibility, inscribed in things once and for all: it is a possibility held captive within an ensemble of signs, but which I can liberate and bring back to life, not in the form of signification aimed at one objective aspect or objective moment of the world or history, but as signification aimed at *me*, because it is *mine*. Glorious or shameful: Tristan and Iseut's love *judges me*; it is the very measure of my soul. *All criticism is decipherment only in order to become confrontation.* Beyond the level of the elucidation of signs, the critical act, like any act that involves our fundamental relations with others, is *a statement of values*. By this I do not mean, needless to say, deciding whether the author ought to have used the subjunctive at such and such a point instead of the indicative, and respected the rules of composition more nicely at such and such another, in the interests of producing a work that conforms to the Canons of Beauty: we can leave

290

that sort of criticism to the seventeenth-century pedants and their imitators in the twentieth. Quite simply, if any great work is an apparition of the Other, insofar as it is proffering me a vision of existence and salvation it is an appeal, from the deepest regions of itself, for my adhesion to that vision. And it is the eminent dignity of the critic that he is free to grant that adhesion or not, in admiration or revulsion, enthusiasm or indifference, love or hate. Although *Tristan et Iseut* judges me, I judge *Tristan et Iseut*. Not as a judge does a case; as a man does a man, to the degree in which every man is the judge of every other man.

Judging, these days, is less than popular; it is even a culpable action; to explain or make explicit, to structure or describe, that is criticism's vocation. "The critic's honor does not lie in praising, the critic's honor does not lie in blaming: the critic's honor is in understanding. . . . In order to understand one must be free. And free, first and foremost, of oneself" (Quoted by R. Fayolle, *La Critique*, p. 329). In a very different sense, we find as it were an echo of this prohibition proclaimed by André Suarès still reverberating in Roland Barthes's latest book: "True 'criticism' of institutions and languages does not consist in 'judging' them but in *isolating* them, in *separating* them, in *paralleling* them" (*Critique et vérité*, p. 14). And it is true that judicature must inevitably become imposture if it is exercised as the sanction of a collective conformism, thereby turning criticism, in any given society, into the watchdog of "right thinking." In this respect Barthes's mistrust is all too often justified.[10] And judgment is also pure humbug if the critic has the unbelievable pretension to believe himself in a position of "superiority" of any kind in relation to the writer. To set oneself up as a judge is, by definition, suspect: in the name of what, and of whom? Judgment, like all things, can be used well or used ill; yet it is impossible to abstain from judgment. De jure, that would be to betray the ethical obligation, imposed by any true work, of responding to its appeal. Entertaining the dream of being a sheet of clear glass, a mirror, or even a magnifying glass, is in the case of the critic an evasion that destroys the very essence of literary communication. De facto, such a neutral vacuum is impossible, and "in order to be subversive criticism has no need to judge; it need only talk about language instead of simply making use of it" (ibid.). What Barthes says is perfectly true, and since all criticism consists precisely in talking about language there is no such thing, as we have observed throughout, as "innocent" criticism. I am nevertheless left with the impression that Barthes's position on this point is equivocal, that his rejection of open judgment is partly conditioned by a personal preference for the covert judgment implicit in the manipulation of an aloof and distant language, which is a means for subjectivity to conceal rather than to reveal itself, a mode of negative revelation one might say, in the sense that we speak of a "negative" in photography. This love that Barthes has for the implicit in literature is something that has long been evident; but in criticism, whose whole endeavor is directed toward the explicit, the personal revelation should be total and open. Insofar as every work is "still to be," a transcendence of the real toward a human possible, I myself make its meaning emerge when I commit myself beyond *what is*, when I compromise myself totally by saying *what ought to be*.

For this reason, the moment when the "global meaning" emerges from the innumerable significations, the moment when we apprehend, through all the variety of its expression, the unity of an intention, that moment at which the author's "vision of the world" is revealed and which it is the aim of all criticism today to capture, is not the mere culmination of a piece of theoretical and detached research: we cannot understand others, as Suarès naïvely believed, "by freeing ourselves from ourselves," but only, as Proust knew, by searching down into the furthermost depths of ourselves. The unification of the meaning is thus a *practical requirement* of the confrontation of two men through a text, a confrontation that occurs at the point when the critic, ceasing his specialist's task of isolating the various structures with his various tools, must finally make a general judgment on the human universe that is calling for his attention; the point when, beyond the technical significations that his investigation has accumulated, he must embrace, in order to give a *yes* or *no*, the profound meaning of an experience that calls the critic himself into question, in his being and in his values. It is this concrete moment that ultimately transcends the rooted ambiguity of the work toward the synthesis of meaning, as the judge in court must go beyond the equivocal nature of human gestures and actions in the unity of his sentence: in his soul, his consciousness, and his conscience, which is to say *at his own peril*. This is what separates the domain of certitudes from that of conviction, theoretical truth from practical truth. If there is a tragedy of criticism, then it does not lie on the plane of knowledge, in the critic's failure to be God, and the failure of his science to be omniscience. If it does, it is simply the tragedy of all cognition, a tragedy of bad faith that is really, in the end, a comedy, which shows us man vainly struggling to transcend his condition. The true tragedy, here, is that of any practical enterprise in which the human condition is, on the contrary, fully assumed; it lies in that inevitable choice in which I pose myself, and if needs be oppose myself, face to face with another; it lies in the *violence* that the critical act — like any act that contains a decision about fundamental values — inevitably requires, and that the "objective" criticisms strive to conceal by shifting the responsibility for it onto knowledge. Thinking, like living, means making one's own choices, taking one's own risks, including that of injustice and error. When man must invent the meaning of his life, the tools of science are no more than useless crutches; it is barehanded, in single combat, man to man, that the critic measures himself against the text in order to measure its worth and in doing so gives his own measure. Listen to Sartre: "The function of the critic is to criticize, which is to say to engage himself for or against and to situate himself by situating" (*Situations I*, p. 231). The writer, as I said earlier, is a man who speaks, in his work, of man to men; the critic is a man who answers him.

But the critic does not answer just anything or just anyhow. Restoring his task to the status and dignity of a personal undertaking does not mean dooming it thereby to being mere impressionism. Impressionism in criticism (and this is its limited truth) is indeed a personal relation to a text, but it is that of the fleeting instinct, of the fragmentary and isolated sensation. Impressionism always tends to be a solipsism: my reactions of mood are of no interest except to myself; or else, at best, they have a simple sociological interest (and this is why they are read) if I am sufficiently representative of a group or class. All the same, there can be no question of a true critic's simply "telling you what he thinks about" a work, like a landlady discussing one of her lodgers; true criticism is not a reflex but reflection. I know of no more exact or profound definition of its ultimate vocation than Baudelaire's: "To be just, in other words to possess its reason for being, criticism must be partial, passionate, political, which is to say made from an exclusive point of view, but from the point of view that opens up the widest horizons." Such is the essential law of criticism: we find in it, as in literature, at the same time and by a simultaneous postulation, a radical subjective rootedness and a demand for permanent universality. How can an "exclusive" point of view "open up the widest horizons"? There is no one point of view that has been miraculously favored, no gift from heaven. This personal and yet open — or, better still, *opening* — point of view is acquired and striven for. One is no more born a critic than one is born a poet: one becomes one by hard work. Not only must criticism integrate all the branches of knowledge pertinent to its object (thus crossing through a "zone of objectivity" and being modified by that process), but it also entails a full consciousness of its effective and affective relations with its object, and through that object with the world. There is therefore a dialectic specific to criticism that goes from the unreflected-upon subject (reading) to the reflected-upon subject (synthesis of meaning), passing through a knowing of the object (various orders of signification) — a dialectic in which impressions are refuted by knowledge to be at once rediscovered and transcended in the final judgment. If the subjectivity that makes the judgment is in theory capable of universalization, which is to say that it has a legitimate claim to the adhesion of others, this is because the critic's self, like the writer's self, is a subjectivity *transformed by its own work process*, and it is in that respect that criticism is, above all, a praxis. The self of the critic "processed" by his work, like the self of the writer, is not an ego turned in on itself and closed around an individual feeling capacity; it is because the *natural* self has been replaced in him by the *cultured* self that the critic is in direct and open communication with another, a communication based on the common foundation of a knowledge and a history fully and lucidly assumed.

The critic therefore does not answer "just anything" to the writer's appeal. Nor does he answer just anyhow. Roland Barthes was quite right to point out that the critic is not an ordinary reader; the critic is answering the writer's works with *another work*. This work-process to which the self subjects itself in order to become a universal subject, this praxis specific to the critic, has already been revealed and described in the writer and is nothing other than his commitment or *engagement in writing*. It is time it was clearly understood, in fact, if it has not been already, that authentic criticism, although it makes use of various types of knowledge, is not itself a special type of knowledge that has literature as its object, but *a particular branch of literature that has literature as its subject*. The critic is very precisely, and in the full meaning of the word, a writer-artist (*écrivain*): a writer who writes about writing as the dramatist and the novelist write about the world. Why this secondary form of writing? And does this mean that criticism is a subsidiary genre of literature, a parasitic literature? The entire development of modern art goes to prove the contrary. Since *Contre Sainte-Beuve*, an essential stage in the creation of Proust's *Recherche*, since Gide's *Les Faux-Monnayeurs* and its accompanying *Journal*, since *Ulysses* and *La Nausée*, we know that there is no longer any literary work that does not contain reflections by the writer on writing, and in which the writing itself does not constitute its own contestation of itself. True, the relations of critic and writer are not those of the writer and his self: but the critic is a writer whose existence is required by the writer, in the sense that writing calls to writing, just as any conscious act calls for an awareness and repetition of itself to occur, in the form of recognition, in another. Literature is in itself an imperative need — which criticism appears in order to satisfy — for that *dialogue* in which each becomes himself by confronting himself with the other, so that the literary work cannot take on its full existence except when it is having its meaning fed back to it by another, except when it is *criticized*. "Existential psychoanalysis," as I said earlier, is in this case psychoanalysis of the psychoanalyist. But we must go further:

it is his "cure." To the degree in which the critic reveals the meaning of a work through the project of its author, he is also uncovering his own "complexes," which he will thenceforward have to take upon himself. The catharsis here is twofold: of literature, as we have seen, by criticism; but also, and conversely, of criticism by literature. Written criticism is the finished form of that intimate and reciprocal contestation that begins with reading.

Naturally there exist false contestations, which lead to pseudo criticism. Although literature, like any human expression, bears the traces of its historical alienations, the authentic creation always succeeds, in a certain way, in transcending them. Criticism, on the other hand, seems to have been for a long while the victim of a radical alienation that has deprived it of its proper end, and of which it is only now beginning to free itself. It is in no way by chance that the relations of criticism and literature present the aspect of a long hostility, or even of a never-ending war. In the seventeenth century, when the pedants, from Malherbe to Boileau, right through the buzzing cohort of Chapelains and d'Aubignacs, claimed the right to rule Parnassus; when at the appearance of every great classical work there was a puffed up hack at hand to denigrate it in the name of good taste and verisimilitude (the "criticism of verisimilitude" is no modern invention), it was only to be expected that Corneille, Racine, Molière, or La Fontaine should eventually hit back. During the eighteenth century, relations were on the whole very little better. In the nineteenth, Hugo, Balzac, Flaubert, and Baudelaire were involved in an unending struggle, which Théophile Gautier sums up rather well: "One thing is certain and easy of demonstration to those who might perhaps doubt it: the natural antipathy of the critic for the poet — of the man who doesn't make anything for the man who does — of the drone for the worker — of the gelding for the stallion." And Flaubert: "Here are the monumentally stupid things: (1) literary criticism of whatever kind, good or bad; (2) the Temperance Society." But how can there not be a "natural antipathy" between criticism and literature, how can contestation not produce resentment, when the criticism is made from *outside*, in the name of good taste, of aesthetic canons, of moral order, of political stability, or on the strength of the ruling

Reason or Science of the day? How can the critic not feel himself emasculated in relation to the writer if he expends all his energy on creations while denying all creativity in himself? Whenever the meeting of literature and criticism is external, or, which comes to the same thing, *partial*, then one of two things is bound to happen: either criticism tyrannizes over literature (as is the case with "dogmatic" criticism of whatever persuasion);[11] or else, and no less unfortunately, criticism suppresses itself as such (as is the case with the celebrated "historical admiration" and also, far too often, with objective approaches).

In order to avoid either murder or suicide, criticism must at last discover the true bond that unites it with literature, a bond that is not a relation of exteriority but an *internal relationship*. If there is alterity, it is of the *alter ego* type: corresponding to the writer's total engagement in his endeavor to reach salvation there is the critic's total engagement in a reciprocal endeavor. And the reciprocity of ends requires a reciprocity of means. Though not autarchic, the critical activity is nonetheless autonomous, and in its turn *creative of meaning*. Like any writer, the critic must first of all create his own language, in a direct and intimate relation of comprehension with the mother work, yet governed by its own internal laws. For it is clear that the language of criticism can never be either that of the original literature or, even less, that of everyday speech. In this respect nothing could be more absurd than the complaint persistently being addressed to the new criticism that it uses "jargon," as though the banality of everyday language — even when fancied up with those phony embellishments that take themselves for "style" and which are to true style what the hip-rolling come-on is to the grace of a natural walk — could ever be the measure of a "clear" and rigorous language; as if literature and criticism, according to their respective needs, were not both perpetually compelled to fight their way out of the clichés of everyday chatter and the worn out phrases of conventional writing. This does not mean, of course, that there are not good and bad critical languages, just as there are good and bad literary languages: to invent a language is always to invent a certain balance between ordinary language and personal utterance. If the second is resorbed by the first, the result is insig-

297

nificance; if it does it excessive violence, then the result is a break-
down in communication and gobbledygook. But in any case, one
can only talk of jargon in relation to a certain internal felicity
in the writing, not in relation to the language of the street or
street corner. (Otherwise one would have to say that Rimbaud's
Illuminations are jargon, and likewise the tortuous periods of
Proust, of whom not so long ago, contemporary lights of "classicism" were saying that he "writes badly." Moreover, just as critical language is not a superproduct of everyday language, so
it cannot be a byproduct of a literary language. Critical literature
can never speak the same language as the original literature,
because they are not saying the same thing; the secondary writing
cannot resemble the primary writing, because their aims are different. Since critical thematization consists in bringing the
thematized literary content into explicitness, the secondary and
primary language are in a reciprocal relation, albeit working in
contrary directions. Whereas literature, brought to bear on the
world, must embody meaning in concrete words, criticism, which
is reconstruction of the same meaning by a reflecting consciousness, must integrate the vocabulary of its reflection into its discourse, which in today's context is the vocabulary of contemporary philosophy and the various human sciences. That this integration poses difficult problems in the writing no one will dispute,
and from this point of view the indignant protests Raymond
Picard has made against Roland Barthes's "style," though they
may be facile, nevertheless raise a real and pressing question.
A question, moreover, that remains the same in the case of Sartre's critical style too, or that of the disciples of Freud, or of
Marx, or of Bachelard. Critical language cannot be ordinary language, or literary language, or philosophic language, or scientific
language; and yet, though irreducible on principle to any of those
various languages, it must invent a synthesis of them. Critical
language is, in consequence, a bastard language, a bizarre language, a strange language — one that not only has utility but
also can and ought to have its own beauty. And in fact there
are already remarkable examples of it in existence, in the work
of Sartre, of Poulet, of Richard, of Starobinski, of Barthes himself,
to name but a few. Only a few nostalgic imbeciles can still believe

that history is immutable, and that "to write well" in 1966 is still to write "like Voltaire."

As with the writer again, however, it is not sufficient for the critic to create a language; he must also, like the writer, embody that language in a *work*, which is to say in a language whose particular texture refers onward to its overall structure in order to be understood. In the work, analytic thought yields pride of place to *dialectic* thought, since the synthesis it offers is in no way of an additive type. One cannot pick up a critical work anywhere along its length, make use of a particular passage, and leave some particular development out of account according to one's own needs. The critical work forms a whole whose parts are not to be understood other than through their internal relations, even though it is also in constant relation to the mother work, just as the literary work itself formed an intrinsic totality even though it continued perpetually to denote the world. Immanent analysis of meaning thus leads to *an immanent meaning of the analysis*: the reality of a critical work is nothing more, and also nothing less, than precisely that. A work, whatever it be — and this is its definition — refers back unceasingly to itself, yet without ceasing to refer outward to something else. This relational circuit, analyzed by Sartre, is that of selfness (*ipséité*) — an interiorization of the world that constitutes a subjectivity. The "truth" of a criticism is therefore not independent of the critic's subjectivity, as we observed even in the case of the "objective" approaches: it is nothing but the movement of that subjectivity at work, or in other words *making a work*. And this work in its turn will be neither a reflection nor a parallel twin of the work it is commenting on: in order to be understood it refers as much to the author of the commentary as to the object commented upon. Since the latter is always an object *revealed* by someone, the quality of the object is indivisible here from the quality of the revealer. Far from the critic's being able to dream of "effacing himself" before the texts, those texts have no existence other than through the intensity of his presence; no totality other than through his process of totalization; no unity other than through the synthesis he constitutes.[12] The critic of Racine takes Racine into his charge; he assumes responsibility for Racine. And if criticism is a total reply, in the critic's work, to the total question posed by the writer's work, then it is clear enough that the coherence of the critical undertaking, like that of the literary creation, is not solely or essentially of an intellectual order but is in fact, above all else, existential. The writer, as we have seen, is a man who finds himself by finding his language; the critic is a man who finds himself and finds us in finding the writer's language. Let us make no mistake: the communication between the critic and his reader is analogous, in its turn, to that between writer and critic; it is communication via a body of knowledge, as earlier via an imaginary world, between one human being and another human being. How? Why? Insofar as criticism is a radically conducted experiment, it becomes, for the reader, a form of self-comprehension, as the literary work was an image of his own condition. Through the critic's commentary on the work of the author, the reader discovers a comprehension of man comprehended by another comprehension, which presents itself to him as the intelligibility that his age gives itself of the past and present of man. And it is because, as Hegel said, the history of thought is always in the present, that the perennial literary work, in order to be all that it can be, calls out at every moment of history for the critical work.

The critical work therefore, like the literary work, is in a sense date-stamped; but, again like the literary work, if it has attained a certain degree of rigor and depth, if its closedness is the living totalization of a concrete experience, and its openness a permanent welcome to other possible experiences, then the authentic critical work must be capable of being transcended without thereby becoming obsolete. Sartre's *Saint Genet* will last as long as the works of Genet himself, even if, in a century or two, man's comprehension of man takes new paths and a different style. It will last because it constitutes, at a certain moment in history, through the fleeting meanings offered to us by Genet's works and existence, a total vision of the meaning of all men's destiny. The value of Sartre's *Genet* is in no way due to the fact that it exhausts Genet (even though the imperialism of the analysis sometimes gives the impression of a total annexation), since the very value of Genet is that of surviving any particular scrutiny, including that of Sartre. Criticism can never replace the reading of the words, as Renan foolishly thought his literary history could. But conversely, the value of Sartre's book would survive a cessation of interest in Genet; since it is an ensemble of the answers that a rigorous comprehension of man makes it possible to bring — in the mid-twentieth century — to the comprehension of one man and his work, the vision of man constituted by Sartre's criticism *as criticism* thereby becomes, for Sartre's reader, an ensemble of questions that call that reader himself into quesion, just as Genet called him into play. It may be said that in taking Sartre as an example I am stacking the cards in my favor, since the critic in this case also happens to be a great writer and a great philosopher. True. But all true criticism, and I am thinking here, out of ten possible examples, of J. Starobinski's *Rousseau*, constitutes in its own way a vision of man embodied in a work and which should be interrogated as such. Sartre, if you like, presents us with a model experiment, but not with a unique one. Directed at the symbolic objects of writing, as the perceptive consciousness is directed at the objects of the real world, the new critical literature is tending little by little to constitute, half way between the original literature and philosophic and anthropological reflection, a particular comprehension of man as he is revealed to himself in the imaginary universe of language. Although it must use the help of the many kinds of knowledge provided by the scientific disciplines and the philosophy of our age, and although it must even constitute, as it were, a *practical synthesis* of them, in the last resort it is solely a literary language of this new type that can reapprehend *from inside* the advent of meaning that all literary creation ultimately is.

And if there is so much unwanted rubbish in the history of criticism, if so many useless volumes encumber the shelves of our libraries, which have become less the museum of criticism than its graveyard, this is ultimately because criticism has come so tardily to an awareness of its true nature and role; it is because, in a word, its history has only just begun. The immense contribution of the new criticism that is gradually constituting itself today, whatever its divergences and inadequacies in other respects, its authentic *newness*, observable in its most noteworthy representatives, is that it has at last shaken criticism out of its age-old lethargy, out of its dogmatic or academic doze, has given it back its vocation, in short, has restored it to literature, at the very moment when literature was instituting itself as criticism. For the first time, hostilities are ceasing between writers and critics, because their experiences now intersect and reflect each other; because the writer is discovering criticism at the heart of his own activity, while the critic is finding writing at the center of his praxis. The critic, having become a writer-artist, can no longer feel a buried envy for the creative writer, nor can the creator, having become a critic, make a show of open contempt for the critic. The literary work and the critical work henceforward share the common will — at different levels of expression — to be an integral cipher of human existence in language. In this respect, they stand in a relation of reciprocal decipherment. A personal universe, beyond the thematization of a body of knowledge, confronting another personal universe in a relation of mutual elucidation that passes through the totality of an historical culture (today, that of the late twentieth century), the critical work in turn calls for its own justification: the recognition and the contestation of its reader. To this movement of perpetual referral and transcendence, to this circular process, there can be no end; no restful halt in the bosom of Truth and Evidence. Criticism draws from literature a meaning that it then uses to evolve its own vision of the world; and from this double meaning the reader's consciousness draws nourishment in his forever uncompleted confrontation with himself through others. Writer, critic, reader: what one finds, invariably, at the starting point as at the destination of this simultaneously shared and inner adventure, is a full and total subjectivity at work.

NOTES

CHAPTER 1

1. It is worth mentioning the opportune republication, under the aegis of Professor Henri Peyre, of certain important and sometimes almost unobtainable pieces of work by Gustave Lanson (Paris: Hachette, 1965).

CHAPTER 2

1. The linguist Spitzer remarked years ago that "Racine peoples his stage with few characters, but he exhausts all the possible relationships between them." *Linguistics and Literary History*, 1948.

2. As George Steiner reminds us in his recent essay *The Death of Tragedy* (New York: Knopf, 1961), "the decline of tragedy is inseparably linked with the decline of an organic vision of the world and of its mythological, symbolic, and ritual context" (p. 212). What makes it even more astounding that Raymond Picard should be capable of writing such ineptitudes is that elsewhere, in his introduction to *Phèdre*, he himself writes: "Like Plato, in *Er* or *The Cave*, [Racine] has put into action on the stage, with the aid of all music and all poetry, a metaphorical explanation of the human condition: truly the tragedy of *Phèdre* is a dramatic myth." But there are not two truths, one for Picard and another for Barthes. *Phèdre* is indeed a "dramatic myth," and Picard is right — thereby putting Picard in the wrong!

3. The patterns isolated by Charles Mauron in his *Inconscient dans l'oêuvre et la vie de Racine* clearly demonstrate the constancy of this double tension between domination and violent escape, both equally frustrated (notably pp. 25–26). Need I point out that this is a description in modern, psychoanalytical terms of a conflict perfectly familiar to seventeenth-century Jansenist thought, and one which is expressed in its own terms? See below, chap. 11, sec. 3, §4.

303

Chapter 3

1. Not that by my eyes alone shamefully ensnared / I love him for his beauty, his much vaunted grace.

2. But to make an inflexible heart yield / To bring pain into a soul without feeling, / To shackle a captive amazed at his chains, / rebelling in vain against a yoke he enjoys; / That is what I want, that is what spurs me on. / Hercules cost less to disarm than Hippolyte, / And since he was conquered more often, defeated sooner, / He offered less hope of fame to the eyes that tamed him.

Chapter 4

1. Raymond Picard chose well when he placed himself under the aegis of the Valéry of the *Préface à Adonis*: "I do not misprize the dazzling gift life makes to our consciousness when it abruptly hurls a thousand memories into the brazier at one throw. But until our own day, never has a momentary inspiration, or an aggregation of such inspirations, ever appeared to constitute a work of art." That is Picard's "the crude" nicely covered. "I have simply attempted to convey the conception that the obligatory meters, the rhymes, the fixed forms, all that arbitrary apparatus we use, adopted once and for all and set up as an adversary to ourselves, as it were, has a sort of clear-cut and philosophic beauty of its own." So much for the "norms and restraints." But Valéry's position is in fact more complex than that. He does not by any means deny the *primacy* of the *primitive*: "The gods, graciously, give us such and such a first line *for nothing*; but it is up to us to fashion the second, which must be in harmony with that first, and not prove unworthy of its supernatural predecessor" (ibid.). The situation could not be more succinctly summed up. And we also know the fame that Valéry ensured for his phrase (colored with infinite shades of attraction and repulsion): "In the beginning came the Fable." It is of dubious wisdom to make Valéry the standard-bearer of this straight-jacketing "classicism" when he palpably bursts it at every seam.

2. The palm for self-satisfied silliness must undoubtedly be awarded here to J.-B. Barrère, whose letter to *Le Monde*, since it is a veritable monument of its kind, must earn quotation: ". . . Forthwith, Pingaud rushes to the rescue with a theory of language. It is these people's hobbyhorse. I can see that it has its place when one needs to explain certain modern writers with reference to something other than what they actually say: it is sometimes desirable, or even necessary. But has M. Pingaud considered the consequences that must ensue from his argument? If Barthes in his turn is saying something other than what he thinks he is saying, can Pingaud be sure of interpreting him correctly? The simple reader, complicating things further, has every right to understand something different from what Pingaud is saying or thinks he is saying about

what Barthes thinks he is saying when he tells us what he thinks Racine meant to say when he said what he thought he was saying. The whole thing would soon fall victim to the guillotine of satire, if laughter still had the power to kill." This last wish is undoubtedly imprudent, and if laughter could still kill we should be seriously worried for M. Barrère's own head. It is to say the least strange to find this critic, with an archness somewhat misplaced at his age, goggling and giggling so gleefully in the face of this extraordinary discovery: that all language, including that of Racine, or Pingaud, or Barthes, is ambiguous, or in other words irreducible to a univocal signification. Moreover he could have spared himself this childlike amazement of his by simply reflecting that there must always have existed some equivocal margin between Racine and his commentators, and among his commentators in their turn, since long before Barthes and Pingaud a great many people, and "serious" people too, had produced absolutely contradictory interpretations of Racine's plays. We can, however, reassure M. Barrère, before his discovery unhinges him quite: there is a difference in the degree of ambiguity existing in the explicit and conceptual language of criticism and that to be found in the implicit and affective language of poetry. So one can (if one tries) understand Barthes and Pingaud perfectly, whereas it will never be possible to grasp Racine in his totality. I should also point out to M. Barrère that reflection on the nature of language is hardly "these people's hobbyhorse"; it so happens that it has been one of the major themes upon which writers as well as philosophers have been meditating since the turn of the century. It takes a critic locked inside a filing cabinet and "retarded," as we now say of children, by fifty or more years not to know that — and to boast as much.

3. Cf. the passage in the letter by J.-B. Barrère quoted in note 2, in which he concedes the possible interest of a "theory of language" "when one needs to explain modern writers by something other than what they actually say." This letter, very much the product of classical art, contains, as it were, a maximum of sillinesses in a minimum of lines.

4. I feel it is worth quoting here, for its entertainment value, another of those letters to *Le Monde* (27 November 1965), whose correspondence columns, like those of the (London) *Times*, constitute an astonishing compilation of idiocies. A certain physician, assuming Barthes to have been dealt a death blow on the subject of Racine, decided, contrary to the deontology of his profession, that it would be a good idea to give him the *coup de grâce* on the subject of Baudelaire. For Barthes, quoting Sartre, had in fact explained that he looked upon Baudelaire's unwritten plays, always being planned but never penned, as a sign of his "vast fund of negativity" and ultimately, the image of his destiny. Desire to write for the theater as a form of self-destruction? Come on

now, the physician cries. And triumphantly quotes one of Baudelaire's letters: "My debts, those the theater will pay off." So if Baudelaire thought about writing for the theater it was simply that he needed money. Isn't that simple enough? Because of course this desire to write impossible plays simply cannot be a wish for money and a wish for self-destruction *at the same time*, and human significations are never ambivalent. The physician in question really ought to go and study for a while with one of his psychoanalyst colleagues. I would not have dealt at such length with this example if it had not been so representative of a state of mind far too prevalent among literary historians, many of whom ingenuously suppose that they have extracted the *true* meaning of a text as soon as they have managed to equate it with some external fact. This is often the procedural method of the "criticism by detail" so dear to the heart of J. Pommier. If Racine invents the character of Aricie, it is because at a Court with Monsieur around, a hero who showed an excessive resistance to women would be suspected of other leanings, and also because, since the tragic hero must never be perfect, Racine was obliged to make Hippolyte fall in love. As though those conditions, by the simple fact of having been integrated into a play, were not thereby transcended, changed in meaning, just as algebraic signs can be. Similarly, we are told that Racine did not need to invent Phèdre's cry of "C'est toi qui l'a nommé" to Oenone, or even adapt it from Euripides, since it already existed word for word in the work of the obscure Gabriel Gilbert. Possibly; but the meaning of this famous hemistich could not possibly be the *same* in Gilbert as in Racine, for the simple reason that meaning does not reside in the mere aggregation of words: it resides in the meaningful relation those words have to the totality of the play, to *Phèdre* as manifestation of guilt as Word, *Phèdre* as utterance of Evil, aspects that Barthes so clearly perceived. There is a whole Racinian context involved here, a context which gives this hemistich a Racinian meaning in which all meanings brought in from other contexts are annihilated.

5. The *tone* in which it is vocalized changes the meaning of a sentence. There is the famous exercise consisting in reading aloud *The Grasshopper and the Ant* twice, once making the grasshopper "sympathetic" and once doing the same for the ant. This is ultimately true of all literature, which is why, in the theater, though the roles may be clearly and totally written out, there always remains the task of *interpretation* for the actors.

6. This is of course a first approximation to, or, if you prefer, a *mode of presentation of*, the literary phenomenon. In fact, as we shall see later in the present chapter and again in chapter 7, the literary work is a false "object."

7. Hence the absurdity of a celebrated formula in English criticism: "A poem does not have to *mean*, it has to *be*." For language, to be and

to mean are one and the same thing. On this point the testimony of a poet as lucid as Yves Bonnefoy seems to me of capital importance: "Now I can begin to define what I mean by poetry. In no way is it, although this is something being constantly claimed these days, the fabrication of an object in which meanings achieve structure. . . . That object does exist of course; but it is the corpse and not the soul or the purpose of the poem. To take account of nothing but that corpse is to remain in the world of dissociation, of objects — of the object that I also am and do not wish to remain; and the more one tries to analyze its refinements, its expressive ambiguities, the greater risk one runs of forgetting an intention of salvation, which is the poem's sole concern. It is not claiming, in fact, to do anything but interiorize reality. It is searching for the links that unite things *in me*." "La Poésie française et le principe d'identité," *Revue d'Esthétique*, 1965.

8. As Jean Rousset put it so perfectly in his study of the relation between imaginative and formal structures: "Corresponding to imaginative structures, with absolute inevitability, there are formal structures. The same secret principles that support and organize the underlying life of a creation also organize its composition. Secret principles: the composition, the action on the forms, the divisions of the presentation, and the technical choices themselves are all governed by the forces and implicit suggestions that obscurely control the artist at his work." *Forme et signification*, xv–xvi.

9. This desire to destroy is admitted, with simultaneous ingenuousness and cynicism, by Renan: The study of literary history is destined to replace to a large degree the reading of the works of the human mind themselves. We may note that the best reply to this is that of Lanson: "With literature as with art, we cannot eliminate the work, which is the depository and the manifestation of individuality. If a reading of the original texts is not a perpetual illustration and the ultimate goal of literary history, then the latter provides us with no more than a sterile and valueless form of knowledge." On this point, unfortunately, "Lansonians" are more often ardent supporters of Renan than of Lanson. The wish to substitute the history of the texts for the texts themselves is always more or less present in literary historians. In a recent newspaper article, Pierre-Henri Simon quotes the following revealing sentence written by an English biographer of Proust: "It may well be asked what people know about *la Recherche* if they know nothing but *la Recherche*." And Simon rightly replied: *the essential*.

10. It now becomes easier to grasp the reason for Picard's curious reticence, noted earlier in this chapter, as to the relation between work and biography, which his intellectualist conception of literature as a consciously willed object should, on the contrary, be particularly suited to elucidate. By a strange fetishism, no doubt due to an excessive reac-

tion against the profanations of the historicists, it is essential, in order to guarantee the aesthetic autonomy of a work, to preserve its virginity. The miracle of literature is that of an "immaculate conception," and the only acceptable biogenesis is parthenogenesis. Historicist on the one hand, aestheticist on the other, creator of either angels or holy virgins, traditional criticism has nothing to offer literature apart from either abortion or sainthood.

CHAPTER 5

1. Academic criticism concerned with Corneille (since we must assume that an academic tradition exists) here joins hands with Racinian criticism: "The richness and diversity of these major plays are such that any effort to establish common characteristics immediately encounters objections; each play, intolerant of generalizations, withdraws into its own individualtiy and isolation." G. Couton, *Corneille*, p. 94.

2. We must of course take into account here the fact that we are dealing not with a general study of Racine's theater but with a series of introductions to his plays, within the framework of a complete edition. That said, we nevertheless have a totally explicit *state of mind* on the biographical level, and one that coincides exactly with the attitudes of Picard's confreres and colleagues — such as Couton — with respect to literary works. See above, chapter 3.

3. Such as this admirable definition of reading from Jean Rousset: "Fruitful reading should be global reading, sensitive to identities and correspondences, to similarities and contrasts, to restatements and variations, as well as to those cruxes and crossroads where the texture becomes denser or unfolds and spreads out." *Forme et Signification*, p. xii.

CHAPTER 6

1. It is Proust, once again, quoted by Spitzer, who has best defined the notion of "structure" when he points out that "finished works of art" are those "in which there is not a single brushstroke isolated from the rest, in which each part receives its reason for being from the others and in return is imposing theirs on them."

2. In this sense, the great philosopher of Structure is Hegel, for whom, as Sartre reminds us, "the structure of the concept is not the simple juxtaposition of invariable elements that could, if the need arose, be associated with other elements to produce other combinations, but an organization whose unity is such that its secondary structures cannot be considered apart from the whole without becoming "abstract" and losing their nature." *Situations III*, p. 145.

3. We are dealing here of course with a difference in level only, not in the nature of the comprehension; our perception of the meaning,

308

even when immediate and fragmentary, remains *structured*; the lines of verse, the successive scenes are comprehended solely through the mediation of that "attraction exercised by the future upon the present, and by the whole, even when it does not yet exist, upon its parts," of which Sartre speaks (ibid., p. 144). The critic's reflexive thought is therefore merely repeating and making more explicit a process begun by the spectator's spontaneous consciousness, by carrying it to its absolute.

4. Translator's note: Since there is nowhere a common root for verbs of reading and binding in English, this argument inevitably loses force in translation.

5. Because at one point, with curious irresponsibility, Picard attributes to Barthes the very attitude that the latter is in fact attacking. Barthes writes: "It is noted that round about 1675 tragedy was supplanted by opera; but this change of mentality is reduced to the rank of *circumstance*." And Picard comments: "But in fact, *he* (Barthes) *immediately corrects us*, it is one of the possible causes of Racine's silence after *Phèdre*" (pp. 71–72). Whereupon Picard goes on to give Barthes a stiff and erudite lecture: in the first place tragedy was not supplanted by opera, and in any case "it is only prudent, when one does not consider a circumstance determining, to avoid the word cause". . . . It is Don Quixote and the windmills! Because here is Barthes's text: ". . . this change of mentality is reduced to the rank of *circumstance*: it becomes one of the possible causes of Racine's silence after *Phèdre*" (*Sur Racine*, pp. 160–61). As it happens, Barthes is not "correcting" anything: it is not, as Picard by some strange misreading seems to think, his own theory that he is expounding, but on the contrary *that of the adherents of traditional literary history*! The latter, in making the transition from "circumstance" to "possible cause", think themselves adequately protected by the prudence of their hypothesis, that "prudence" so dear to Picard's heart. So all Barthes means — and he is totally in the right — is that "this prudence is already a systematic attitude": this prudence is not employed, as its adherents ingenuously believe, *without reference to any system. There can be no more or less except within a given system of reference.* In this case, then, to argue that the rise of the opera can be one of the possible causes of Racine's silence — as traditional critics, *not* Barthes, do — is to constitute that *possibility* on the basis of an interpretative schema such that, when certain historical circumstances on the one hand, and certain psychological dispositions proper to Racine on the other, are given and placed side by side, then we obtain, as a possible effect of this "cause", Racine's silence. The degree of probability introduced into this causality principle in no way changes its *nature*: it remains what it is: a metaphysical postulate, and an absurd one to boot, but in any case a global method of explaining the relations of man and literature to reality.

As systems go, Barthes also makes it plain in the incriminated passage, he prefers deeper and more highly evolved ones — and who can blame him?

CHAPTER 7

1. "I have often dreamed of a peaceful coexistence between the critical languages, or, if you prefer, of a "parametric" criticism that would modify its language in relation to the work confronting it, not of course in the conviction that these languages in aggregate would eventually exhaust all the truth in the work for all eternity, but in the hope that these varied languages (albeit not infinite, since they are subject to particular ratifications), might give rise to a general form, which would be the intelligible form itself that our age gives to things. . . . In short, it is because there would then exist, in us, a general form of analyses, a classification of classifications, a criticism of criticisms, that the simultaneous plurality of our critical languages could be justified." *Essais critiques*, p. 272.

2. "Critical discourse — like logical discourse moreover — is never anything but tautological: it consists ultimately in re-stating after a time-lag, but confining itself wholly within that time-lag, which for that reason alone is not insignificant: Racine, is Racine, Proust, is Proust . . ." *Essais*, p. 256. But Barthes's "time-lag" in no way breaks the tautology: it *doubles* it, one might say.

3. "The syntagmatic consciousness is consciousness of the relations that link signs together at the level of the discourse itself, which is to say, essentially, consciousness of the sign's restrictions, tolerances, and liberties. This consciousness has left its mark on the linguistic researches of the Yale school, and also, outside linguistics itself, on the researches of the Russian formalist school." "L'imagination du signe," in *Essais critiques*, p. 209.

4. In a penetrating article — "L'Homme et les signes," *Critique*, 1965 — devoted to Barthes, G. Genette shows very clearly that the latter's "semiological" preoccupations betray, in reality, an "existential choice": in opposition to the "redundant and overfed" significations of language, Barthes, Genette says, is trying to restore to signs an original purity disencumbered of "visceral" connotations. We recognize here, on the critical plane, the selfsame obsession that Robbe-Grillet displays on the level of fiction: in both cases, "the determination to weigh down signification with the maximum guarantee provided by nature provokes a kind of nausea" (*Mythologies*); in both cases we meet, to use the expression Genette applies to Barthes, an "ascesis" or a "catharsis" intended to liberate the object or sign from the meanings superimposed upon it by History — and, we would also add, by the poetic imagination. Barthes's desire to "demythologize" the world is therefore the exact

310

counterpart of Robbe-Grillet's wish to "detragify" reality. As far as I am concerned, this "existential choice" seems in both cases to be inauthentic, and to betray both a hoodwinking of the consciousness in its relations with the world and a historical alienation of technocratic civilization.

5. "The child's power of speech, assimilated as the child learns its mother tongue, is not the sum of that tongue's morphological, syntactical, and lexical significations: such knowledge is neither necessary nor sufficient for the acquisition of a tongue, and the act of speaking, once acquired, does not presuppose any comparison on my part between what I wish to express and the notional arrangement of the means of expression I employ." M. Merleau-Ponty, "Sur la phénoménologie du langage," *Signes*, p. 111.

6. It is this "visionary" aspect of style that Proust so admirably caught: "It [style] is the revelation, impossible to achieve by direct and conscious methods, of the *qualitative difference* that, if there were no art, would remain the eternal secret of each individual. By art, and by art alone, we are given the power to emerge from ourselves, to know *what another sees* of this universe that is not the same as ours . . ." (my italics). *Le Temps retrouvé*.

CHAPTER 8

1. Certainly worthy of note in France, nevertheless, is Gilbert Durand's *Le Décor mythique de la Chartreuse de Parme* (Corti, 1961), which distinguishes, in literature, between the form — to which the "sciences of literature" (stylistics, syntax, rhetoric, etc.) are applicable — and the content; and then goes on to discern in the latter "that primordial semanticism of the human soul that overflows all semiologies in an immediate datum, not of the individual and reflexive consciousness, but of the universal communication of consciousnesses" (pp. 11–12). This leads to an archetypal approach to the literary "myths."

2. And since such communication must, nevertheless, be imagined somehow, here is the model of intelligibility we are offered: "The work of art, grafted onto the unconscious, is an equally unconscious self-knowledge" (*L'Inconscient*, p. 181). A reflection of the unconscious becoming unconscious knowledge of itself; an unconscious unconscious, transforming itself into *consciously unconscious* unconscious: this schema of a double unconscious is merely a double absurdity.

3. Nor is the Lacanian variant of French Freudianism calculated to make me change this opinion. If Mauron had made use of Lacan's structuralist terminology instead of Freud's mechanical vocabulary, he would no doubt have brought himself into line with current fashion, but philosophically nothing would have been changed. If you wish to convince yourself of the truth of this, you need only read Jean Reboul's

311

theoretical study "Jacques Lacan et les fondements de la psychanalyse" (*Critique*, December 1962), written in the somewhat oracular style characteristic of the Lacan school, whose sibylline tone makes one yearn for Freud's brutal frankness. Simply replacing "impersonal psychological laws" by a "formalism dominating human behavior and realizing itself in that behavior without its knowledge" or, as Reboul puts it, by "a formality that finds itself there without having been formalized by anyone"; simply changing the Id into the "locus of language's being," and that hypostatized language into "an unconscious symbolic structure, transcendent in relation to man," does not change in any way at all the fact that "*man is no longer at the center of himself*" (which is why we observed that Racine's theater, as it appears in Mauron's study, is a totality whose circumference is clearly defined but whose center is nowhere). Lacan can at least be given credit for saying out loud what every Freudian thinks under his breath: "I think where I am not, I am where I do not think." And Reboul adds the comment, intended as a criticism of zealous adherents to that "security blanket" the *ego cogito*: "From the *Discourse on Method* to the *Science of Dreams*, no bridge is thinkable: we have to leap . . ." Well, for my part I refuse to "leap," because such a leap is merely risible. Any interpretation of man incapable of providing an account of that Cogito which remains untranscendably the primary evidential fact of human existence, and the only way it has of apprehending itself *concretely* (the unconscious, let us remember, being a hypothesis of the conscious, so that we ought to apply here the Roman proverb on maternity and paternity: the unconscious is a matter of probability, the consciousness, of certainty), any interpretation that ousts the subject from centrality in favor of some kind of material or formal "laws," is simply in error and a betrayal of experience itself, which is the sole basis upon which science is possible. But this error is not "innocent": it is merely manifesting the fundamental *nihilism* of Freudian thought, the triumph within it of the death wish over the life force. It is the arch-Freudian and Lacanian Reboul who tells us so: "Man is not at the center of himself, and the locus of his desire is the chasm of the unattainable "thing," forbidden and incapable of verbalization, besieged by metaphors and sublimations that exhaust their energies clogging and concealing it without ever arriving at anything better than the ultimate traps (among them beauty, fallen from its function as truth's splendor) veiling, while also unveiling, the death wish. . . . Here we join the profound intuitions of Sade, of Nietzsche, of Georges Bataille, on death in hubris and the terminal ejaculation with which the *libido* crowns its end on the final summit that annihilates it. . . . Hence the affirmation of an ethic of desire not unrelated to that dionysiac pessimism foreshadowed by Freud." This psychoanalysis, whose "scientific truth" eventually leads to a metaphorical apprehension of the reality of which it began as a theoretical travesty, itself cries out for psychoanalysis.

4. It is worth pointing out, however, that practical problems of therapy are forcing the theory to modify itself; hence the proliferation of psychoanalytic schools, notably in the U.S.A., where, with the neo-Freudians and the existential psychoanalysts, the theoretical horizons have been widened to a remarkable extent. My criticism is aimed solely at the determinist philosophy animating Freudian psychoanalysis, which, until something happens to change the situation, is still, if not the only school, certainly the largest.

5. What is true of the patient, whose trouble is precisely that he is *alienated* [*aliéné* is the French word for one who is mentally ill], far from providing a useful schema for explaining the acts of the free man, can only be understood insofar as it is in contradiction to them. "Psychological determinism" does not render human freedom illusory; it is itself no more than the *moment* of that freedom frozen into immobility.

6. Goldmann was later led to reflect urgently and in detail on both the complementary and mutually exclusive relations between psychoanalysis and Marxism. We shall see how and why later.

7. "The possibility of understanding them [empirical facts] and of elucidating their laws and signification is the only valid criterion for judging the value of a philosophic method or system." *DC*, pp. 13–14.

8. This grouping is particularly odd (and unfortunate) in that the phenomenological position consists precisely in denying any causal interpretation of the phenomena of consciousness. This is therefore quite simply an error.

9. Auguste Cornu too, in his *Essai de critique marxiste*, makes the transition, quite *naturally*, from the plane of knowledge to that of action, from the realm of study to that of the norm, without even commenting on the radical leap involved in such a transition: "Essentially oriented toward action, Marxist criticism does not limit itself to this mode of precise analysis of the works of the past, for that would be to reduce revolutionary thought to an attempt at comprehension without any practical bearing, to a contemplative exercise without influence on the process of artistic and literary creation. Integrating itself into the body of revolutionary thought Marxist criticism sets itself as its object not only the evaluation of a work's content with constant reference to the class relationships that determine it, but also and above all the contribution it can make to the creation of new works directed toward the future" (quoted by R. Fayolle, *La Critique littéraire*, 1964). Please understand me: I do not for a moment criticize Marxist criticism for being *engaged*; it is criticism's very vocation to be that — and on this point Cornu has the merit of being more straightforward than Goldmann. My criticism is of the fact that it travesties the nature of its engagement by making

engagement into a corollary of knowledge; this is to lay fraudulent claim to *certainties* when all you in fact have is *convictions*.

10. "The tragedy of rejection, expressed in the writing of Pascal, Racine, and Kant . . ." (*DC*, p. 57). Or again: "The writings of Sophocles, Shakespeare, Pascal, Racine, and Kant are together with those of Homer, Aeschylus, Goethe, Hegel, and Marx, summits of classical art and thought" (p. 52). Art and thought, it's all one and the same thing — in theory. In practice, however, it is no coincidence that the analyses Goldmann devotes to Pascal are of considerably better quality than those dealing with Racine. Philosophic thought, which like his method also works from the concrete to the abstract, accommodates itself without difficulty to the sociologist's procedural method; artistic creation, which works from the clear to the ambiguous, just as naturally tends to slip through his net.

11. Whereas, as we saw earlier, a true phenomenological analysis would have consisted in ascertaining first of all, by means of an attentive scrutiny of the works, whether there is indeed a Jansenist meaning of Racine's plays and what its real importance is in the inmost organization of the whole.

12. "It is she whom I have above all striven to express to the full, and my tragedy is no less that of Aggripine's fall than that of Britannicus's death."

13. "There remains for me to mention Junie."

14. *In theory*, of course, "although Marxism . . . relates any spiritual movement to the development of the forces of production and of the social relations determined by the latter, it does not try to relate them exclusively to that development and to establish an absolute parallelism between the two tendencies" (Cornu, *Essai de critique marxiste*). But it is nevertheless odd that *in practice* "dialectical" materialsim automatically falls back on the schemas of "mechanistic" materialsim. The reason is that since no philosophy of subjectivity, no *Cogito*, has been integrated within that dialectic, *no real rhythm can be found in the processes of thought*. Though postulated, it remains undiscernible, and that is to be expected; as long as (Lenin *dixit*) thought is a reflection of the brain, the superstructures will continue eternally to reflect the infrastructures.

15. Having long persisted in talking about "socialist science" and "capitalist science" under Stalin — just as under Hitler there was talk of "Jewish science" with reference to Einstein and Freud — it appears that today's Marxists have definitively abandoned such nonsense. There is only one kind, one body, of scientific knowledge, whose applications can, it is true, be different under different political regimes, and whose progress can be hastened or delayed by them, but which, in its specific nature, in no way depends upon the historical mode of its appearance in the world.

314

16. Lucien Goldmann emphasizes that the particular situation of the human sciences derives from the fact that there is a "partial identity of the subject and the object of its research." More precisely, this identity can never be anything but *partial* in any scientific research: but in concrete reality, as in philosophic and literary expression, it is *total*.

17. Do you remember that marvelous passage in which Péguy guys the "scientific" pretensions of criticism in his day: "Have we been set the task, or set outselves the task, of studying La Fontaine? Good; instead of beginning with the first fable we turn to we begin with Gallic humor; the French sky; soil; climate; food; ethnology; early literature; then the man; his way of life; his tastes . . . then the writer; his gropings toward classicism; his Gallic escapades; then the writer (continued); opposition in France between culture and nature . . . and all that makes up part one; on to part two . . . French society in the seventeenth century and in La Fontaine; the king; the court; the nobility . . . finally part three . . . comparison between La Fontaine and his predecessors, Aesop, Rabelais, Pipay, Cassandre; the expression; the picturesque style; accuracy of vocabulary; colloquial expressions . . . lastly, theory of the poetic fable; nature of poetry . . . finis; and I am left wondering in panic where, in all that, I am to find the fable itself . . ." *Passim* (quoted by R. Fayolle, in *La Critique Littéraire*). With traditional scholarship one is so bogged down by sheer erudition that one struggles in vain to fight one's way through to the text itself. With Goldmann it is the opposite: one starts from the text, but the constantly accelerating centrifugal impetus of his method soon has one hurtling out in bewilderment through ever vaster and vaster frames of reference. One feels as though one has been caught up in one of those anguished guests that Ionesco characters go in for, at one moment desperately attempting to reach their objective, at the next practically rupturing themselves trying to get away from it.

18. "In general, good criticism should be wary of individuals and not accord them too large a share of its attention. It is the mass that creates, for the mass possesses to an eminent degree, and a thousand times more spontaneously, the moral instincts of nature . . . Geniuses are no more than editors of the crowd's inspirations. . . . To laud them for their individualtiy is to debase them." The style apart, it is clear that Renan's scientism didn't wait for Goldmann's structuralism to say exactly the same thing, and for the same reasons: to objectivist thought the individual is always *de trop*.

19. This is something Sartre makes very clear in his *Critique de la raison dialectique*, in which he attempted to provide Marxist dialectic with a solid basis in the form of the individual praxis, just as Marxist dialectic had previously provided Hegel's idealist dialectic with a solid basis in the concrete. Whether or not he succeeded is another matter.

315

20. Cf. Sartre, *L'Être et le néant*; pp. 484–503. Translated by Hazel E. Barnes as *Being and Nothingness* (London: Methuen), part 3, chap. 3, sec. III, "Being-with" and the "We," pp. 413–33.

21. "Individuals . . . manifestly appear, if not as the last, at least as the immediate, subjects of the behavior in question" (*SR*, p. 214).

22. "The essence is the insertion of the abstract individual fact within the ensemble of its relations by the process of conceptualization that *concretizes* it" (*DC*, p. 107). Hence the proliferation of phrases such as "to concretize" human facts by means of a "dialectical conceptualization" (p. 14), etc.

23. A passage from Renan, so monstrous in its silliness, and for so long a dead weight on French literary studies, must be quoted here: "Absolute admiration is always superficial; no one admires Pascal's *Pensées*, Bossuet's *Sermons* more than I. But I admire them as works of the seventeenth century. If these works were to be published today they would scarcely merit notice. True admiration is historical." I will not insult Goldmann, who more than anyone has a sense of the permanence of certain values and has so admirably demonstrated the modernity of Pascalian dialectics, by identifying his attitude with that of Renan. What is unfortunate is that though he departs from Renan in practice, when it is a matter of *comprehension*, he is incapable of dissociating himself from him in theory, when he concerns himself with *explanation*.

CHAPTER 9

1. On the work of Leo Spitzer, generally little known in France, see J. Starobinski's article "La Stylistique et ses méthodes: Leo Spitzer," *Critique*, July 1964; Maud Bodkin, *Archetypal Patterns of Poetry* (Oxford, 1963); G. Durand, *Les Structures anthropologiques de l'imaginaire* (1960); P. Delbouille, *Poésie et sonorités* (1961). Needless to say, this is intended neither as a bibliography nor even as the beginnings of a bibliography. I merely offer a few examples that seem to me significant.

2. Robert Castel, in his study "Méthode structurale et idéologies structuralistes" (*Critique*, November 1964), is led to ask himself the same question apropros of Lévi-Strauss's structuralism: "The structuralist — one who employs the structuralist method — is in *the first place*, in this sense, a 'scientist' who is inquiring and also inquiring into himself as such. Can he be *at the same time* an 'ideologist' without playing the double game of science and philosophy, of strict objectivity and pathos, which elsewhere he claims to condemn? Or are there two scales of measurement, so that when his strict objectivity has successfully been used to refute others, thus assuring him of a good scientific conscience at other people's expense, he can still rely on having a certain good philosophic conscience in reserve, derived from a naïve affirmation of the unimpeachable foundations of his own system?" Clearly the problem is strictly identical for all the human sciences.

CHAPTER 10

1. I have given an account, rapid but not unjust I think, of what I take to be the psychoanalyst's "complex" or, rather, "complexes." It would not be difficult to show also upon what affective grounds Goldmann's sociological criticism is constructed, in particular his "hatred of the individual." The individual human being is being-for-death, the untranscendable tragic; the human as collective being is, on the contrary, the transcendence of the tragic by dialectics (the leitmotif of *Le Dieu caché*), which opens up to humanity the dimension of the future refused to the individual. We find the same theoretical and practical obsession in the Sartre of *Les Mains sales* and *La Raison dialectique*. But as the same Sartre makes admirably clear in *Le Mur*, faced with the twelve bullets of a firing squad the future closes, and man becomes again what he had never ceased to be: an individual. And that this criticism of mine, in its turn, reveals *my* "complexes" is also quite certain; the only difference is that my theory exists for precisely that reason, as a means of taking them into account and integrating them into my thinking.

CHAPTER 11

1. This theoretical necessity is encountered by the various forms of empirical investigation in their different domains as "barriers" of fact: for psychocriticism, the work of art is a self-analysis, but an unconscious one that never succeeds in achieving full consciousness of self; for the sociology of Lukács and Goldmann the traditional novel presents the biography of a "problematic" hero, which is to say a hero whose existence and values confront him with problems he can neither solve nor fully grasp because of his historical alienation.

2. In the days when the existentialist vocabulary had still to be invented, Buffon said quite simply: "Style is the man himself." Some may feel nostalgic for such simplicity. I don't. Today's terminology, though more cumbersome, can be precise about things that the "classical" style left vague.

3. It is a dream expressed once by André Suarès: "On every side the same conclusion is reached: one must first and foremost efface oneself. In the attempt to create any work of value, the same law governs the critic's talent and the tragic poet's genius: the first point is that one must withdraw from oneself and leave pride of place to the object." As though Racine's plays were not the presence of his being in his work in its most concrete form! The same law does indeed govern the critic's talent and the poet's genius: first and foremost, he must exist.

4. These levels differ not only in accordance with the *mode* of perception, which is to say the duration specific to the consciousness (cf. the first paragraph of chapter 6), but also according to the *richness* of that perception, which is to say to the individual culture and intelligence serving as refractive index. If the critic is the "developer" of the work,

the work is revealed all the more clearly when that developer is a good strong solution.

5. See chapter 6. There are precise reasons for this factual situation. If the work is indeed a mode of the apparition of the Other, on the one hand there is never evident knowledge of the Other (there cannot be evidence other than from self to self, and in this sense mathematical evidence has as its correlate an ideal object constructed by the consciousness); on the other hand, the knowledge of the Other engages me totally, in my being and my values: my judgment judges me. This is why, in criticism, the "evidence" is not detachable from the individual, as it can be in the sciences.

6. The reader must evaluate as he will the letter to *Le Monde* (13 November 1965) in which E. Guitton castigates the guilty Pingaud in these terms: "Let him only turn to the introductions in the Pléiade edition: he will see what an informed and perspicacious mind, without any ideological ambition of any sort, feels it has the right to say in order to prepare possible readers for a reading of Racine." The example is on the whole an unfortunate choice. Alas! In order to have no "ideology of any sort" it would be necessary *to stop thinking altogether*. Though one must allow that Mr. Guitton, who was dreaming earlier of "effacing himself in the presence of the texts," hasn't got far to go.

7. It should be noted that the authentic critical experience is more often than not *fortuitous in character*, which comes to the same thing as saying that it is *concrete in character*. Spitzer quite rightly says: "Why do I affirm that it is impossible to give the reader a systematic method, to be applied point by point to the work of art? It is because, for a start, the first step, from which all else depends, can never be predicted; it must already have taken place. This first step is the awareness of having been struck by some one detail, followed by the conviction that this detail is linked to the work's essence" (*Linguistics and Literary History*, pp. 26–27). And Jean Rousset observes, again rightly: "The critical tool must not precede the analysis. The reader must remain open and responsive, but with his sensibility perpetually on the alert, until the moment when the stylistic signal appears, the unexpected and revealing structural fact" (*Forme et signification*, p. xii). This does not mean that the critic must himself be unprovided with what I shall term "theoretical structures of reception," and thus fall back into pure impressionism. But it does mean that theoretical elucidation, in criticism, can never be a mechanical procedure, a rule to be applied, a reference grid that can be moved from one author to another; the instrument we use can never be anything if not supple. In a word, *theoretical comprehension must be an inner framework to support the meaning, never a corset*. (Robert Kanters, please note.)

8. For an analysis of the look in painting, see Jean Paris's study *L'Espace et le regard* (Paris: Le Seuil, 1965).

9. Renan was logical enough to follow this philosophic positivism through to its inevitable conclusion: "To praise this or blame that is the mark of the small-minded method. The work must be taken for *what it is*, perfect of its kind, eminently representing what it represents, and not blamed for lacking what it does not have. The notion of inadequacy is misplaced in literary criticism. . . . All works are not equal, of course, but a play is in general *what it can be*" (*L'Avenir de la science*, my italics). At least Renan has the honesty to draw the conclusion that by imprisoning criticism within the realm of factual knowledge you inevitably exclude from it all consideration of values.

10. "As long as the traditional function of criticism was to judge, it could not be other than conformist, which is to say in conformity with the interests of the judges" (*Critique et vérité*, p. 14). In this respect it is tragic to see a certain kind of "socialist" criticism taking over the baton from men like Nisard and Maurras.

11. It may reasonably be asked how exactly a "criticism of judgment" such as I have just proposed and championed against the pure criticism of "comprehension" or "description" is differentiated from dogmatic criticism. As folows: dogmatic criticism shelters, by definition, behind a *dogma*, that is, an objective and collective norm and code of laws (good taste, good manners, bourgeois order, socialist legality, etc.), which are applied to literature from without. Whereas true judgment, on the contrary, entails a personal and total responsibility on the critic's part; it is exercised inside literature itself, precisely in the name of the human requirements that it has taken upon itself.

12. So far we have dealt exclusively with written criticism. It is clear that this also applies, mutatis mutandis, to the living, spoken criticism of the university lecture, in which the *presence* of the professor plays an essential role. A good lecture had never been a kind of central clearing house for information, facts, documents, statistics, etc.; it is not of an "informational" order (for that, textbooks are quite adequate — until machines are perfected). A good lecture is one in which the person of the professor is *irreplaceable*, because it brings the text to life and *makes it exist* as the synthesis of a lived experience, which it strives to communicate to others.

INDEX

INDEX